Ethiopians in an Age of Migration

The migration of Ethiopians across international borders is a recent phenomenon because of the limited integration of the country and society to the global economy. Since it was never colonized – aside from the Italian occupation of 1936–1941 – Ethiopia's economy and society were not directly impacted by the ebb and flow of the global economy, and thus never generated international migration. Beginning in the 1970s, due to factors such as famine, rural poverty, civil war and political repression, an unprecedented number of Ethiopian migrants began to leave their country in search of better, more secure lives. Today, this diaspora constitutes a distinctive community dispersed across the world, but bound by a common feeling of collectiveness and a shared history of the homeland.

The contributors to this volume draw their work from a wide variety of interdisciplinary fields and provide new critical insight on Ethiopian migrants and their diaspora communities. What has emerged from these scholarly works is the recognition that the Ethiopian diaspora – although separated by oceans and nations, by politics, ethnicity, class, gender and age – is carving out a social and material world born out of their particular circumstances both 'here' and 'there'. This book was originally published as a special issue of *African and Black Diaspora: An International Journal*.

Fassil Demissie is a faculty member in the Department of Public Policy at DePaul University, Chicago, IL, USA. He is the co-editor of *African and Black Diaspora: An International Journal*.

Ethiopians in an Age of Migration

Scattered lives beyond borders

Edited by
Fassil Demissie

LONDON AND NEW YORK

First published 2017
by Routledge
2 Park Square, Milton Park, Abingdon, Oxon, OX14 4RN, UK

and by Routledge
711 Third Avenue, New York, NY 10017, USA

Routledge is an imprint of the Taylor & Francis Group, an informa business

© 2017 Taylor & Francis

All rights reserved. No part of this book may be reprinted or reproduced or utilised in any form or by any electronic, mechanical, or other means, now known or hereafter invented, including photocopying and recording, or in any information storage or retrieval system, without permission in writing from the publishers.

Trademark notice: Product or corporate names may be trademarks or registered trademarks, and are used only for identification and explanation without intent to infringe.

British Library Cataloguing in Publication Data
A catalogue record for this book is available from the British Library

ISBN 13: 978-1-138-28082-3

Typeset in Myriad Pro
by diacriTech, Chennai

Publisher's Note
The publisher accepts responsibility for any inconsistencies that may have arisen during the conversion of this book from journal articles to book chapters, namely the possible inclusion of journal terminology.

Disclaimer
Every effort has been made to contact copyright holders for their permission to reprint material in this book. The publishers would be grateful to hear from any copyright holder who is not here acknowledged and will undertake to rectify any errors or omissions in future editions of this book.

This book is dedicated to all those Ethiopian migrants who have lost their lives in search of fulfilling their hopes and dreams.

Contents

Citation Information	ix
Notes on Contributors	xi
Living across worlds and oceans – an introduction Fassil Demissie	1
1 Emigrants and the state in Ethiopia: transnationalism and the challenges of political antagonism Solomon M. Gofie	10
2 Somewhere else: social connection and dislocation of Ethiopian migrants in Johannesburg Tanya Zack and Yordanos Seifu Estifanos	25
3 Trafficking of Ethiopian women to Europe – making choices, taking risks, and implications Anne Kubai	42
4 Determinants of diaspora policy engagement of Ethiopians in the Netherlands Katie Kuschminder and Melissa Siegel	60
5 Ethiopian taxicab drivers: forming an occupational niche in the US Capital Elizabeth Chacko	76
6 Ethiopian female labor migration to the Gulf states: the case of Kuwait Faiz Omar Mohammad Jamie and Anwar Hassan Tsega	90
7 'Deported before experiencing the good sides of migration': Ethiopians returning from Saudi Arabia Marina de Regt and Medareshaw Tafesse	104
8 The return migration experiences of Ethiopian women trafficked to Bahrain: '…for richer or poorer, let me be on the hands of my people …' Adamnesh Atnafu and Margaret E. Adamek	119

CONTENTS

9 Migration, gender, and mobility: Ethiopian–Israeli women's narratives of career trajectories 133
Yarden Fanta-Vagenshtein and Lisa Anteby-Yemini

10 Bole to Harlem via Tel Aviv: networks of Ethiopia's musical diaspora 150
Ilana Webster-Kogen

11 'No place like home': experiences of an Ethiopian migrant in the host country and as a returnee to the homeland 166
Adamnesh Atnafu and Margaret E. Adamek

Index 179

Citation Information

The chapters in this book were originally published in the *African and Black Diaspora: An International Journal*, volume 9, issue 2 (July 2016). When citing this material, please use the original page numbering for each article, as follows:

Introduction
Living across worlds and oceans – an introduction
Fassil Demissie
African and Black Diaspora: An International Journal, volume 9, issue 2 (July 2016) pp. 125–133

Chapter 1
Emigrants and the state in Ethiopia: transnationalism and the challenges of political antagonism
Solomon M. Gofie
African and Black Diaspora: An International Journal, volume 9, issue 2 (July 2016) pp. 134–148

Chapter 2
Somewhere else: social connection and dislocation of Ethiopian migrants in Johannesburg
Tanya Zack and Yordanos Seifu Estifanos
African and Black Diaspora: An International Journal, volume 9, issue 2 (July 2016) pp. 149–165

Chapter 3
Trafficking of Ethiopian women to Europe – making choices, taking risks, and implications
Anne Kubai
African and Black Diaspora: An International Journal, volume 9, issue 2 (July 2016) pp. 166–183

Chapter 4
Determinants of diaspora policy engagement of Ethiopians in the Netherlands
Katie Kuschminder and Melissa Siegel
African and Black Diaspora: An International Journal, volume 9, issue 2 (July 2016) pp. 184–199

CITATION INFORMATION

Chapter 5
Ethiopian taxicab drivers: forming an occupational niche in the US Capital
Elizabeth Chacko
African and Black Diaspora: An International Journal, volume 9, issue 2 (July 2016)
pp. 200–213

Chapter 6
Ethiopian female labor migration to the Gulf states: the case of Kuwait
Faiz Omar Mohammad Jamie and Anwar Hassan Tsega
African and Black Diaspora: An International Journal, volume 9, issue 2 (July 2016)
pp. 214–227

Chapter 7
'Deported before experiencing the good sides of migration': Ethiopians returning from Saudi Arabia
Marina de Regt and Medareshaw Tafesse
African and Black Diaspora: An International Journal, volume 9, issue 2 (July 2016)
pp. 228–242

Chapter 8
The return migration experiences of Ethiopian women trafficked to Bahrain: '…for richer or poorer, let me be on the hands of my people …'
Adamnesh Atnafu and Margaret E. Adamek
African and Black Diaspora: An International Journal, volume 9, issue 2 (July 2016)
pp. 243–256

Chapter 9
Migration, gender, and mobility: Ethiopian–Israeli women's narratives of career trajectories
Yarden Fanta-Vagenshtein and Lisa Anteby-Yemini
African and Black Diaspora: An International Journal, volume 9, issue 2 (July 2016)
pp. 257–273

Chapter 10
Bole to Harlem via Tel Aviv: networks of Ethiopia's musical diaspora
Ilana Webster-Kogen
African and Black Diaspora: An International Journal, volume 9, issue 2 (July 2016)
pp. 274–289

Chapter 11
'No place like home': experiences of an Ethiopian migrant in the host country and as a returnee to the homeland
Adamnesh Atnafu and Margaret E. Adamek
African and Black Diaspora: An International Journal, volume 9, issue 2 (July 2016)
pp. 290–301

For any permission-related enquiries please visit:
http://www.tandfonline.com/page/help/permissions

Notes on Contributors

Margaret E. Adamek is the Director of the PhD Program in Social Work, Indiana University, Bloomington, IN, USA.

Lisa Anteby-Yemini is based at the Women's Studies Research Center & Israeli Studies, Brandeis University, Waltham, MA, USA.

Adamnesh Atnafu is an Assistant Professor at the School of Social Work, Addis Ababa University, Ethiopia.

Elizabeth Chacko is an Associate Professor of Geography and International Relations at The George Washington University, Washington, DC, USA.

Fassil Demissie is a faculty member in the Department of Public Policy at DePaul University, Chicago, IL, USA. He is the co-editor of *African and Black Diaspora: An International Journal*.

Marina de Regt is an Assistant Professor in Social and Cultural Anthropology, VU, Amsterdam, The Netherlands.

Yordanos Seifu Estifanos is based at the University of Oldenburg, European Masters in Migration and Intercultural Relations (EMMIR) Consortium, Oldenburg, Germany.

Yarden Fanta-Vagenshtein is a Senior Associate Fellow at Brandeis University, Waltham, MA, USA.

Solomon M. Gofie is an Assistant Professor in the Department of Political Science and International Relations, Addis Ababa University, Ethiopia.

Faiz Omar Mohammad Jamie is based at the Center for Peace and Development Studies, University of Bahri, Khartoum, Sudan.

Anne Kubai is an Assistant Professor of World Christianity and Interreligious Relations at the Department of Theology, Uppsala University, Sweden.

Katie Kuschminder is a PhD Fellow in Migration and Development at the Maastricht Graduate School of Governance, United Nations University, Maastricht, The Netherlands.

Melissa Siegel is an Associated Researcher at the Maastricht Graduate School of Governance, United Nations University, Maastricht, The Netherlands.

NOTES ON CONTRIBUTORS

Medareshaw Tafesse is a Lecturer and Researcher at Ethiopian Police University College, Sendafa, Ethiopia.

Anwar Hassan Tsega is based at the Center for Peace and Development Studies, University of Bahri, Khartoum, Sudan.

Ilana Webster-Kogen is a faculty member at the School of African and Oriental Studies, University of London, UK.

Tanya Zack is based at the Planning Department, School of Architecture and Planning, University of the Witwatersrand, Johannesburg, South Africa.

Living across worlds and oceans – an introduction

Fassil Demissie

DePaul University, Chicago, IL, USA

'I have no future in Ethiopia, … I've seen Europe on TV, and it's better.'*

The movement of people across national frontiers both voluntary and involuntary is reshaping societies and politics across the world and has emerged to be one of the most contentious and challenging issues in the contemporary world. Given the different projections of the number of international migrants, no one for sure knows how many international migrants are there. The United Nations Population Division estimated that for mid-year 2005, the number of international migrants stood at 191 million. By 2007, the figure approached 200 million or approximately 3 percent of the world's population of 6.5 billion people. The number of migrants who live outside their country of birth is projected to reach 230 million by 2050 (United Nations 2006, 9). In addition, there are hundreds of million more people who been displaced within their countries of origin. According to the estimates by the United Nations, the total number of international migrants in Africa rose from 9 million in 1960 to 16 million in 2000. The largest increase occurred between 1960 and 1980, when the number of international migrants in Africa rose from 9 million to 14 million (United Nations 2003a, 2003b).

Today, migration of people across borders and demographic mobility lie at the core of the ongoing process of globalization. Globalization has come to describe the trends and initiatives aimed to restructure the global economy and the free flow of capital, information and technology but not labor. Given the vast literature on the topic of globalization, one approach is to characterize the process as 'the widening, deepening and speeding up of the worldwide interconnectedness in all aspect of contemporary life' (Held, McGrew, and Perraton 1999, 2). A fundamental component of the process of globalization is a rapid increase in cross-border flows of all sort, starting with finance and trade, but also democracy, good governance, cultural and media product, environmental pollution and – most importantly – people (Castles and Miller 2009, 5). A multitude of factors are involved that push people to move temporarily or permanently, nationally and transnationally, individually or in groups, return to their countries of origin, or migrate to another country, or move cyclically between two or more countries. Furthermore, migration is no longer limited to particular clearly identifiable human groups as in the past: the range of the types of persons who involved in those migration affects the social reproduction of their families and the development of their communities of origin is increasingly broad, and in their places of final

---

*Abdirizak Mohamed Mohamoud. Accessed January 21, 2016. http://www.irinnews.org/report/94279/ethiopia-cautionary-migration-tales-are-no-deterrent.

destination, they establish links with diverse social groups, build temporary and complex networks of contacts which stretch across transnational borders, and use different social, political and economic strategies and means for their movements, enhancing the ability of migrants and diaspora groups to live simultaneously both 'here' and 'there'.

The causes of these population movements across national frontiers or within regions and between countries are driven by a complex set of factors, including the impact of globalization, civil war, poverty, and environmental degradation affecting more countries in the global South which has dramatically increased the number of people migrating in search of new opportunities and a better life, which takes many different forms: people migrating as manual workers, highly qualified specialists, entrepreneurs, refugees or as family members of previous migrants (Castles and Miller 2009, 4). The migration patterns of these individuals and groups are far more complex and it is no longer possible to draw a simple trajectory between points of departure and arrival of migrants or to classify countries as desired destinations.

In the last three decades, the Horn of Africa has been transformed into the epicenter for Cold War rivalry, prolonged civil war, poverty, environmental degradation, and political, economic and food crises, compounded by repressive governments resulting in migration of people on an unprecedented scale across national borders. Writing for *Foreign Affairs*, Prendergast and Thomas-Jensen (2007) noted that the Horn of Africa (Ethiopia, Southern Sudan, Eritrea, Sudan, Djibouti, Somalia, Kenya and Uganda) has emerged to be 'the hottest conflict zone in the world … [where] … violent wars of the last half century have ripped the region apart' generating a massive displacement of people both nationally and internationally. As of March 2013, there were over 9 million refugees and internally displaced persons in the region (IMO 2014). Apart from the migration and refugee population originating in each of these countries, some of the countries have also been host to large refugee populations from other neighboring states.

The migration of Ethiopians across international borders is a recent phenomenon because of the limited integration of the country and society to the global economy. Unlike other colonized countries, Ethiopia was never colonized (except for a brief Italian occupation during 1936–1941) and its economy and society were not directly impacted by ebb and flows of the global economy to generate international migration. Much of the population movement in Ethiopia was due to a complex set of factors beginning in the nineteenth century. However, the gradual incorporation of the country into the global economy particularly since the postwar when Emperor Haile Selassie began a modernization program aimed at opening the economy and society through the introduction of Western education and the flow of foreign capital in the incipient industrial, commercial, and agricultural sectors. The period also saw the gradual restructuring of the Ethiopian state to facilitate the activities of foreign capital and for managing and streamlining the activities of the bureaucracy. This particular process rested on two pillars; Zewde (1984) argued that two factors were critical in the formation of the modern Ethiopian state during the postwar period: first, the decisive role of Western imperialism which facilitated the rise of the Ethiopian 'modern state' and second, the coercive capacity of the state to carry out repression against the local population. Both these factors facilitated Ethiopia's integration into the orbit of global economy.

ETHIOPIANS IN AN AGE OF MIGRATION

The intensification of commodity production and exchange and the growth in communication within the country as a whole began to undermine the traditional system of power relations in rural areas leading to the concentration of power in the emerging urban-based oligarchy whose economic and political interest coincided with the new political economy of the country (Hiwet 1975).

During this long period (1940–1970), no measurable international migration of Ethiopians took place until the early 1970s. For example, the late Sociologist, Levine (1965) has estimated that only 35 Ethiopians migrated to the Europe and North America between 1876 and 1922. Although the figure appears to be low for the period, there is no national or international data available to indicate the extent of Ethiopian migration across international borders. To streamline the staffing of the emerging new state, the Emperor took active interest in sending Ethiopian students, primarily drawn from the landed aristocracy and nobility to study in American and European Universities. These individuals were carefully selected from loyal members of the aristocracy and upon their return; they occupied key positions within the new state. Similarly, young members of the Ethiopian armed forces and police were also sent to American and European elite military institutions for further training as part of the institutionalization of the new state. Levine (1965, 45) notes that between 1941 and 1974 an estimated 20,000 Ethiopian left the country to pursue high education abroad who were mostly men and the number of Ethiopian seeking political asylum abroad during the period was very limited. Between 1951 and 1960, US immigration statistics indicated that only 61 Ethiopians were granted asylum status and for the next decade, 1961–1970, only two Ethiopian were granted asylum (Terrazas 2007). For the most part, the number of Ethiopian international migration or seeking asylum abroad was very limited until the demise of Emperor Haile Selassie in 1974.

Ethiopia is one of the countries with a large number of diaspora in North America, Europe, and the Middle East. The UN 2008 Revised Population Database shows that 546,000 Ethiopian migrants live in different parts of the world. This estimate is very small compared to the official estimation given by the Ministry of Foreign Affairs of Ethiopia which put the number of Ethiopian migrants to be about 1 million (Teferi and Bruk 2009) (Table 1).

Table 1. Ethiopia's migrant stock from 1970 to 2010 (in thousands).

Indicator	1970	1975	1980	1985	1990	1995	2000	2005	2010
Estimated number of international migrants at mid-year	395	392	404	584	1,155	795	662	554	548
Estimated number of refugees at mid-year	21	9	11	180	42	371	228	108	91
Population at mid-year	30	34	37	43	48	57	66	75	85
Estimated number of female migrants at mid-year	171	175	184	268	548	376	312	261	258
Estimated number of male migrants at mid-year	223	217	220	315	607	419	351	293	290
International migrants as a percentage of the population	1.3	1.1	1.1	1.3	2.4	1.4	1	0.7	0.6
Female migrants as percentage of all international migrants	43.4	44.7	45.5	46	47.4	47.3	47.1	47.1	47.1
Refugees as a percentage of international migrants	5.2	2.2	2.7	30.9	64.2	46.7	34.4	19.6	16.6

Source: Cited in Assaminew et al. (2010), p. 5.

Internal migration

The first large-scale population movement within and out of Ethiopian began in the aftermath of the 1974 military overthrow of Emperor Haile Selassie and the famine of 1973–1974 which created a unique circumstance in the country's history for mass displacement. Although famine is not new to the country's long history, periodic famine generated by lack of rain, antiquated land-use system, deforestation, overgrazing, and the inability of subsistence agriculture to generate sufficient surplus often led people to migrate to other parts of the country (Pankhurst 1985). The confluence of these factors in 1973–1974 produced the worst famine in the county's history killing an estimated 300,000 people in the northern part of the country, particularly in Wallo, Tigray, Northern Shoa, Eritrea, Harerghe, and Begemindir, and displacing hundreds of thousands of people.

The massive displacement of Ethiopians, internally by famine, war, and rural poverty was followed by a campaign of political repression by the military government popularly known as the *Derge* which launched the 'Red Terror' program in response to a series of political assignations carried out by one of the main opposition parties – the Ethiopian People's Revolutionary Party (EPRP) – to its rule. Human rights abuses, arbitrary arrests, torture, and murder on a scale unknown were carried out both in the main cities most notably in Addis Ababa and rural areas. It was one of the most systematic uses of state power to eliminate political opposition to the military rule. The exact number of people who perished in *the Red Terror* campaign as well in the assignations carried out by the EPRP remains unknown. Although the number is in thousands, those killed by the government were far greater than those killed by the EPRP. Subsequent developments in the country further led to dislocation of people in the Eastern and Central Ethiopia because of the war between Ethiopia and Somalia, which erupted in 1977. The secessionist war in Northern Ethiopia also accelerated the cross-border movement of people to neighboring countries, especially Sudan and Yemen. Hundreds of thousands of people fled war-torn areas (Tiruneh 1993).

The military government's ill-conceived and poorly planned villaglization and resettlement programs of rural peasants beginning in 1985 compounded the dislocation of the local population in the Northern and Eastern part because of the civil war. Estimate varies as to the actual number of rural peasants who were forced into the villagization and resettlement programs. The objectives of these programs were to group scattered farming communities throughout the country into small village clusters in order to promote rational land use; conserve resources; provide access to clean water and to health and education services; and strengthen security. Critics of the military regime suggested that these policy measures were primarily designed as a counterinsurgency measure program to deprive the various ethnic-based insurgency in northern and eastern Ethiopia for their operations. As the *African Watch Report* (1991, 4) noted,

> The Ethiopian case stands out as particularly destructive because of the extraordinarily prolonged level of sustained violence and the frequent lack of any compensatory assistance to the relocated and restricted population. Because of the fragile rural economy and the dependence of rural people on mobility and a range of economic activities, this was particularly damaging, and a major contributor to famine (de Waal 1991).

Due to international criticism, deteriorating security conditions, and lack of resources doomed the program to failure. On the eve of the military government's demise, the regime announced that it is abandoning villagization and would now adopt new economic policies of free-market reforms and a relaxation of centralized planning.

A number of problems complicated the resettlement program of the military government. Rahmato (2004) sums up the challenge faced by the regime in the following way.

> During the period 1984–1986, the *Derge* resettled some 600,000 people mostly in the lowlands of western Ethiopia. In this same period, some 33,000 settlers lost their lives due to disease, hunger, and exhaustion, and thousands of the families were broken up.

In 2010, the Ethiopian People's Revolutionary Democratic Front (EPRDF) which replaced the military government commenced an ambitious villagization program to settle 1.5 million individuals, who primarily subsist on (agro-) pastoralism and shifting cultivation. This program is taking place in the four 'emerging' regional states: Afar, Benishangul-Gumuz, Gambella, and Somali. The current villagization scheme is unfolding at a time of considerable interest in the intensification of large-scale commercial agriculture. Local and international opponents of the scheme argue that what is taking place is a 'forced relocation' of indigenous people from their ancestral land in Gambella, South Omo, and other lowlands of the country (especially in Afar, Benishangul-Gumuz, and Somali). Despite the local and international resistance against the villagization scheme by human rights organizations, the government has accelerated the implementation of the program and by mid-2013; it was reported that the villagization targets were met in Gambella, with more than 90 percent of the 45,000 households relocated into new villages (Erda 2014).

Mass displacement and emergence of Ethiopian diaspora

As indicated above, the internal political, economic, and social crisis within Ethiopia largely accounts for the cross borer flow of Ethiopian migrants, refugees, and the formation of the diaspora. The dichotomy between migrants and refugees has become increasingly blurred, as it is increasingly difficult to distinguish between people to migrate to escape poverty, and those who are fleeing because they fear for their life due to war or ethnic conflict. At a time of increased economic growth, massive infusion of international capital, and the desire of the EPRDF to achieve a middle-income country status, more people are fleeing the country to neighboring countries, including South Africa, Middle East, Gulf States, Europe, and North America. As Magill Dyess Martini argued,

> the Ethiopian government has maintained a claim of double digit growth for the last decade while the number of young migrants has increased year after year. In any real-world situation when a country experiences exponential growth gainful employment and income must also increase. If this were truly the case then one would expect to see the numbers of undocumented migrants decrease. It is difficult to eliminate migration all together, but it would have to decrease if economic opportunity were to increase. The truth is that there must be something wrong with how this growth has translated for the working youth.

The migration of young despite the 'double digit growth' rate in Ethiopia originates as Magill Dyess Martini from the fundamental contradiction of what she calls the 'impact of the glitz economy'. While the economy was booming, opportunities for the country's young people are very limited especially for those who are not members of the ruling party.

> Young people unfairly see new recreation centers, new homes and new hotels but they can't afford them. They see luxurious cars but they cannot even afford taxis or buses and the like. This dilemma can damage the psychology of the new generation and as a result, they may wish to escape to a world where opportunities are accessible. So again, this type of growth might be a reason for young people to make the dangerous journey abroad. (Martini 2015)

Table 2 provides some indication of the number of Ethiopian refugees who receive assistance from the UNHCR.

Table 2. Ethiopian refugees – January 2009 by host countries.

Country	Total number of refugees in a country	Assisted by UNHCR
Kenya	23,500	23,500
Somalia	5,600	5,600
Sudan	16,523	10,050
Yemen	800	800
Other countries	37,160	
Asylum seekers	1,667	
Total	85,250	

Source: UNHCR (2009). Cited in Fransen and Kuschminder (2009).

Apart from the consequence of high unemployment, especially among the youth (Mains 2012) that is plaguing the country, demographic mobility and human displacement have been provoked by other factors including authoritarian rule and the accompanying political repression. Critics of the government point out that human right violation, lack of freedom of expression, monopoly of power, and control of businesses by entities affiliated with the ruling party, often create a climate of hopelessness, and encourage people to migrate seeking better opportunities elsewhere. Indeed, international migration from Ethiopia is a particular coping strategy for family members to generate resources to support the family and enable them to make investments in education, health, and housing reducing vulnerability. In addition, migration could also be considered as improving the social status of families (ICMPD 2008, 14).

Ethiopian diaspora

One major consequence of mass migration in the era of globalization is the emergence of the Ethiopian diaspora located primarily in Europe, North America but also in Australia and other parts of the world. While a significant percentage of Ethiopians in this category who have fled from political persecution could aptly be described as 'refugees', and others would more appropriately be classified as 'economic migrants'. Even those who have applied for political asylum in Western countries following their escape could hardly classify themselves as 'refugees' – a clear indication of the complexities of human displacement in the age of globalization.

The Ethiopian diaspora constitutes a distinctive community dispersed and living across worlds and oceans bound by a common feeling of collectivity and shared history of homeland. The majority of the Ethiopian diaspora are concentrated in North America, Europe, Middle East, Australia, and New Zealand. Members of the Ethiopian diaspora could also be found in such places as Ghana, Uzbekistan, Guinea, Serbia and Montenegro, and South Africa.

International trafficking of domestic workers

In the last two decades, the migration (both legal and clandestine) of Ethiopian female domestic workers to globalizing cities of the Middle East and Gulf States particularly, to Dubai, Beirut, Riyadh, Abu Dhabi, Doha, Sana'a, and Cairo has increased dramatically because of the promise of globalization and neoliberal economic policies which ushered in increased free trade, deregulation, and privatization. Pushed by poverty and destitution, Ethiopian female domestic workers face hardship, violence, and abuse by their employers (Anbesse et al. 2009, 560). One graphic illustration of the plight is the number of female bodies returning to Addis Ababa because of suicide from such cities as Jeddah, Dubai, and Beirut.

The exact number of Ethiopian domestic workers in the Middle East and Gulf States is not known. However, an estimated 20,000–25,000 Ethiopian domestic workers live and work in Lebanon, a significant number of whom are trafficked. Women trafficked to the Gulf for domestic labor go via legal or illegal employment agencies. With illegal agencies, often women are introduced to agents via family or friends, they usually pay some of the agent's fee in advance, and the rest is deducted from their pay once they begin work (GTZ 2003).

Table 3 illustrates the source of Ethiopian domestic workers and the number of female domestic workers has increased dramatically over the years with Saudi Arabia and Kuwait absorbing the highest number of labor migrants, respectively. Compared to other regional states, the city of Addis Ababa shows a relatively lower increasing rate in the number of migrating domestic workers. Given the dire economic circumstance in the rural areas as well as sharp increase in poverty among rural households, the majority of migrant domestic workers now come from regional states other than the capital.

The collection in this special issue of *African and Black Diaspora: An International* (ABD) grew out of discussions with colleagues in the USA, France, and Ethiopia regarding the need to bring scholars from different fields together for a critical reflection about Ethiopian migrants and diaspora in different parts of the world at a time when globalization is creating new complexities of human displacement. What has emerged from these scholarly works in recognition that Ethiopian migrants and diaspora although separated by

Table 3. Regional distribution of domestic workers 2008–2013.

Region	September 2008–August 2009	September 2009–August 2010	September 2010–August 2011	September 2011–June 2012	July 2012–February 2013
Tigray	949	573	1,582	8,592	4,966
Amhara	3,551	1,952	10,769	62,836	33,831
Oromia	3,600	2,757	10,430	64,431	39,185
Southern Nations, Nationalities and Peoples	1,981	1,300	4,547	23,392	13,813
Addis Ababa	7,251	6,860	11,813	26,774	11,472
Total	17,332	13,442	39,141	186,025	103,267

Source: Woldemichael (2013).

oceans and worlds and their lives crisscrossed by politics, ethnicity, class, gender, and age are carving out a social and material world born out of their particular circumstances both 'here' and 'there'.

Acknowledgements

I would to extend my special thanks and appreciation to Kim C. Damian and the Production Staff of ABD at Taylor and Francis.

Disclosure statement

No potential conflict of interest was reported by the author.

References

Anbesse, B., C. Hanlon, A. Alem, S. Packer, and R. Whitley. 2009. "Migration and Mental Health: A Study of Low Income Ethiopian Working in Middle Eastern Countries." *International Journal of Social Psychiatry* 55 (6): 557–568.

Assaminew, E., Getachew Ahmed, Kassahun Aberra, and Tewodros Makonnen. 2010. "International Migration, Remittances and Poverty Alleviation in Ethiopia." Working Paper No 1/2010 Ethiopian Economics Association/Ethiopian Economics Policy Research Institute.

Castles, Stephen, and Mark Miller. 2009. *The Age of Migration: International Populations Movements in the Modern World.* 4th ed. New York: Guilford Press.

Erda, Fana. 2014. "Social Engineering or Forced Relocation in Ethiopia's Lowlands." In *African Up Close.* Accessed February 1, 2016. https://africaupclose.wilsoncenter.org/author/fana/

Fransen, S., and Kate Kuschminder. 2009. *Migration in Ethiopia: History, Current Trends and Future Prospects.* Maastricht: Maastricht Graduate School of Governance.

GTZ. 2003. Study on Trafficking in Women in East Africa: A situational analysis including current NGO and Governmental activities, as well as future opportunities, to address trafficking in women and girls in Ethiopia, Kenya, Tanzania, Uganda and Nigeria.

Held, D., A. Goldblatt McGrew, and J. Perraton. 1999. *Global Transformations: Politics, Economics and Culture.* Cambridge, MA: Policy.

Hiwet, Addis. 1975. *Ethiopia: From Autocracy to Revolution.* London: Review of the African Political Economy.

ICMPD (International Centre for Migration Policy Development). 2008. *Gaps and Needs Analysis Country Reports: Libya, Ethiopia and Kenya.* Vienna: ICMPD.

Levine, David. 1965. *Wax and Gold: Tradition and Innovation in Ethiopian Culture.* Chicago, IL: University of Chicago Press.

Mains, D. 2012. *Hope is Cut: Youth, Unemployment and the Future in Urban Ethiopia.* Philadelphia, PA: Temple University Press.

Martini, Magill Dyess. 2015. "Ethiopia and Horn of Africa Migration: Push or Pull?" In *MADOTE*, http://www.madote.com/2015/05/ethiopia-and-horn-of-africa-migration.html

OECD (International Migration Outlook). 2014. Accessed January 30, 2016. http://www.oecd-ilibrary.org/docserver/download/8114101e.pdf?expires=1455067372&id=id&accname=ocid56017179&checksum=34848646451E00BDBD37260BCE20713B

Pankhurst, Richard. 1985. *The History of Famine and Epidemics in Ethiopia Prior to the Twentieth Century.* Relief and Rehabilitation Commission.

Prendergast, John, and Colin Thomas-Jensen. 2007. "Blowing the Horn." *Foreign Affairs* 86 (2): 59–74.

Rahmato, D. 2004. *Searching for Tenure Security? The Land Policy and New Initiative in Ethiopia, Forum of Social Studies.* Addis Ababa.

Teferi, M., and A. Bruk. 2009. "Remittance Inflows and Country Experience: The Practice and the Potential for Improvements." In *Proceedings of the Sixth International Conference on the Ethiopian Economy, Volume I*, edited by Getnet Alemu. Addis Ababa: Ethiopian Economics Association.

Terrazas, Aaron Matteo. 2007. "Beyond Regional Circularity: The Emergence of an Ethiopian Diaspora." In *Migration Policy Institute*. Accessed February 8, 2016. http://www.migrationpolicy.org/article/beyond-regional-circularity-emergence-ethiopian-diaspora

Tiruneh, Andargachew. 1993. *The Ethiopian Revolution, 1974–1987: A Transformation from an Aristocratic to a Totalitarian Autocracy.* Cambridge: Cambridge University Press.

United Nations. 2003a. *World Population Prospects: The 2002 Revision*, Vol. I: Comprehensive Tables, E.03.XIII.6.

United Nations. 2003b. *Trends in Total Migrant Stock: 1960–2000*, 2003 Revision, POP/DB/MIG/Rev.2003.

United Nations. 2006. *Trends in Total Migration Stock: The 2005 Revision, CD-ROM Documentation.* Department of Economic and Social Affairs Division.

United Nations High Commission on Refugees (UNHCR). 2009. Accessed January 15, 2016. http://www.unhcr.org

de Waal, Alex. 1991. *Evil Days: Thirty Years of War and Famine in Ethiopia.* New York: Human Rights.

Woldemichael, Selamawit Bekele. 2013. "The Vulnerability of Ethiopian Rural Women and Girls: The Case of Domestic Workers in Saudi Arabia and Kuwait." Unpublished MA Thesis, Uppsala University.

Zewde, Behru. 1984. "Economic Origins of the Absolutist State in Ethiopia (1916–1935)." *Journal of Ethiopian Studies* 17 (November): 1–29.

Emigrants and the state in Ethiopia: transnationalism and the challenges of political antagonism

Solomon M. Gofie

Department of Political Science and International Relations, Addis Ababa University, Addis Ababa, Ethiopia

ABSTRACT
Since the fall of military-socialist government in 1991 in Ethiopia, the Ethiopian Peoples' Revolutionary Democratic Front (EPRDF) has embarked on the total restructuring of the state. It has presented 'Nations, Nationalities, and Peoples' as an 'organizing principle' and it has been working towards the rebuilding of the Ethiopian state along this line. The focus of this paper is EPRDF's policies and practices of engagement of Ethiopian emigrants. The analysis is based on information and interviews with government officials in Addis Ababa and with Ethiopian migrants in Washington DC during February–May 2013. This study indicates that the EPRDF government gradually started to focus its attention on Ethiopian migrants around the world, mainly due to the growing economic significance of their transnational engagement in Ethiopia. The study also shows the circumstances in which political debates about the conditions in Ethiopia has been permeating interactions within Ethiopians emigrants.

Introduction

Emigration in the case of Ethiopia since the modern times has taken place in the context of the wars of conquest, modernization, and centralization drives of the imperial state since the late nineteenth century. Resistance to imperial rule by regionally based groups may have induced more and more outmigration of political dissidents during the late 1890s and early nineteenth century (Bahru et al. 2010; Gebru 1996). Christian and Muslim religious pilgrims to Jerusalem and Mecca, the Italian invasion in 1930, the desire to pursue modern education, added to the dynamics of emigration during the period of the 1940s–1960s (Bahru et al. 2010).

The emergence of political groups that challenged the feudal order in the 1970s and the repressions that followed led to the formation of Ethiopia's early 'political diaspora' in the Western countries. Among others, an organization of dissenting Ethiopian students – named the Ethiopian Students Union in North America (ESUNA) – was formed in the early 1970s in America (Alem 1990). This was followed by the departure in large number of Ethiopians during and after the revolution that brought the monarchy to its end in 1974. The 'Red Terror' unleashed by the military-socialist regime – the Derg against those it considered its political enemies, in which thousands were killed – gave rise to what has been popularly called the 'first generation' of Ethiopian migrants in North America and Europe.

The change of government in 1991 and the subsequent separation of Eritrea from Ethiopia brought about a new context for emigration in the post 1991 period. Following the Ethiopian Peoples' Revolutionary Democratic Front's (EPRDF) and its allies overthrow of the Military-socialist government, 'Nations, Nationalities, and Peoples' became an 'organizing principle' of the state in Ethiopia. This led to two mutually reinforcing and at times contradictory trends. First, since the fall of the military-socialist government in May 1991, the discourse of 'ethnic' identity has guided the political strategy which is equated with an 'organizing principle' of the state. The formalization of such through a federal system in which 'Nations, Nationalities, and Peoples' supposedly reign supreme has become the major feature of political dynamics in Ethiopia currently. And the 1995 Constitution (Art. 39) provides for 'the right to self-determination including and up to secession'. Secondly, the reorganization of the state in Ethiopia along these lines has set in dynamics of far-reaching consequences, featuring prominently in the state's strategies of engaging individuals and groups within the Ethiopian society at home and abroad in its 'peace, democracy, and development' agenda. Essentially, the political framework based on 'ethnic-linguistic' criteria being institutionalized requires individuals to identify themselves, with one of 'the Nations, Nationalities, and Peoples'. This means that in the transnational dealings of the Ethiopian government, emigrants of Ethiopian origin would be encouraged to organize along the ethos of 'Nations, Nationalities, and Peoples' (Merera 2003). This brought about new dynamics of belongings of Ethiopian emigrants in a transnational context.

As the EPRDF kept working on consolidating its power domestically, it gradually started to engage with Ethiopian migrants abroad. It appears that one of the first such opportunities to engage Ethiopians from abroad in large number arose during the Ethio-Eritrean war (1998–2000). The conflict created a situation where the government was forced to mobilize people and resources within the country as well as from outside. Delegations composed of government officials, academics, and renowned individuals were sent to the USA, Europe, and the Middle East, visiting different cities and conducting series of meetings with 'the diaspora' on how to help the government's war effort. In the aftermath of the war, the government introduced as one of its foreign policy purposes what is called 'economic diplomacy'. While the scope of the purported 'economic diplomacy' of the government is broad in scope, this could possibly involve public relations activities in the form of promotion of Ethiopian produces such as coffee, investment promotion, providing information about the availability of land and other economic resources for overseas investment. It also links with the search for financial resources in the form of investment, trade, foreign aid and loans. This followed periods of liberalization, privatization, and market economy dispensations of the regime during its first decade in power. It appears that the discourse of 'economic diplomacy' links well with the perspective that presents migrants or the 'diaspora as resource' that has gained prominence in recent times, following similar discourses taking place at the continental and international level (MOFA, March 2002). Such an understanding of the role of emigrants is predicated on the assumption that economic development is non-political, an arena of potential consensus between the government and those who politically oppose it, especially those in North America and Europe. In other words the language of economic development, investment, and poverty reduction are understood on the part of the state and its proponents as an approach to dissuading migrants from politically opposing the incumbent, and to persuade them to join 'the forces of peace, democracy and development' (Merera 2003).

Nevertheless, political instability has continued to give rise to significant migration out of the country in the post 1991 period. This is the case where thousands of former Ethiopian army members as well as officials and their families had to flee the country as the combined forces of Tigrian People's Liberation Front (TPLF)/EPRDF and Eritrean People's Liberation Frontforces took power in Addis Ababa and Asmara, respectively. The mass airlifting of Ethiopians to Israel and the fallout between the incumbent EPRDF and its allies such as the Oromo Liberation Front that brought about the downfall of the former military-socialist regime in Ethiopia have led to outmigration of tens of thousands of Ethiopians to the outside world in the post Derg period. The Ethio-Eritrean war of 1998–2000 leading to the departure of tens of thousands of those identified as Eritreans, the US diversity visa program, and economic hardships and perceived opportunities abroad and the post 2005 elections crisis set in motion new dynamics for outmigration from the country. The youth have continued to leave the country at an alarming rate despite the risks evidenced by recent tragic incidents involving this category of the Ethiopian population. Thousands of young people traverse Sudanese, Egyptian, and Libyan deserts to reach the Mediterranean a gateway to Europe. Djibouti, Somalia, Somaliland, Kenya, and Uganda are gateways to the Arabian world and to Southern Africa. Many lives have been lost on the high seas, the Arabian Peninsula, and in south eastern Africa. Many of those who arrived at places such as Yemen have been subjected to untold human suffering at the hands of their captors.[1]

Conceptual clarifications

This section briefly discusses some conceptual issues relevant to the discussions in this study. Migration and transnationalism are the key conceptual themes of analysis here. To begin, migration (human) refers to a 'change of usual place of dwelling which can be across city, regions or international boundary lines' (Adamnesh 2008, 1). Migration denotes not only the movement of individuals from one place to another but also it conjures images of a very complex history of movement of masses of people over centuries. While, rural–urban migration has been the most common aspect of internal migration, international migration which is the focus of this study refers to varying circumstances in which individuals or groups of people flee or leave their countries of origin and seek to work or settle in another country. According to Hear (1998), the term migrant encompasses diverse groups of people including settlers, temporary contract workers, professionals, refugees, and asylum seekers. In differentiating two closely related terminologies, emigration denotes the act of fleeing the country of origin, whereas immigration refers to entering a destination country. In the context of this study, the term emigrant is applicable in characterizing Ethiopians who left the country in different periods and are now residing in different countries around the world; and those in Washington DC area are the focus of this study.

Diaspora is a concept that is closely related to migration. According to Hear 'diasporas comprises of individuals, and communities that may have migrated several times; they include people who carry the historical baggage of migration, sojourns who have accumulated substantial migratory cultural capital' (1998, 51). Here, it is worth noting that the term in the Ethiopian context today while increasingly becoming common, is no longer used in its conventional sense. Traditionally, the concept of diaspora was used to describe a specific group of people denoting the circumstances of their historic dispersal as well as survival, for instance in the sense of 'the Black Diaspora' or 'the Jewish Diaspora'. In Ethiopia, nowadays the term is synonymously used with the term emigrants, referring to anyone of an Ethiopian origin living or working abroad. Consequently, the term diaspora is widely applied and it has come to include those who very recently left the country, including those through the US government Diversity Visa program popularly known in Ethiopia as DV. Such unwarranted reference to the term is not limited to its use by the general public in Ethiopia. State officials, academics, International Government Organizations/ Non-Government Organizations are all disposed to employ the term without any qualification.

In addition to the above, there are various perspectives on migration informed by the discourses of globalization. One of them, new economic theory of migration maintains that 'family decision making' and 'risk diversification schemes' are central to the dynamics of modern migration (Bijak 2006). Another theory of recent import-cumulative causation theory understands migration as an evolutionary process contributing to development dynamics in countries of origin as well as countries of destination (Faist 2000). It argues that emigration fosters positive economic development in countries of origin while helping to fill the labor force supply gap in countries of destination (Massey et al. 2011). There is also a 'network theory' of international migration. As a relatively new perspective of migration, network theory focuses on the ties connecting migrants-kinship and shared experiences wherein interpersonal ties play considerable roles in sustaining the practices of migration (De Haas 2008).

It is understandable that no single theoretical perspective on migration or diaspora fully captures the dynamics, the nature of state policies, transnational migrant belonging, and practices. In the context of this study, however, it requires thinking beyond mainstream theories or perspectives on migration mentioned above some of which relate to recent discourses on globalization. It would require an approach capable of capturing the key issues of discussion in this paper. As observed from the cursory reference to the various theoretical perspectives on migration, there seems to be one thing in common, that is, the interaction of political and economic forces underlying the whole notion of migration (Bush 2008). In this respect, the concept being currently widely used in the studies of migration, as in many areas, is transnationalism. In the social science literature, especially in political science and its sub-field international relations, it appears that the use of the term 'transnational' has superseded its predecessor –'international'. It could be stated that the proliferation of actors, the wider recognition of non-state actors especially since the 1990s, has given rise to the frequent use of the term 'transnational' (Henderson 1997). We have come to see a situation where the term transnational is being viewed as more inclusive of ideas, institutions, actors, their interactions and the outcomes thereof. The multiplicity of actors in the international system and the complex interactions mean that emigrant communities or the diaspora are increasingly understood as actors in transnational relations. Such an approach enables us to identify the key actors involved, their purposes and interests, the forms of interaction among them, the outcomes and the broader implications. It is in this framework that the paper attempts to explain the strategies and policies of the state in Ethiopia in its dealings with migrants and the exploration of the latter's belonging and practices in a transnational context.

From dissociation to active engagement of migrants: developments in state policies and institutions

In the post Derg period, the immediate focus of the EPRDF regime was the maintenance of power it took from the former military-socialist regime and the consolidation of the same by deploying various strategies in dealing with the different sections of the Ethiopian population domestically. Far away emigrants were not a factor of immediate concern, compared to the task of maintaining power and dealing with myriads of issues of domestic, regional, and international ramifications for the regime. Therefore, during its early years in power, for the EPRDF government the situation was more of dissociation than actively engaging Ethiopian emigrants across the board.

Gradually, however, the ruling EPRDF began to encourage groups and individuals, especially those who were active supporters and members of the TPLF/EPRDF during the war with the military government, to return and take part in its 'peace, democracy, development' dispensations (Bahru et al. 2010). The demise of the military-socialist government in 1991 means that some of the individuals and groups who left the country mainly because of the repression could return. As mentioned previously the realization on the part of the regime of Emigrants' economic, political, and social roles in Ethiopia was apparent in the post Ethio-Eritrean war of 1998–2000.

The Ministry of Foreign Affairs (MOFA) has been at the forefront of representing the government in its dealings with Ethiopian migrants abroad. Its main function, in this respect, was:

> to serve as a liaison between the different Ministries and Ethiopians abroad, to encourage the active involvement of expatriates in socio-economic activities of Ethiopia to safeguard the rights and privileges of Ethiopians abroad and to mobilize Ethiopians abroad for sustained and organized image building. (MOFA 2001)

High-level state officials often made frequent visits to different cities around the world, especially those hosting large number of Ethiopian migrant population. During some of his recent visits to places such as Washington DC and London, the current Foreign Minister, Dr Tewdros Adhanom, has been calling for active participation of the migrant population in the country's development and called on them to stand united in promoting the country's interest.[2]

As a reflection of the government's emphasis on engaging the Ethiopian emigrant population, it inaugurated the Ethiopian Expatriate Affairs General Directorate at MOFA in 2002. According to information from the Ministry this section was opened with the aim to liaise between different ministries and 'the diaspora', promote their active involvement in economic activities of the country, and for the purpose of building the country's image (MOFA, Diapora Policy 2012). Various manuals, rules, and regulations towards enhancing diaspora engagement have been issued by the government since the inauguration of the Directorate.[3]

Besides MOFA, there are various government bodies that have been working in implementing policies targeting the Ethiopian emigrant population. According to Mr Getnet,[4] in all most all 21 federal government ministries, there is a separate office or coordinating unit of diaspora issues. The Ministry of Labor and Social Affairs (MLSA) is one among several of them. According to an interview with the official of MLSA, there are activities involving the ministry in regards to migration and diaspora engagement since 2011, following the establishment of diaspora office within the Ministry.[5] The Civil Service Ministry has also been involved in mobilizing the diaspora and resources for capacity building and for poverty alleviation. The Ministry of Health has its own diaspora office in order to engage the diaspora in health sectors and the same applies for most of the federal ministries.

According to information from Mr Mulugeta,[6] the government's realization of the growing economic role of this category of the population in development and emigrants increasing transnational activities necessitated the formulation of a policy concerning the diaspora, popularly known as Diaspora Policy announced in December 2012. According to Mr Mulugeta stated that the policy is 'more reliable and comprehensive and urges for more diaspora engagement in national development'. It was stated that this shows that 'the diasporas issue has become important and that the government is giving due attention to it'.[7]

The developments in state institutions and policies came at a time when remittances have emerged as the major sources of hard currency. In recent times this has been recognized to be at the top of all sources of foreign currency earning. While it is difficult to determine the exact amount, there is an understanding that it stands at something more than a billion, which was estimated to have been only about US $359 million in 2007 (Fransen and Kuschminder 2009). Such an estimate takes into account only the formally recorded inflow of remittances.

To insure the inflow of remittances the government has been promoting the provisions for International Remittance Services (IRS) (MOFA, Diapora Policy 2012). The emphasis on economic engagement of migrants prompted the government to introduce various forms of incentives and privileges that have been publicized to bring the same to the attention of Ethiopian emigrants abroad. Among other things the government introduced what has been called 'Diaspora Bond'. The diaspora therefore are among the primary targets of treasury bonds towards financing the construction of the hydro-electric generation dam across the Nile River, also popularly known as the 'grand renaissance dam/GERD' (MOFA 2012). The government has also been offering what has been called the Ethiopian origin identity card to enable emigrants of Ethiopian origin to have access to a range of 'services and privileges' (MOFA 2001). 'Between 1992 and mid-2009, over 1800 Ethiopians living abroad were issued investment licenses by the Ethiopian Investment Agency, more than a third (39%) of whom were reported to be residents or citizens of the USA' (Chako and Price 2009, 11). A substantial proportion of this group is based in the Washington Metropolitan Area. The bulk of their investment in Ethiopia was reported to be in real estate development and small-scale manufacturing industries. The opening of foreign currency accounts in Ethiopia by members of the diaspora has also been promoted to enhance the inflow of finance and investment from the diaspora and to 'support the international foreign exchange reserve and ease the balance of payments problem of the country' (MOFA 2012).

In sum, the political economy of engaging emigrants revolving around the notion of 'diaspora as resource' brought into the picture actors beyond the institutions of the state, and the International Organization for Migration (IOM) is one of them. The organization has an Ethiopian office working on migration and diaspora engagement among its various activities. According to interview made with Ms. Firehiwot,[8] the Ethiopian-based office of IOM has the objective to implement programs such as Migration for Development in Africa (MIDA), an initiative that took off in 2001 as part of what has been stated as 'demand-driven institutional capacity building program', to facilitate the transfer of skills and resources of the African diaspora to their countries of origin. In light of this, the IOM Ethiopia office undertakes a variety of activities which in one way or another can supplement the government's policies and strategies of diaspora engagement. Among them, development takes a larger share, which includes enhancing institutional capacity and assisting the Ethiopian government development plans.[9]

The discussion in this section focused on developments in state policies and institutions of state engagement of emigrants. Since Ethiopian emigrants in Washington DC were the focus of this paper, about 40 individuals were interviewed in Washington DC, in addition to interview with officials in Ethiopia. The discussion in the next three sections is based on the interviews in the Washington DC area. As it is discussed later in detail in this paper, the policy of engaging emigrants or 'diaspora as resource' has led to the downplaying of the transnational political role of emigrants. This converges with the lack of transformation of antagonistic state-society relations in Ethiopia that has come to profoundly affect the nature of political debates within Ethiopian emigrant population and proscribed their transnational role.

Ethiopian emigrants' belongings, perceptions, and perspectives

There are possibly several perspectives about the forms of belonging among the Ethiopian Emigrant population in the Washington DC area. Professor Mohammed Moen of Howard University, an Ethiopian emigrant with more than 40 years of experience in the USA, does not take it lightly as far as the distinction between the concept of migration and diaspora is concerned.[10] For him, the applicability of the notion of diaspora that is now being used widely without qualification requires a critical scrutiny. He critically reflects on the loose application of the concept of diaspora to all categories of Ethiopian emigrants in the DC area and elsewhere. He suggested the use of the term 'naturalized Ethiopian' or 'new Africans' rather than using the term diaspora. He classifies Ethiopians who emigrated at different times. There is the first generation who originally went to the West for the purpose of education, some of whom went back home as 'nation builders'. The second generation refers to a mass of migration during and post the regime change period (1974) in Ethiopia, identified as 'first settlers', 'political refugees' who became entrepreneurs, whom the professor describes as the 'ethiopiawinet' group. The third generation refers to emigrants of the current period, encompassing political activists, and those who fit within the DV lottery category, which Professor Moen termed as a 'payback generation'.[11]

Others classify immigrants into two categories: first generation and second generation. The perception here is that those in the first category are resistant to change, who strongly identify themselves with Ethiopia, and for whom integration into the culture and the way of life of the population of the host society are also challenging. There is second generation who are thought to be adaptive to the new environment.[12] Some of the interviews are of the impression that the second generation are more preoccupied with employment and job-related issues.[13]

Then there are those who look into the generational issue from the perspective of the unfolding dynamics of Ethiopian politics. For the 'EPRP generation' who arrived in the USA about 35 years ago as political refugees, there is a difference between them and those who migrated at about the same time as students, as entourage and dignitaries of the royal family and the landed aristocracy – some of whom were married and integrated, as going back in the post-revolutionary period became remote.[14]

Mr Dereje of ZeEthiopia (a Washington-based media organization) defines Ethiopian emigrants in the USA as Ethiopian-Americans. He believes that this is the case as long as they have to participate in every aspect of the host country's activities, and obey US laws. He noted that Ethiopian emigrants in the DC area do live and work in the USA not just as Ethiopians but also residents or citizens of the USA. This means that they have to exercise their obligations and rights, as residents and or at US citizens and 'technically' serve two countries. Concerning the level of visibility/presence of Ethiopian emigrants, Mr Dereje mentioned that Ethiopian emigrants are far from being a strong community, and not settled yet. He rather believes that they have to do a lot as a community which he characterized as not connected-scattered.[15]

There are several organizations or institutions of Ethiopian emigrants in Washington DC area providing one or another form of belonging to the emigrant population. The organizations are of various forms – community, cultural, religious, business, and those who are active in activities such as tournaments, and so on. Ethiopian community associations are one of the most widely known organizational forms of Ethiopian emigrant belonging. The Ethiopian Community Center (ECC) that was established in 1979 has the objective of helping or supporting Ethiopians who continue to migrate and live there. It started functioning at the time when more Ethiopians were migrating to the outside world, especially to the USA following a period of political instability in Ethiopia in the 1970s and 1980s.[16] ECSDC – Ethiopian Community Services and Development Council – is another community association established in 2002 by Ethiopians in the Washington DC area. The director of the Center, Mr Dawit, stated that the association has been providing various services to Ethiopian emigrants. The center helps in facilitating access to free health insurance, running orientation sessions for new migrants, helping with immigration applications, computer and skill training, job placement programs, helping the homeless, and organizing after-school and summer-youth program. The director mentioned that the Association has more than 12,000 members.[17] Mr Dawit observes that 'most Ethiopian emigrants actually help each other since Washington DC has become the 'second city' of Ethiopia- one-stop centre for Ethiopians.'[18]

Ethiopian Student Association (ESA), at the University of Maryland, provides another form of belonging of people of Ethiopian origin in the Washington DC area. The student representatives interviewed view it as a rapidly growing association that started with a couple of people and grew into hundreds in a short period of time. In the eyes of the student representatives, the student body is a mix of first (parents) and second (students) generation. They characterize the relationships within the student association as political and sensitive. This broadly relates to the concern that the divisions within the student body along the lines of identity politics is affecting their interrelationship and the modalities of allocation of funding by philanthropic organizations.[19] There is also a

Young Ethiopian Professionals (YEP), an association created by young people of Ethiopian origin. From the interviews with YEP leaders 'finding spaces that overlap in order to collaborate and fill gap or any lack of platform for Ethiopian professionals, break barriers' and to create avenues or opportunities to connect are two primary goals.[20]

Religious institutions create by far the most resilient form of belonging for a significant section of Ethiopian emigrants. The presence of a number of churches established by members of Ethiopian emigrant population in the Washington DC area is a widely felt phenomenon. Among the possibly various religious formations of the diverse Ethiopian emigrant population residing in the DC metropolitan area, the Ethiopian Orthodox Church is highly visible. Interviews with church goers and observations of the congregations at a time of fieldwork in May 2013 clearly attest to the role of religious formations in creating a powerful sense of belonging among member of the community. Hundreds attend the weekly sermons, and this could grow into thousands during special occasions. The diversity of the attendees in terms of age, sex, and background is impressive. The demographics vary from very elderly to adult and small children, from those who have lived there for decades to new arrivals, from the well-educated to those who have less formal education. During the interviews, Likeseyuman Getahun stated that there are more than 11 Ethiopian orthodox churches in the DC area. While the churches primarily aim at spiritual belonging, 'self-actualization and spiritual nourishment', they mean a lot for those who migrated from Ethiopia in different times and for different reasons. He describes the community as 'a melting pot' of people of all walks of life. He mentioned that the churches play a prominent role within the community. Individuals interviewed have emphasized that the churches have been at the 'forefront' of providing support to the community, and has been actively engaged in humanitarian aid, development activities, and maintenance of the monasteries in Ethiopia.[21] Moreover, interviewees are fully aware of the significant cultural role of the church, whereby it is underlined that the Ethiopian Orthodox Church sermons have long been great cultural attraction for the population of the host country.

The centrality of politics in Ethiopian emigrants' transnational interaction

In the words of Professor Moen, politics has become 'the profession' in permeating discussions relations among a considerable section of Ethiopian emigrants. Other interviewees also concurred with this view in observing the circumstances in which politics plays a major role. They see a situation in which there are groups in the Ethiopian communities in the Washington DC area whose views shape the political discourses. For instance, a student interviewed at Maryland University believes that there is an 'extremely loud group of Ethiopian emigrants' who tend to dominate the discourses that gives a semblance of unified resistance, for instance, by staging protests at the Ethiopian embassy, US State Department, at the UN in New York, and so forth.[22]

In further strengthening the argument for the centrality of politics in Ethiopian emigrant discourses, An interviewee from Ethio-American (business organization) has the following to say:

> We're not settled yet politically, there is instability -ethnic & political issues. Here people are free, they're not controlled, and there is no fear because the government is not here. There

is a lot more expression; we are in the honeymoon of expression. The opposition is very vocal here; your opinion is governed by the opposition. The majority of people are silent –it's not easy to organise oneself, you have to be a part of it or you have to stay out of it ... It's very hard for the Ethiopian government to mobilize the diaspora ... they are effectively banned from the community by the vocal groups, the government can't fully participate they are always opposed by other groups. They only go to the -embassy just for passports, visas.[23]

'Ethnic' discourse takes many different forms, such as branding the government – pointing to some of the politicians and other times arguing about the role of larger or dominant groups in Ethiopia. Overall there is a striking consensus that the politicisization of identity in Ethiopia has directly contributed to the reproduction of the same in the USA where 'you can't express it, but you can feel it', in the words of one of the interviewees.[24] Interviewees observe a situation where one cannot underestimate the role of political discourses in the transnational engagement of emigrants and in development in Ethiopia.[25]

Thus, the major finding of this study is that the political dynamics in Ethiopia in which the politicization of identity takes a central place has affected the institutions of and interactions within the Ethiopia emigrant population. The various organizations of Ethiopian emigrant population including religious formations are not immune from this particular dynamics of Ethiopian politics. Without going into the details, while religious formations and churches such as the Ethiopian Orthodox churches in the DC area do create a powerful sense of belonging, a source of spiritual nourishment, including the socialization of the young siblings, they are not immune from the political dynamics in Ethiopia. There are those who feel that while the religious space is not as divided as the others, there are moments of tensions affecting community and associational life. In the words of one of our interviewees

> ... ethnic conflicts are not by merely (by individual) people, they are by organised people-if there is an element of organisation to agitate or mobilize, then people become aware of ethnic conflict-ethnic conflict therefore becomes largely institutionally constructed-institutions can put forth an ideology which overtime starts to become the belief of different people, ethnicity becomes visible through moments of opposition and promotion.[26]

Equally important, the politicization of identity has made the community's relations with Ethiopian government representatives in the USA highly problematic. Interviewees believe that the Ethiopian diplomatic mission has little or no meaningful connection with the Ethiopian emigrant population. According to the views of several of the interviewees, this is related to the politicized nature of the relations, discouraging the Embassy from actively engaging with the community, and to make it virtually absent in such a place where large number of Ethiopian live.[27]

Despite these, the interviews also show the impact of diaspora in Ethiopia, and members of the Ethiopian migrant population have been involved in various activities in Ethiopia-building hotels, hospitals, schools, and bringing in new business ideas.[28] Such an observation has led some to advocate that diaspora should be included as an important community in Ethiopia. Mr Yohannes cites an example where countries like India are providing voting rights and dual citizenship to the emigrant population. He stated – 'If you're contributing more money than actually the whole country can generate from taxes and export, you should have a say in how the country is run and developed.'[29] In general while the interviewees argued that the diaspora is always an extension of the home country, the institutionalization of 'ethnic' politics has become inescapable, and a situation has been created where every person in Ethiopia is forced to identify his/her ethnic origin is a source of concern.

However, it would not help to overlook the fact that there are equally important topics of political discussion of Ethiopian emigrant population. The rule of law, human rights, democracy, and the general business environment in Ethiopia are among the key issues. The focus on 'ethnicity' is rather an indication of that particular dynamic revolving around the politicization of identity in Ethiopia having the capacity to permeate relationships of Ethiopian emigrants with state authorities, as well as the latter's relations with the various categories of Ethiopians at home.[30]

In connection with the argument for the centrality of politics among Ethiopian emigrant discourses, Mr Brigety (US state Department) mentioned that the state department does not actively engage with the Ethiopian Embassy on diaspora issues. He was of the opinion that the US government is aware of the fact that there are 'obviously political fissures' within the Ethiopian diaspora in the USA that mirror many of the political divisions inside Ethiopia, and therefore the US government is trying to stay out of it. The fact of coming from 'a history of repression negatively bears on the willingness to share/ network which could be greatly decreased because of these memories of fear',[31] he commented.

Overall the members of Ethiopian emigrant community believe that politics is central to their concerns under the current circumstances. This has affected the communities in the sense that it prevented them from speaking in the same voice, making it difficult for them to be taken seriously to whoever they appeal concerning the challenges and the practices in their country of origin.[32]

Nevertheless, interviewees also acknowledge some of the positive developments in the country in the areas of infrastructure, energy, health facilities, etc.[33] There were some who stated that government's engaging of Ethiopians in Washington DC on economic issues is relatively better. The fact that the Ethiopian government has been working to create interest among emigrant communities by publicising the various economic investment opportunities back home has also been noted. The uses of internet media and broadcast services from Ethiopia and DC, on Ethiopian issues have allowed them to closely follow developments in Ethiopia.[34]

The challenges of political antagonism

In contrast to the practices of slow level of engagement with emigrants in the 1990s, the leadership of the state in Ethiopia since the 2000, especially following the 2005 has been projecting its agenda of economic engagement of migrants and image building as its priorities. The government's discourse of 'Nations, Nationalities, and Peoples' and the use of the same as a strategy of mobilization and organization of society at home lead to the pragmatic use of the same in its dealings with various sections of the Ethiopian migrants abroad. In addition to appealing to Ethiopian migrant communities across the board for their participation in development in Ethiopia, there has been a practice of viewing Ethiopian individual and groups abroad as belonging to one or another members of the 'the Nations, Nationalities, and Peoples'. This practice and its use as a mechanism of mobilizing support mean further consolidation of the boundaries of identity and belonging, which could have its own impact on the interrelationship among members of Ethiopian migrants/communities in the Washington DC area and beyond. Besides the banner-'economic diplomacy' put at the forefront, the political dynamics prompted the EPRDF government to give attention to a growing transnational involvement of the bourgeoning migrant population, especially in the aftermath of the 2005 elections crisis. While the strategy on the part of the state was to disrupt the political influence of sections within the diaspora mobilizing and supporting opposition against it, the EPRDF government may have gradually realized that this would be a formidable task.

As Lyons (2007) observed, the leaders of EPRDF as well as opposition political organizations 'regularly send delegations to sensitize the various sections of migrant communities in North America' and in similar other places. Lyons also observed that the EPRDF government that has for long been reluctant to recognize the political role of migrants, except when they come out clearly in manner supportive of its policies, has continued to sensitize the communities to achieve a level of political support by at the same time aiming to neutralize the 'vocal diaspora'. This is in as long as the proponents of the government's position maintain that the 'vocal diaspora' in the process of politically opposing the government back in Ethiopia has also been accused of depicting the negative image of the country to the outside world.

Moreover, the interviews and discussions conducted with members of the Ethiopian migrant communities in Washington DC in May 2013, indicate that the project of organizing Ethiopians as part of 'constituency building', as support base for the government is far from being a success, precisely because of the political resistance from within the community. Interviewees invariably are of the opinion that the government through the Embassy in Washington DC has no observable engagement with them, hinting to the inability on the part of government representatives to engage adequately with members of the immigrant population. One can simply look at today's YouTube videos and various social media concerning the scale of disruption of Ethiopian government officials' meetings with members of Ethiopian emigrant population while at the same time Ethiopian diplomatic missions in North America and Europe becoming the sites of protest.[35]

Interviews with government officials show that the government largely views the political role of the migrant population a problematic area. Mr Mulugeta[36] in his discussion during the interview in Ethiopia divided the Diaspora abroad into three categories on the basis of their political positions. These are 'dutiful supporters' (possible to define these as EPDRF affiliated); 'opponents' and 'the silent majority'. The later categories or the silent majority are considered as either potential contributors of Ethiopian development if the government is keen to actively work on persuading or attracting them or they could be considered passive depending on situations. He said 'these groups are Diasporas who cannot confidently speak about Ethiopia on different events and mobilize others that keep silent but contribute and engage in development'.[37]

Conclusion: the limits of transnationalism and state policies of engagement of emigrants

The recognition of emigrants' economic role is the logical outcome of the political economy of state building and strategies of power in the aftermath of the fall of the military-socialist regime in Ethiopia. Such an approach has also been bolstered by the discourses of globalization at the global and continental (AU) level, and the liberalization and privatization dispensation in Ethiopia during the 1990s. While the economic interest is at the forefront of state policies of engagement of Ethiopian immigrants, in the words of one the informants, Ethiopian migrant communities in the Washington DC area have for long been gripped by 'politics as profession'.[38] This is in reference to the circumstances in which political debates about the conditions in Ethiopia has been permeating various forms of expressions of Ethiopian emigrants. The concern about the political conditions in Ethiopia has been reflected in the discussions with most of the informants during the fieldwork in Washington DC in May 2013. Central to the concerns and the controversies is the political structure in Ethiopia in the post 1991 period centered on the total reconstruction of the state. The term 'vocal diaspora' has been used by the state authorities in Ethiopia not only in designating the politically active members of Ethiopians in Washington DC but also to ridicule its political opponents who have been working to mobilize opposition to it. Therefore, the political aspect is the most challenging aspect of state interpellations of migrants which also in a very profound manner impacted the forms of transnational involvement of emigrant population of Ethiopian origin, and not least relations among migrants in the Washington DC area. Its impact on the relations among migrant communities goes beyond interaction at group or individual levels but also has affected associational life. Community self-help associations, religious formations, and sport activities are not immune from the onslaught of the phenomena of politicized identity.

Finally, transnationalism as applied in this study offers a framework of analysis of state policies of engagement and migrants own experiences across time and space. Transnationalism is now a days being widely applicable in describing various phenomena including the nature of contemporary migration. However, the Ethiopian government's conception of the role of Ethiopia emigrants which recognizes their increasing economic role and at the same time distrusting their political role limits the applicability of the notion of transnationalism in its holistic sense. It could therefore be concluded that political tensions following decades of politicization of identity, the government's strategies of mobilizing emigrants as resources, and emigrants' experiences will remain an important feature of state polices of engagement of Ethiopian emigrants, their belonging, and their transnational practices.

Disclosure statement

No potential conflict of interest was reported by the authors.

Funding

This work was supported by the research project entitled 'at the limits of the diverse nations: migration and the plurinational projects of Ecuador and Ethiopia', Faculty of Social Sciences, Quito, Ecuador.

Notes

1. Explaining the Ethiopian outmigration: Incentives or Constraints? By Seid Hassan and Minga Negash December 20, 2013.
2. 'Ethiopia Foreign Minister, Dr Tedros Adhanom meets Ethiopian Diaspora in DC', Tigrayonline, 29 April 2013, http://www.tigraionline.com/articles/tedros-adhanom-meets.html, accessed May 2014.

3. Mr Mulugeta, General Director of the Diaspora Engagement Affairs Directorate General, interview, May 2013, Addis Ababa.
4. Mr Getnet, Officer, Ministry of Civil Service and Diaspora Coordinating office, interview May, 2013, Addis Ababa.
5. Officer at the Diaspora affairs office at the Ministry of Labor and Social Affairs, Interview May, 2013, Addis Ababa.
6. Mr Mulugeta, the General Director of the Diaspora Engagement Affairs Directorate General, Interview May 7, 2013, Addis Ababa.
7. Mr Mulugeta, Interview.
8. Program Assistant, International Organization for Migration, Ethiopian Office, Interviewed, May 7, Addis Ababa.
9. Ms. Firehiwot, Interviewed, May 2013, Addis Abba.
10. Received ECDC (Ethiopian Community Development Center) distinguished service award.
11. Professor Mohen, Howard University, Interview, May 2013, Washington DC.
12. Mr Dawit, Director, ECDSC, Interview, May 2013, Washington DC.
13. Mr Dereje, ZeEthiopia (media organization), Interview May 2013, Washington DC.
14. Mr Paulos, Private Physician, Interview, May 2013, Washington DC.
15. Mr Dereje, Interview.
16. Ms. Hermela, ECC Director, May 2013, Washington DC.
17. Mr Dawit, Interview.
18. Mr Dawit, Interview.
19. Interviews with Ms. Taera Asrat – University of Maryland Ethiopian Student Association-Incoming President, Mr Tedros Bitew – University of Maryland Ethiopian Student Association-Public Relations Representative, Mr Kirubel Tadesse-University of Maryland, Baltimore County Ethiopian-Eritrean Student Association-Incoming Vice-President, May 2013, Maryland, see also, http://www.umbc.edu/studentlife/orgs/eesa.
20. Interview with Lulit Ayne & Shimelse Mekonnen, Co-Founders + Vice-President and Executive Vice-President, respectively, Young Ethiopian Professionals, Washington DC, see also http://www.yepnetworks.org.
21. Likeseyuman Getahun, Interview, May 2013, Washington DC.
22. Interview with leaders of Ethiopian Student Association at Maryland University, May 2013.
23. Interviewee Ethio-American (business organization), Interview, May 2013, Washington DC.
24. Mr Yohannes, Interview.
25. Mr Dereje Interview.
26. Mr Dereje, Interview.
27. Mr Dawit, Interview.
28. Mr Yohannes, Interview.
29. Mr Yohannes, Interview.
30. Mr Paulos, Interview.
31. Mr Bregity, US State Department, African Affairs, Interview, May 2013, Washington DC.
32. Dr Dawit Teklu, Strayer University, Interview, May 2013, Washington DC.
33. Likeseyuman Getahun, Interview.
34. Mr Alemayehu, Interview, May 2013, Washington DC.
35. The most dramatic recent incident is allegations of protesters attempting to enter the Ethiopian Embassy in Washington DC, and the subsequent firing of a gun by the Embassy Security Guard.
36. Mr Mulugeta, Interview, 7 May 2013, Addis Ababa.
37. Mr Mulugeta, Interview.
38. Interview with Ethiopian emigrants in Washington DC, 25 May 2013.

References

Adamnesh, Atnafu. 2008. "Facets of International Out-Migration and Return: The Case of Ethiopia." A Conference Paper, Raeye Ethiopia.

Alem, Asres. 1990. History of the Ethiopian Student Movement (In Ethiopia and North America): Its Impact on Internal Social Change, 1960–1974, University of Maryland.

Bahru, Zewdie, Gebre Yintiso, and Kassahun Berhnau. 2010. "Contribution of the Ethiopian Diaspora to Peace-Building: A Case Study of the Tigray Development Association (TDA)", University of Jyväskylä, Diaspeace Project, 2010.

Bijak, Jakub. 2006. "Forecasting International Migration: Selected Theories, Models and Methods." Working Paper 4/2006, Central European Forum for Migration Research, Warsaw, Poland.

Bush, Kenneth. 2008. "Diaspora Engagement in Peace Building." In *Whose Peace? Critical Perspectives on the Politcal Economy of Peace Building*, edited by Michael Pugh and Neil Copper, 191–206. New York: Palgrave.

Chacko, Elizabeth, and Marie Price. 2009. "The Role of the Diaspora in Development: The case of Ethiopian and Bolivian immigrants in the USA." Conference paper, George Washington University, October 02.

De Hass, Hein. 2008. "Migration and Development: A Theoretical Perspective", Working Papers 9, University of Oxford, International Migration Institute.

'Draft Diaspora Policy'. 2012. Ministry of Foreign Affairs of the Federal Democratic Republic of Ethiopia (*Hidar* 2004: EC, in Amharic).

Faist, Thomas. 2000. "Transnationalization in International Migration: Implications for the Study of Citizenship and Culture." *Ethnic and Racial Studies* 23 (2): 189–222.

Fransen, Sonja, and Katie Kuschminder. 2009. "Migration in Ethiopia: History, Current Trends and Future Prospects", Maastricht School of Governance (Paper Series).

Gebru, Tareke. 1996. *Ethiopia: Power and Protest, Peasant Revolts in the 20th Century*. Trenton, NJ: Red Sea Press.

Henderson, Conway W. 1997. *International Relations: Conflict and Cooperation at the Turn of 21st Century*. Pennsylvania: McGraw-Hill.

Lyons, Terrence. 2007. "Conflict Generated Diaspora and Transnational Politics in Ethiopia." *Conflict, Security and Development* 7 (4): 529–549.

Massey, Douglas, Joaquin Arango, Graeme Hugo, Ali Kouaouci, Adela Pellegrino, and J. Edward Taylor, eds. 2011. "Theories of International Migration: A Review and Appraisal." *Population and Development Review* 19 (3): 431–466.

Merera, Gudina. 2003. *Competing Ethnic Nationalisms; the Quest for Democracy*. Addis: Ababa University Press.

Ministry of Foreign Affairs. 2001. "Basic Information for Ethiopians in the Diaspora", Diaspora Engagement General Directorate, September 2001.

Minsitry of Foreign Affairs. 2002. "Ethiopian Foreign Affairs and National Security Policy and Strategy and its Success".

Van Hear Nicholas. 1998. New Diaspora: Mass Exodus, Dispersal and Regrouping of Migrant Communities. Seattle: University of Washington Press.

Somewhere else: social connection and dislocation of Ethiopian migrants in Johannesburg

Tanya Zack[a] and Yordanos Seifu Estifanos[b]

[a]Planning Department, School of Architecture and Planning, University of the Witwatersrand, Johannesburg, South Africa; [b]University of Oldenburg, European Masters in Migration and Intercultural Relations (EMMIR) Consortium, Oldenburg, Germany

ABSTRACT
The meaning of personal relationships for Ethiopian migrants to Johannesburg is shaped by individual connections, by imported social networks that are adapted in the host city, and by the particular conditions of livelihood creation in the emerging Ethiopian entrepreneurial enclave of 'Jeppe'. In their migration individuals experience both rupture and reconnection – with relatives, as well as through relationships and networks that constitute social capital in Johannesburg. The social world of Ethiopian migrants in this entrepreneurial enclave is complex. Many social connections and dislocations are affected by the life choices in which income generation and economic relations are the primary aim and social relations are necessarily secondary. Others are influenced by the strength of informal social networks that serve the needs of Ethiopian migrants. And, far from 'here' and 'there' being connected through the use of technology and advanced connectivity, 'home' and Johannesburg are experienced as quite separate and different places.

Introduction

The meaning of personal (and not-so-personal) relationships for Ethiopian migrants to Johannesburg is shaped by individual relationships, by the imported social networks that are adapted in the host city, and by the particular conditions of livelihood creation in Johannesburg.

In their move from Ethiopia to Johannesburg individuals experience both rupture and reconnection – with relatives, as well as through relationships and networks that constitute social capital in Johannesburg. To explore these experiences of social disconnection and connection, interviews were conducted during 2014 with 22 Ethiopian migrants in the inner city of Johannesburg in 'Jeppe' – an area that is an emergent ethnic entrepreneurial enclave.

DuFoix (2008) has postulated that migrants use a number of approaches to manage proximity notwithstanding distance through. He intimates that the Internet and other communication technologies have created the possibility of making distance independent of time, that is, have enabled the possibility of achieving 'here' and 'there' at the same time. This paper in part interrogates the experience of Ethiopian migrants to Johannesburg in managing proximity through the use of technology in order to explore the ease or complexity of such a dual presence for these particular migrants.

The interviews relied on a random selection and the willingness of respondents. Open-ended, semi-structured interview questions were posed to interviewees, and in most cases interviews were conducted in the home language of interviewees.[1]

In terms of the experience of leaving, the questions focused on who migrants had 'left' behind, on who they had followed or brought to South Africa, on who they missed, and on how they maintained contact. The technologies used were also explored. They were asked what important life experiences they had personally had while in Johannesburg or what they had been absent from while in Johannesburg and how the separation from home, at these times, had been experienced and managed.

In terms of social experiences in Johannesburg they were asked who their community was and what formal and informal social structures they were affiliated to. They were asked about their experiences of support and of social life and about the comparisons between their social worlds in Johannesburg and those back home. They were asked to reflect on how their migration had impacted on their families.

The findings of these interviews are narrated below. However, before moving onto their stories, this paper describes the migrant situation of the respondents and of the research context.

Background

Drivers of Ethiopian migration to South Africa

South Africa is a major destination country for African asylum-seekers and migrants aspiring for better opportunities. The United Nations High Commission for Refugees (UNHCR) estimated on its website that in 2013 South Africa hosted 67,500 recognized international refugees and 233,100 asylum-seekers, making it the country with the largest single concentration of urban (non-camp) refugees and asylum-seekers in Southern Africa (UNHCR 2014). Although most migrants to South Africa are from Southern African countries, there are also large numbers of migrants from East Africa, particularly Somalia and Ethiopia (IOM 2013).

> [But] it is more than likely that no one knows how many Ethiopians, Somalis and Kenyans journey to RSA through irregular means each year. Like that of other irregular, illicit and clandestine activities, information on smuggling is not collated. (IOM 2009, 7)

Ethiopians are amongst the most significant of the migrant populations that have become established in South Africa, and particularly in Johannesburg. While much of the immigration from Ethiopia is undocumented and irregular (Kanko, Bailey, and Teller 2013), thus far at least three migration drivers have been identified. The first recent noticeable migration of young Ethiopians to South Africa came about in the early 1990s with the coincidence of the fall of the military Dergue regime in Ethiopia and the rise of democracy in South Africa, particularly noticeable beginning in 1991 (Messay 2005; Sinedu 2009).

However, the fact that the 'Kembata-Tembaro' and 'Hadiya' ethnic groups from southern Ethiopia dominate the migration to South Africa begs further explanation, as individuals also played a role. Although the role of individuals in establishing international network migration is rare, it is not totally non-existent. Jacqueline Hagan describes the role of an individual in instigating and perpetuating the Mayan Migration to Houston (Hagan 1998), and a former Ethiopian ambassador to South Africa created job opportunities for some youth from his Kembata-Tembaro birthplace in the early 2000s (Kanko, Bailey, and Teller 2013). These youth found job opportunities around major South African cities such as Johannesburg and Pretoria, worked there for some years and then returned home with the money they saved. Their apparent success has motivated other youths in the area, thus creating a feedback loop among former migrants, return migrants, and potential migrants as assumed in the networks theory of migration. The theory claims that once started, an established social network perpetuates migration and reproduces more migrants over time and space, even when opportunities at the receiving end are exhausted (Massey et al. 1998). Human smugglers are also a key factor in expediting migration into South Africa.

A further wave of migration was evident following major events in Ethiopia and South Africa. The politically unstable period in Ethiopia leading up to and following the third-round of national elections conducted in 2005 led some Ethiopians to South Africa (Kanko, Bailey, and Teller 2013), while the 2010 FIFA World Cup in South Africa attracted others. Many of the young Ethiopians who came to Johannesburg in these waves of migration and who continue to enter the city, find themselves in 'Jeppe'.

'Jeppe' – Johannesburg's 'Ethiopian Quarter'

The context for this enquiry is 'Jeppe'. Located in a north-eastern segment of inner-city Johannesburg, 'Jeppe' is a retail area that has been created and expanded over a 20-year period, mostly by Ethiopian migrants (Zack 2013). These migrants have transformed what were unused and underutilized office buildings into a plethora of small shops and stalls, predominantly selling discount fashion and footwear imported from China.

Medium- and high-rise modernist buildings have been appropriated for this retail use and function as internalized shopping centers. The enterprise of these migrant entrepreneurs has stretched over many buildings on more than six full city blocks and has extended down many streets in the inner city.

In addition to the dominant offering of low-cost clothing and shoes, home ware products, groceries, and mobile phones are available in 'Jeppe'. Shoppers to this precinct are hawkers who on-sell goods in neighboring former black townships, in rural areas of South Africa and in towns and villages of sub-Saharan Africa. They buy both small quantities and bulk amounts of goods in 'Jeppe'. The goods are sourced from Chinese wholesale merchants who mostly operate from warehouse-type shopping centers.

'Jeppe' has matured from a place in the early 1990s where a few ground-floor shops began to be occupied and subdivided by Ethiopian merchants. Over the following years spaces within buildings were incrementally converted into retail spaces, to what is now a retail cauldron dominated by thousands of mostly young Ethiopian male migrants. Over time the demand for Ethiopian music, clothing, spices, food and coffee in the area has increased. Many buildings now offer these goods as Ethiopian migrants cater to the needs of fellow migrants. In addition, social institutions offering particular or community-wide needs, whether for security, political activism or welfare exist in the area. Business, travel, and monetary services are also present.

These responses to the growing ethnic enterprise in the area suggest some mimicking of an ethnic enclave. However, while the success of ethnic entrepreneurialism in 'Jeppe' does rely both on the size of the ethnic and consumer populations – preconditions for ethnic enclaves, as noted by Aldridge and Waldinger (1990), it is not primarily driven by a dependency on an Ethiopian customer base. Wilson and Portes (1980) also describe a dependency on ethnic customers in the early stages of the development of ethnic enclaves. By contrast, most Ethiopian entrepreneurs in 'Jeppe' rely on a customer base that is external to this community. The clustering of Ethiopian entrepreneurs in 'Jeppe' is more important for the social capital role it plays than for its role as a consumer base (Zack 2015).

Experiences of disconnection and connection

The promise of South Africa

Most Ethiopians cite limited economic opportunity at home as the main driver for their migration (IOM 2009; Gebre, Maharaj, and Pillay 2011). Some potential migrants even noted that they would prefer to migrate to South Africa than to complete their studies at home, noting that education is not their final destiny (Kanko, Bailey, and Teller 2013).

In this regard Tadiwos Hailemariam[2] was no exception. His family was extremely poor and his sole aspiration was to work in a government institution in Ethiopia as a route out of poverty. He studied hard and focused only on this ideal. One day, however, his hope shifted toward migration. He saw a recording of a televised sermon being shown in a petty shop in his village. A pastor was preaching in South Africa and Tadiwos Hailemariam noticed that the Ethiopians in the scene looked rich and healthy. He also heard stories of Ethiopian migrants' success in South Africa and saw pictures that these migrants sent home – of themselves posing with (their) cars. These images gave him new hope, and he immediately started making a plan to go to South Africa.

Disconnection and reconnection

Like many other young men Tadiwos Hailemariam would leave his family and head south. He would follow his elder brother on a well-trodden route in a culture where the eldest child carries the responsibility for contributing to the family well-being and is thus the most likely to migrate first. Kanko, Bailey, and Teller (2013) found that a high proportion of migrants from southern Ethiopia to Johannesburg were first borns in their families and that they provided experiential information to younger siblings to migrate. Sara Alemu is also the eldest child in her family and came to South Africa for medical treatment. Afterwards she stayed on to study, and eventually married and settled in Johannesburg where she ran a shop in 'Jeppe'. But her birth order not only burdens her with economic responsibilities. She also spoke of loss. As the eldest in the family, she had emotional responsibilities to hold the family together. Her absence was thus a big loss for the family.

While most migrants follow someone or join relatives, friends or people who are connected to someone they know, there are those who do not immediately enter a network. 'I arrived alone,' said Mulualem Gebru who had been in Johannesburg for 14 years and had never been back to Ethiopia. In Ethiopia he was a soldier. He fled with no means of support and no money. He came straight to 'Jeppe'. But he said:

> when you come here you find people and they guide you. One Ethiopian guy gave me a place to sleep and food. He showed me how to sell belts and wallets. I bought from 'Jeppe', and I sold in townships.[3]

From there his progression was not an unusual route for Ethiopian migrants as he went on to buy a shop in a town east of Johannesburg and later opened an Ethiopian restaurant in 'Jeppe'. His story also reveals a bittersweet disconnection and reconnection.

Mulualem Gebru was not married before he left Ethiopia. But he was in a committed relationship and he had a child of 18 months. He sent money home to his girlfriend and daughter every two or three months and at holiday times. And he often phoned them. But he also became involved in a new relationship in South Africa and six years after leaving Ethiopia he had a child with his South African girlfriend. Although the love relationship did not last, Mulualem maintains contact with his child. After 14 years in South Africa Mulualem brought his first girlfriend and his eldest child to Johannesburg. To his surprise his girlfriend was pregnant when she arrived. 'She had fallen in love with another man and didn't want me,' he said:

> But she also had my 15-year-old daughter with her so I was happy. What can I do? I cannot be angry. I had another girlfriend. Look for how many years I was here. She did not know if I would ever go back or we would ever be together. Now her new man has come to live here too. I see her as a sister. And I get to have my child with me a lot.

And his connection with his daughter had been maintained over many years, both through technology and through the strength of his family connections in Ethiopia.

> We get along well and because I used to talk to her a lot and send photos. We were not strangers when she arrived. In Ethiopia she also had a lot of contact with my brothers and sisters so she is part of my larger family too.

Several interviewees talked of the many years of disconnection from close relatives and friends. Addisalem Gobena said she had been totally disconnected from her many friends who emigrated to the USA and to Europe. During his 12 years in Johannesburg intermediary[4] Admassu Mulugeta has neither visited Ethiopia nor had visitors from home. He was unmarried but in a committed relationship when he left Ethiopia – and he had a daughter. His girlfriend has since died in Ethiopia and Admassu's mother now takes care of his child. His father died three years ago. He is still unmarried. He says that in both times of loss the Ethiopian community in 'Jeppe' comforted him.

In spite of his eagerness to find opportunity in South Africa, Tadiwos Hailemariam talked of the wrench of leaving home. He said departing from his mother was traumatic. He had to be physically pulled apart from her. And seven years after his arrival he was processing documents in the hope that he could visit Ethiopia, and see his mother 'while she is still alive'.

Perhaps the most extreme disconnection is that experienced by Ashenafi Mamo. An only child, he was born into poverty in the rural south of the Hossana region. He says he left home, as a young child, after his father died and his mother had no means of supporting him. After years on the streets of Addis he moved to Kenya where he managed to get a low-paying job. He then came to South Africa where he lives a marginal existence of depending on favors and handouts of fellow Ethiopians. He last saw his mother 25 years ago and has no way of contacting her. 'I don't know if she is alive,' he says:

> Dereje Hussen summed up the complex experience of loss faced by those living away from their homeland: 'Migration strengthens your physical endurance, but spiritually, you are weakened.'

Respondents also told of reconnection. It is less usual for married people to migrate, according to Kanko, Bailey, and Teller (2013). Embedded social ties and responsibilities generally bind them. Jemal Abdela, who was married when he migrated in 2000, said 'I missed my daughter the most'. He came alone at the age of 31. 'My child was two years old when I left and I was separated from my daughter and wife for more than 13 years. They came to Johannesburg in 2013.' He spoke of the loss of the years lived apart. 'The changes in my daughter made me feel that I am lost. But I give thanks to God that my family is beside me now.'

Phoning home

Like most international migrants Jemal Abdela maintained contact with his family through calling. Madianou and Miller (2011) have examined the importance of technology in communication for migration. The means to communicate with relatives and those from whom migrants are separated is pivotal to maintaining interpersonal connections. The smart phone age has made such communications easy and possible, once the initial costs are covered. This is true also for the respondents in this enquiry. Sara Alemu maintained contact with US and European-based friends through social media, mobile applications, and direct phone calls. But she said the connection to Ethiopia is 'still weak' and her main contact with her relatives is by telephone.

Most of Sara Alemu's cohort of school leavers migrated out of Ethiopia. They live in the USA and in Europe and she maintains contact with them via Facebook, and the video call application Tango. In order to keep in contact with his family, Tadiwos Hailemariam bought mobile phones for each close relative, 'both to keep in contact and because it's a status symbol to have a phone there – they all wanted one'. Endriyas Desta talks on the phone and writes letters to his parents and his little sister in Ethiopia, 'because my mother and father don't have [an] email account'.

Marta Agonafir said she talked and sent pictures to her family on her phone. She also uses WhatsApp. She used the service provider that offers the most competitive rates for connecting to Ethiopia from South Africa. And she often went to Internet cafes to communicate with her relatives or friends by email and Facebook. Addisalem Gobena avoided having a smart phone because of the threat of theft in Johannesburg, and so did not use mobile phone applications to contact her family. 'Cell C is relatively cheap,' she said of her service provider. 'With R25 I can call home.'

Following others

Following the networks theory of migration that define migration in terms of the interpersonal ties that connect migrants in networks of friendship, kin and shared origin (Massey et al. 1998), respondents were asked about their experience of bringing or following friends or relatives. Dereje Hussen said a few friends followed him when they heard of his success. Also, Helen Zewde followed her brother to South Africa. She came six years ago and her brother paid for her trip. He also found her a job in a shop in 'Jeppe' and helped another sister to go to school because of the remittance he sent home.

Most of the migrants either followed older siblings or brought younger ones to South Africa. Some of them followed their relatives or friends, and others come without knowing someone, but find one in South Africa. And has any relative or close friend joined Sara Alemu? In spite of her role as the first born, and the roots she is apparently planting in this city through employment and marriage. 'No one came to join me, and never will I let anyone to come,' she says of Johannesburg – offering the first glimpse of the complexity of this particular city as a place of arrival.

Social capital in Johannesburg

Social institutions are part of this social capital in 'Jeppe'. Amel Yimer (2012) compares the Ethiopian quarter in Johannesburg with Ethiopian enclaves elsewhere in the world and notes that Ethiopians bring to these spaces a strong sense of tradition as well as centuries-old institutions that are recreated in the host society. Her research examines transformations that occur in Ethiopian social institutions when brought into South Africa. She explores the workings of two social institutions that emanate from Ethiopia: Idirs[5] or funeral clubs and Mahbers[6] or social clubs. These are the vehicles through which 'members essentially interact with one another and reinforce their belonging to that society' (Yimer 2012, 14). She posits that when Ethiopian migrants leave their home country they leave a social environment, including such social institutions that sustain and validate them within networks of people including neighbors, friends, co-workers, churchgoers, etc.

Some Ethiopian migrants to 'Jeppe' access ethnically oriented organizations that range from trade and support organizations to support political organizations. These independent organizations offer various services or network opportunities to individuals, to particular trading groups, or to ethnic minorities.

When asked about social networks many respondents referred to churches, social clubs, and the practice of 'helping one another'. They intimated that Ethiopians go to church together, celebrate weddings together, and create an Ethiopian way of life here. Eskindir Alemu said he had made many friends in Johannesburg and felt that fellow Ethiopians help one another in times of need. Ketema Teshome agreed: 'When someone has problem with money we help; when he is sick we visit him.' Besides, every denomination of Ethiopian church is represented in Johannesburg. Dereje Hussen commented:

> As an Ethiopian wherever you go you try to keep your culture, religion and social ties. You cannot totally isolate yourself from society in the destination country. It is impossible. You may also live near Ethiopians so that you can communicate and spend time together. So you do recreate the social life back home here. But its never the same quality or depth.

Mulualem Gebru felt 'the Ethiopian community is my community'. He had first-hand experience of community help when his mother died in 2011 and his father died six months before we interviewed him. He had not seen either parent since he left Ethiopia in 2000. He said that although he had not been a member of an Idir 'they comforted me. They visited and sat with me to help me forget'. In Johannesburg, the period of mourning was shortened to a few days. 'In Ethiopia they sit for longer but here you cannot afford that time because you must get back to your shop,' he added. He also enjoyed socializing with Ethiopians:

> At night I go to places where you can get Ethiopian food. There is a flat where we meet a night. It's like a social club. Saratoga Gardens. It's like being in Addis. That social time is good. Its time to talk football and politics.

But Misganaw Goshu said:

> I don't think I only belong to the Ethiopian community. I live with different nationals. South African, Zimbabwean, Malawian and others and these are all part of my community. I have two countries. Ethiopia and South Africa.

The talk of community was not universal. There are some signs of the geographies of home impacting on social networking in Johannesburg, as ethnic affiliations affect some interactions. Mulualem Gebru said, 'someone from another ethnic group cheated me. But I didn't get help from the elders. Some ethnic groups protect each other. Villages will protect each other here in "Jeppe"'. And Abraham Ashagre said he had difficulty getting orders for samples he brought to 'Jeppe' because he is one of the Tigrayans in 'Jeppe' who are associated, by some, to the ruling class in Ethiopia. 'Others don't support me,' he said of his business dealings.

Loss and longing

Some respondents when asked what they missed most spoke of the country as a whole. Jemal Abdela said, 'Ethiopia is my home. I am only here because of political problems. I am not happy about my life here. I miss everything, the rivers and the mountains.' Ketema Teshome said, 'Ethiopia is in my blood. On each and every celebration I miss home.'

Many respondents echoed a longing for home and loved ones that are associated with celebrations. With the simplification of important holiday celebrations to four times a year Dereje Hussen calculated that he had missed 40 special holidays while living in Johannesburg. Sara Alemu said it is her family tradition to celebrate Saint Gabriel. Several feasts and rituals were held in honor of the saint in her family home, and she missed these events. She had timed her few visits back home to coincide with the ritual. Even now, she said, 'I am waiting for a friend to bring me special food that was prepared for the most recent Saint Gabriel celebration.'

'I miss my kids the most,' Mulatu Tekle said. He was 29 when he left his wife and three children in Ethiopia. That was nine years before we interviewed him. He had not seen any of them since. He talked to them on the phone and sent letters and photos. Marta Agonafir did not mention her father until we had almost completed the interview with her. Then she said, 'I miss my father the most.' She told us that he had been deported to Eritrea in 1999. She had not seen him in 14 years. He returned to Ethiopia after she had left home. Marta had sent money to fund the costs of smuggling him back into Ethiopia via Sudan. 'But I haven't seen him myself,' she said of her 77-year-old father.

Dereje Hussen said:

> I left my family and my girlfriend behind. The last time I saw my family was ten years ago. I missed all of them, my mom, my brother, my sisters ... and also the neighbours. I miss the Ekub, the Idir, the gatherings, and the way we celebrate religious occasions.

He said he missed his girlfriend the most. 'But I have stayed here for ten years now, and I have lost her already. She has married someone. No one can wait you for ten years.'

Arega Hailu had to flee Ethiopia as he was a political activist and under threat. His approach to the loss he felt was to avoid things that reminded him of home.

> I do not celebrate Ethiopian events. It's too painful for me. I don't want to remember things from home. If I celebrate Ethiopian things I long too much, so I would rather not do that here. I also don't socialize here. Only my body is in South Africa. My mind is not here. I am not at peace here.

Life events in absentia

Some respondents had missed out on both happy and sad life events since having left Ethiopia. On the flip side, migrants' relatives had also missed out on important moments that the migrants had experienced in Johannesburg. 'My sister died while I was here and I could only phone home. It's not a good way to mourn,' said Dereje Hussen. He also regretted the stunted mourning period in Johannesburg that results from the urgency to get back to work. 'Back home, you learn a lot while sharing and comforting one another. You share life experiences, beyond comforting. It is real emotional sharing.'

Shemsu Shiferaw had missed the weddings of two of his sisters. He married an Ethiopian woman in Johannesburg and his family missed his wedding. Marta Agonafir said her younger sister got married and she missed that event. She sent money for the wedding. Misganaw Goshu said, 'My dad passed away last year and my little sister got married and there are more occasions that I have missed. Sometime I cry ... ' He added, 'I met my wife during the Ethiopian millennium celebrations in Johannesburg and married her here.'

Tadiwos Hailemariam spoke of the pain of not having his mother at his wedding and of how hard it was for her. He explained that weddings are special for Ethiopian parents. 'It's something they want to see. Parents may even push their children to ensure they marry before they die.' Addisalem Gobena agreed. She married an Ethiopian migrant in Johannesburg. Her family missed her wedding. This especially upset her mother. She explains that families put a lot of emphasis on their children's weddings and it was a big loss for them to miss this ceremony. She sent a video of the proceedings and her family watched it and held a celebration in honor of her marriage while they watched the video.

Some respondents also indicated that they had been able to maintain traditions transnationally. Sara Alemu met her husband in Johannesburg. His parents back home sent elders to her parents, as is customary in traditional marriage proposals. The families agreed to the marriage terms. In Johannesburg Sara did not move to the home of her would-be husband until their families had agreed on the marriage. Afterwards the couple went to Ethiopia to celebrate their engagement and to register their marriage in an Ethiopian court. Her family also celebrated her life events in absentia. Before Sara gave birth to a child her female relatives celebrated the anticipation of the birth, in

Ethiopia, in the traditional way of entertaining and cooking for friends and in particular of sampling the porridge – genfo.[7]

Finding community – or not

Respondents were asked about the roots and networks they had established in Johannesburg. Belahcew Niguse was 20 years old when he came to South Africa. His brother later joined him. Belahcew is married to a South African woman and has two children. He felt that he had 'grown up' in South Africa. 'Johannesburg is my community. I work with locals, with Zimbabweans, with Chinese and so on. I also help any Ethiopian guy who has a problem. Ethiopia is my first home, South Africa is my second.'

Endriyas Desta had been in South Africa for 11 years. At the age of 19 he followed his brother to South Africa. He was married and his wife joined him. But, they divorced and he married a Xhosa woman. Yet he said, 'My community is the Ethiopian community. We help each other with money and ideas and so on. And I am Ethiopian. My home is Ethiopia.' Zerihum Mengistu arrived in Johannesburg in 2003 at the age of 29. He married a South African woman and they have visited Ethiopia together. 'She is my first point of comfort,' he said. But he added that the Ethiopian community was very important to him, 'we do anything to help with money, ideas, and information'.

Respondents reported mixed experiences of social networking in Johannesburg. Sara Alemu had made many friends, had a sociable husband who also had several relatives in the city, and she had an established social life. She felt that her relationships with fellow Ethiopians were often unstable. 'Some Ethiopians here are unpredictable,' she said. 'Today they may greet you and tomorrow avoid you. Loyalty cannot be taken for granted.' 'I strategized,' she added, 'I made best friends with Zimbabwean and Malawian women. I taught them some Ethiopian cultural practices such as sharing food and making coffee ceremonies. They are my closest friends, for now'. 'Nevertheless,' she sighed, 'the social world at home is irreplaceable'.

Social capital in a work-dominated environment

The dominance of work in this Ethiopian entrepreneurial enclave is overwhelming. Much of the social capital in this area is informed and inspired by economic connections. Yimer notes that the proximity of businesses in the area where Ethiopian migrants spend long hours allows them a physical closeness to and ongoing interaction with one another. Yet she finds that 'the relationships formed in this community do not extend to more than knowledge of one another's basic background information such as city of origin, religion or marital status' (Yimer 2012, 38). Indeed she notes that ' (i)n the case of Ethiopian migrants who come to South Africa seeking better financial opportunities, their communal virtues are replaced by competition, cash, and conflict' (Yimer 2012, 34). These findings were borne out in the interviews conducted for this study.

Dereje Hussen repeated his sense of having lost a lot by moving to Johannesburg. Some of this is the absence of shared personal history even with fellow Ethiopians.

> There is nothing satisfying or that makes you happy here. You can smile but you are not 100 per cent happy. You live together and communicate with friends but it's just superficial. Social

> life here is not real. You are here to just work. And in your spare time, you talk to friends. You gather and you talk but you are thinking of somewhere else.

He has a metaphor for this sense of inauthenticity. 'Life here is like pp,' (per procurationem) he says, as if he could equate his life here with the act of signing on behalf of someone else. Dereje's major point of comparison between his hometown and Johannesburg is the work style.

> Back home you work Monday to Saturday morning. On Saturday afternoon you gather with friends and enjoy life. On Sunday you go to church and go visit relatives. But here life is busy. You work Monday to Monday. You can't tell whether you are fulfilling your dreams or not because every day is busy ... you are not satisfied here. At home you can be satisfied in small ways. Here it takes a lot to get satisfied. Even though we now hear that the cost of living back home has increased and life is harder, but people support one another there.

Mulualem Gebru said that as a soldier in Ethiopia he had lived in fear of dying. His stress now is work focused. He said there were too many shops in 'Jeppe' and business was tough. He was constantly worried that he would not succeed. Marta Agonafir said 'Johannesburg is not home. We are only here to work and there is no social life. I have few friends here. I only have people to talk to about business.'

Similarly, Tadiwos Hailemariam said:

> When you come to Johannesburg money has power. It is what works here ... You don't have real friends. Everyone's relationships are mostly about money. And the competitive and sometimes clandestine nature of the job and environment makes you cautious and suspicious.

Social impact of risks faced in Johannesburg

The host city presented other obstacles to peace of mind. High levels of crime circumvent social freedom in Johannesburg, said Tadiwos Hailemariam. 'It is stressful. There are high risks. You could be attacked if you go out at night.' And so he says, 'You have your freedom, but you can't exercise it.'

Eskindir Alemu added that crime against foreign migrants was a major threat. He said the problem with being in South Africa was xenophobia –'if something goes wrong in the country, all eyes are on migrants,' he said. He always felt tense outside of 'Jeppe' and away from his fellow countrymen. He said that even during the 2010 FIFA World Cup ordinary people insulted him and other Ethiopians, telling them they should leave the country. He said, 'although business is good, we are not welcome here'.

Gemechu Bedassa owned a supermarket in a township west of Johannesburg. He was attacked and shot there. 'I was shot in both legs,' he said. He had very little assistance. Although he was taken to hospital and one bullet was removed, another one remains in his leg and he is never given assistance at the state hospital he attends monthly. On another occasion he was mugged. 'I lost my front teeth,' he says as he removes three false teeth 'they hit me in the face with the butt of a gun.' Gemechu added 'I think Joburg is temporary. It's not my home. I am scared to stay here. I want to go anywhere else. To a sane country.'

A recent book on the xenophobic attitude toward migrants in South Africa indicates that:

> The simultaneous demonization of mobility and the practical impossibility of controlling it have elevated migration and migrants to an official and popular obsession in which they become a convenient scapegoat for poor service delivery, crime, and other social pathologies. (Landau 2011)

Regarding this, Addisalem Gobena said the crime in Johannesburg was frightening. 'You are not even sure if you will reach home safely.' Several interviewees echoed a sentiment that is often expressed in 'Jeppe' – that Johannesburg has a bad spirit. Addisalem says 'they say there is a bad spirit here. I don't know if its money or demons, or crime or corruption, but it has a bad spirit'. She wondered if some problems lingered for so long and then transformed into a bad spirit across the area. Another respondent made this point more directly: 'this is a devil's place'.

Benefits and costs of migration for relatives 'Back Home'

In terms of the benefits of migration, most respondents talked of remittances they sent home. But these benefits were offset by the emotional hardship of separation. Tadiwos Hailemariam said that while his family had saved the expenses of taking care of him, they missed his love and company. They had benefitted financially as he sent regular remittances, and pays for fertilizer expenditures – a costly commodity back home. 'I also brought my younger brother,' he says, 'so they are getting extra remittances from him'.

Addisalem Gobena said that by emigrating she became her family's hope:

> There is the hope that if my parents fall ill, I will cover medical costs. Also help them if something bad happens. So, it's not just the money I can send them. More important is that they have a daughter in Johannesburg.

She indicated that if necessary relatives could be brought to Johannesburg. 'But,' she added, 'they miss us a lot. Whenever there is a celebration my mother will always say, "if only we were together"'.

Respondents reiterated that the monetary benefits of migration were neither automatic nor immediate. Shemsu Shiferaw said that in the first five or six years of his life in Johannesburg his family didn't benefit financially. It took him time to settle in business. He also said that because he is the eldest in the family he carried a lot of responsibility at home and his departure meant that the family lost those benefits. He had worked in a private company in Addis and had a good salary.

Social freedom and vigilance

Tadiwos Hailemariam said that the Ethiopian community moderated the increased social freedom in Johannesburg. He said, 'You are watched by fellow Ethiopians and people will still admonish you if you misbehave. You can say "voetsek,"' he said, evoking a South Africanism of reprimand usually reserved for chasing away a dog. But he added that the social control could not be escaped. It was necessary to watch each other and to keep people on track because, 'it's possible to fall out of the system if you do not keep working properly'.

Addisalem Gobena noted, 'for various reasons you have to be reserved. Everyone knows the details of everyone else's life here. There are no secrets. If you do well you will be identified in the community. And there are suspicions', referring to the Ethiopian community. 'You may not dress up or display anything. The environment doesn't allow that. We only dress up on celebrations and weddings.'

Sara Alemu hinted at rivalries and jealousies within the ethnic business enclave, 'People watch whether you change in Johannesburg. If you show off or wear flashy clothes you can be identified for making a fortune here.' And this vigilance was not restricted to fellow Ethiopians. She said the identification of Ethiopians as wealthy and the specific risk that this brings in a city with an astronomical crime rate is linked to the public display of success that was afforded Ethiopian migrants during the African Cup of Nations. Sara says Ethiopians who dressed well and celebrated lavishly at that time were identified and targeted as successful migrants.

Addisalem Gobena indicated that suspicions within the enclave of 'Jeppe' could become very personal. She said, 'When you are away and alone you feel too much.' She says social life is difficult.

> It is difficult to build trust. Even with your husband. Because its not only between you and your husband. Others watch you. If you stay outside late at night they talk to him. They say why do you give her so much freedom. People interfere. Unless God gives you a good husband, relations here are very difficult.

The people who Addisalem met in 'Jeppe' were not friends beyond the workspace. 'Even though we eat together, these are not real friends.' She may also have been reflecting the gendered relations in 'Jeppe' where, Yimer (2012) finds, women are caught up in the day-to-day operations of running a business and unlike the men have limited access to socialize and to opportunities to interact on a non-business level with fellow Ethiopians. Addisalem expressed loneliness and a lack of trust in the community. She said she coped by 'closing my door and praying' and by receiving counseling from a church elder. She says her sister is her best friend.

Gender violence and risk

Helen Zewde described her experiences of abuse as a woman migrant. The shop owner she worked for was good to her. When he asked her to marry him she agreed. Her life changed dramatically. When she first arrived and worked in 'Jeppe' as a single woman she had been able to send money home to help her family. Her husband stopped that. He put restrictions on her, including banning her from using Skype to connect with her family. 'So for years I couldn't see what they looked like when I talked with them,' she said. When she fell pregnant he became physically and verbally abusive. The abuse continued for two years and was often linked to his accusations that she was seeing other men in the workplace. When she was interviewed for this study she was filing for a divorce. She said the suspicion and the abuse was one of the difficulties of being a woman in this overwhelmingly male-dominated business environment. She added that she had few friends to turn to, as relations in 'Jeppe' were business focused. She said that after work hours she was alone, 'It's just me, my baby and God'.

Askale Dagnachew who came to Johannesburg alone at the age of 25 said living alone as a woman in Johannesburg and in the Ethiopian community was very tough, 'When you need something they want something from you,' she said of the pressure she was constantly put under for sexual favors. She wanted to return home.

Keeping up appearances

The interviews highlight the pressure to succeed that migrants experience both in Johannesburg and from their families in Ethiopia. Several respondents indicated that there was a family expectation that the migrant would achieve success in the host country and that it was a matter of honor to prove that success. It would be shameful to return home without having been materially successful. Addisalem Gobena said that her mother became ill and she and her sister visited even though they had not yet made money in Johannesburg. 'We came here to make a better life and our family expects us to be in a better position,' she said. 'Many people stay abroad waiting to make a success, even though they want to return home,' she said.

Conclusion

The narratives presented here demonstrate widely varied and individual experiences of Ethiopian migrants' separation and of connection with relatives and others who they have left behind, as well as of social capital available and social connections forged in the host city of Johannesburg. While the narratives are not intended to offer generalizations, they do offer insights that highlight features of social disconnection and connection that are particular to the Ethiopian migrant experiences in the Johannesburg context.

The irregular nature of migration to Johannesburg as well as the route to regularization – that of seeking political asylum places heavy restrictions on the probabilities of migrants' returning to or visiting Ethiopia once they have left. Respondents in this study expressed the palpable emotional rupture of loss of contact with home, family, and friends. Several respondents expressed the experience of living physically in Johannesburg while longing emotionally for home. Loss and severe disconnection with close relatives was reported.

There is evidence of a substantial network of formal as well as informal social institutions that are designed to import Ethiopian tradition and social apparatus to the host society. The centrality of religion in the tradition of Ethiopians has been accommodated and most migrants working in 'Jeppe' observe celebrations. All the major Ethiopian faith-based denominations are present in the city and are frequented by Ethiopian migrants. These are sites not only of worship but also of socializing and support. Formal institutions and non-profit community organizations have been set up in response to the needs of individuals or particular groups within the Ethiopian community. Traditional Ethiopian social institutions have also been imported and adapted for the needs of migrants. Funeral clubs and social clubs are common and the practices of these have been adapted to suit the life and work style of migrants. Meeting places are often not in the home and mourning periods are restricted to accommodate the need to return to work as soon as possible.

The web of social capital in this dense ethnically dominated enclave is thus significant. Yet respondents report that there are social ruptures within the space that undermine the support possible in this area. A sense of disconnection within the broader network of connection was evident as people spoke of loneliness and mistrust. The social capital is further influenced by the overwhelming role of 'Jeppe' as a place to make money. This dominates all social interaction within the Ethiopian enclave and makes this it, in the first instance, an entrepreneurial enclave. There is enormous competition and high economic risk in the saturating entrepreneurial enclave of 'Jeppe'. Thousands of small-scale traders are vying for the same goods and the same customers. In this cauldron of near-perfect competition the risks of failure are extreme. There is a transparency of information in this economic cluster where business operates in small highly visible shop fronts. There are few business secrets. And social interaction is constrained by the features of business interaction that include competition and suspicion, which, at times, turn into conflicts among these migrant entrepreneurs. This latter point has been raised in research on migrant entrepreneur in other contexts (nDeon et al. undated).

The move to a more modern context of Johannesburg did not necessarily offer respondents unqualified social freedom. Respondents expressed both the pressure to conform and the freedom not to abide by strictures of Ethiopian society in Johannesburg. High levels of economic, social and personal vigilance amongst fellow Ethiopians were noted and respondents reported widespread suspicion amongst fellow Ethiopians. Mistrust is linked not only to business competition but also to vigilance over displays of wealth and to patriarchal practices toward women.

The context of Johannesburg impacts on social connection. Crime and the threat of xenophobia loom over the lives of migrants. Socially the danger of being mugged, robbed or killed limits migrants' movement and socializing as it restricts movement and hours spent in the public domain. Migrants may opt for modest attire in order to lessen the risk of being targeted as successful and so threatened with theft.

In terms of the notion of dual presence the responses in this research do not support the idea that technology has eased the possibility of being both 'here' and 'there' at the same time. While it has undoubtedly enabled connection and degrees of continuity in relationship, technology has not translated into a sense of dual presence. Respondents speak categorically of Johannesburg and of their source country or neighborhood as distinct places. They convey a string sense of 'home' being irreplaceable. While several express the sense of a longing for Ethiopia the experience is more one of feeling split between two contexts rather than having integrated a co-existence of the 'here' and 'there'. Home is decidedly separate and is the source and host contexts are 'somewhere else'.

In summary, this research explored the nature of social networks that exist for Ethiopian migrants whose mainstay in the host city of Johannesburg is making money. The social world of Ethiopian migrants in this entrepreneurial enclave is complex. Many social connections and dislocations are affected by the life choices in which income generation and economic relations are the primary aim and social relations are necessarily secondary. Others are influenced by the strength of formal and informal ethnic social networks that serve the needs of Ethiopian migrants.[8]

Disclosure statement

No potential conflict of interest was reported by the authors.

Notes

1. Research assistance in the form of some direct interviews and translation for some interviews conducted by Tanya Zack were provided by Abraham Tsegaye (at his request, his name has

been changed for the purpose of this paper). Yordanus Seifu conducted interviews in the home language of respondents.
2. At the request of most interviewees, the names of all respondents have been changed for the purposes of this paper.
3. Former black residential areas on the outskirts of Johannesburg.
4. In 'Jeppe' intermediaries earn a living by sourcing clothing samples from Chinese outlets to show to Ethiopian traders in order to obtain orders. They insert a small profit into the final sale amount.
5. An Idir is a funeral group that plays a supportive role to grieving relatives at a time of death through regular visits and through assistance with funeral and other arrangements.
6. Mahbers are social clubs originally connected to the Ethiopian Orthodox church and are vehicles for the monthly celebration of patron saints. Members meet at one another's homes to feast and socialize.
7. Genfo is a stiff porridge served for breakfast in Ethiopia. It is traditional for relatives and friends to come together to eat genfo to celebrate the birth of a baby.
8. Interviewers: Yordanos Seifu (YS), Abraham Tsegaye (AT) and Tanya Zack (TZ).

References

LIST OF INTERVIEWEES
1. Tadiwos Hailemariam (male), interviewed by YS, 5 September 2014
2. Sara Alemu (female), interviewed by YS, 4 September 2014
3. Mulualem Gebru (male), interviewed by TZ, 11 September 2014
4. Addisalem Gobena (female), interviewed by YS, 28 August 2014
5. Admassu Mulugeta (male), interviewed by AT, 14 August 2014
6. Ashenafi Mamo (male), interviewed by TZ, 22 September 2014
7. Dereje Hussen (male), interviewed by YS, 26 August 2014
8. Jemal Abdela (male), interviewed by AT, 17 August 2014
9. Marta Agonafir (female), interviewed by TZ, 20 September 2014
10. Endriyas Desta (male), interviewed by AT, 13 August 2014
11. Helen Zewde (female), interviewed by TZ, 1 September 2014
12. Eskindir Alemu (male), interviewed by YS, 26 August 2014
13. Ketema Teshome (male), interviewed by AT, 14 August 2014
14. Misganaw Goshu (male), interviewed by AT, 13 August 2014
15. Abraham Ashagre (male), interviewed by AT, 17 August 2014
16. Mulatu Tekle (male), interviewed by AT, 14 August 2014
17. Arega Hailu (male), interviewed by TZ, 22 September 2014
18. Shemsu Shiferaw (male), interviewed by YS, 5 September 2014
19. Belahcew Niguse (male), interviewed by AT, 17 August 2014
20. Zerihum Mengistu (male), interviewed by AT, 15 August 2014
21. Matiyas Solomon (male), interviewed by TZ, 28 August 2014
22. Askale Dagnachew (female), interviewed by AT, 15 August 2014

Aldridge, H. E., and R. Waldinger. 1990. "Ethnicity and Entrepreneurship." *Annual Review of Sociology* 16: 111–135.
Dufoix, S. 2008. *Diasporas*. Berkeley: University of California Press.
Gebre, L. T., P. Maharaj, and N. K. Pillay. 2011. "The Experiences of Immigrants in South Africa: A Case Study of Ethiopians in Durban, South Africa." *Urban Forum* 22: 23–35.
Hagan, J. 1998. "Social Networks, Gender and Immigrant Incorporation: Resources and Constraints." *American Sociological Review* 63 (1): 55–67.
IOM. 2009. *In Pursuit of the Southern Dream: Victims of Necessity, Assessment of the Irregular Movement of Men from East Africa and the Horn to South Africa*. Geneva: International Organization for Migration.

IOM. 2013. *The Wellbeing of Economic Migrants in South Africa: Health, Gender and Development*. Working paper for the World Migration Report.

Kanko, T. D., A. Bailey, and C. H. Teller. 2013. "Irregular Migration: Causes and Consequences of Young Adult Migration from Sothern Ethiopia to South Africa." Paper presented at the XXVII International Population Conference, Busan, South Korea, August 26–31.

Landau, L. 2011. *Exorcising the Demon Within: Xenophobia, Violence and Statecraft in Contemporary South Africa*. Johannesburg: Wits University Press.

Madianou, M., and D. Miller. 2011. *Migration and New Media: Transnational Families and Polymedia*. London: Routledge.

Massey, D. S., J. Arango, G. Hugo, A. Kouaouci, A. Pellegrino, and J. E. Taylor. 1998. *Worlds in Motion. Understanding International Migration at the End of the Millennium*. Oxford: Clarendon Press.

Messay, M. 2005. *Debub Africa: Ye Tesfayitu Midir*. Addis Admass Gazeta Qitse 5 Hidar 13 to Yekatit 30: 8. ["South Africa: The Dream Land." *Addis Admass Magazine* November 22 to March 10: 8.]

nDoen, M., C. Vrije, P. Vrije, and P. Vrije. Undated. "Ethnic Entrepreneurship and Migration: A Survey from Developing Countries."

Sinedu, H. 2009. "Tikuret yemiyashawu hige-wot ye-sewochziwuwur" [An Irregular Migration of Men that Needs Focus]. *Addis Zemen Megazine*, November 15: 11.

UNHCR. 2014. *2014–2015 Global Appeal South Africa*. Report from UN High Commissioner for Refugees. Accessed August 12, 2015. http://www.unhcr.org/528a0a2916.html.

Wilson, K., and A. Portes. 1980. "Immigrant Enclaves: An Analysis of the Labor Market Experience of Cubans in Miami." *The American Journal of Sociology* 86 (2): 295–319.

Yimer, A. M. 2012. *The Ethiopian Clubs: The Development of Social Institutions and Identities amongst Ethiopians in Johannesburg*. Unpublished MA thesis, University of the Witwatersrand.

Zack, T. 2013. "Seeking Logic in the Chaos Precinct – 'Jeppe'." In *Rogue Urbanism: Emergent African Cities*, edited by E. Pieterse & A. Simone, 283–291. Johannesburg: Jacana Media & African Centre for Cities.

Zack, T. 2015."'Jeppe' – Where Low-End Globalisation, Ethnic Entrepreneurialism and the Arrival City Meet." *Urban Form* 26 (2). doi:10.1007/s12132-014-9245-1.

Trafficking of Ethiopian women to Europe – making choices, taking risks, and implications

Anne Kubai*

Department of Theology, Uppsala University, Uppsala, Sweden

ABSTRACT

This piece focuses on the Ethiopian women victims of trafficking – the agency of these women in the whole trafficking process, and issues of choice – 'trying a chance', or just taking a risk to get out of poverty or difficult social circumstances, considering that they are lured, tricked, coerced, or even forced into the hands of traffickers by a wide range of circumstances and people, including family and friends. Traffickers target girls with economic, social, and family problems. Most of the trafficking of women and girls from Ethiopia is carried out through the use of service 'agencies' and human smugglers who facilitate the process of migration through a number of routes. Many of those who use the 'desert route' often begin from Sudan to North Africa from where they cross to Europe. The data for this contribution were generated in a study – 'Captured in Flight: Experiences of violence among African women in Sweden' – funded by the Swedish crime prevention agency (Brottsoffermyndgheten). The research for the project has been carried out in Sweden, but the women whose case studies are presented here have been in the Middle East, Turkey, Italy, Finland, and Greece before coming to Sweden.

Introduction

In the last decade, scholars have paid attention to migration and investigated factors, patterns, trends, economic aspects, impact on communities of origin, and citizenship and integration issues in the countries of destination. Simply defined, migration is the action or process of changing the place of residence permanently or temporarily. Migration can also be voluntary or involuntary, though as some scholars would like to argue, very few people would take the risk of leaving their countries or communities and migrate to unknown places without being forced to do so by circumstances that are usually beyond their control. Often the line between migration that is motivated by a sense of adventure and the search for greener pastures is blurred. However, it is evident that for majority of Africans who seek to migrate to Europe, America and other places do so largely in order to seek refuge from conflicts, poverty, repression, and related challenges. Whatever the causes and though migration has always been there, there is no doubt that it is one of the most phenomenal globalization trends of our time. Globalization has increased not only the flows of immigrants but also their diversity. Ali (2013), relying on the World Migration Report (2011) points out that, about a billion people (that is one in seven of the world's population) are immigrants. According to official World Bank statistics, 30 million Africans have migrated outside the continent and these figures are expected to grow significantly in the coming decades (2011a).

The Horn of Africa has been ravaged by conflicts for more than three decades, and as we shall illustrate below these have triggered migration flows particularly from Ethiopia and Somalia. The prevailing state of repression, conflict with Ethiopia, and political violence in Eritrea are the major causes of the current wave of migration from that country. These are not peculiar to the Horn of Africa; they are part of the global causes of migration which have become generally widespread.

History provides useful insights, especially when we recall the phenomenon of slavery and slave trade that linked Africa with the rest of the world through a horrific trade in human beings. Here we would like to recall the images of slave ships that are now relics seen only in photographs in museums, and question whether they have any semblance with the rickety boats overloaded with human cargo perilously floating across the Mediterranean Sea in the service of international modern slavery and slave trade that is euphemistically referred to as human trafficking. Why would human traffickers find a market for humans as commodities in contemporary societies, which pride themselves in the protection of human rights and gender equality? Buying and selling is a two-way process/interaction. It is assumed that goods which have no commercial or other value cannot be sold or bought. From this perspective, the explanation for human trafficking must reside in the dominant ideas and ideals of the day about the values of persons – those that underpin social and structural factors both in the countries of origin and destination. This also implies a paradigm shift in the re-interpretation of the notion of demand and supply with regard to human trafficking. It implies a reversal of prevailing perspectives in the way of looking at the economic factors – poverty in Africa – as the main driver of human trafficking; and looking at the global economic pull factor from the perspective of entrepreneurship and profitability.

There is no doubt that Ethiopia has experienced tremendous displacement of people for decades. Ethiopia is known for its 'complex challenges of food insecurity, overpopulation, drought, political instability, and ethnic conflict. In addition to these issues, Ethiopia faces large challenges with respect to migration flows' (Fransen and Kuschminder (2009, 4). The volume, direction of the flows, and the character of migration from Ethiopia have gone through a number of changes over the last four decades (Andersson 2014) due to these and other factors, which include geopolitical and economic developments in the Horn of Africa region. A rough periodization of Ethiopian migration puts it into four phases: first, the flows of migration shaped by the pre-1974 dynamics of the Cold War which engendered a revolution that overthrew the Emperor and installed a Marxist military regime that became known as the *Derg*, forced many, largely the educated elite to seek asylum in Europe and the USA. Second, the 'red terror' of the Derg (1974–1982) drove thousands of Ethiopians out of the country. A third wave of migration in the form of family re-unification in the Western countries took place between 1982 and 1991. Fourth was the politics of ethnic federalism since 1991, which prompted a new exodus of people fleeing ethnic violence and political repression in Ethiopia (Terrazas 2007). A closer examination of the combination of factors behind of these waves of Ethiopian migration reveals a clear link between local and global trends of the Cold War era.

It is illustrative for our purpose to note that in these waves of Ethiopian migration, in 1992, 'women become the dominant group' to Sweden and 'especially in 1994 and 1995 the female dominance over the males is striking' (Agnarson 2006, 18).

In addition to political migration, Ethiopia has experienced periodic severe draughts and these too have contributed to migration flows Thus in the earlier years Ethiopian migrants were fleeing conflict and famine, but in the 'later years the motives ... to flee their country shifted to more economic motives' (Fransen and Kuschminder 2009). A quick look at the demographic characteristics of Ethiopia shows that it is one of the African countries with the largest national population (80 million in 2009), coupled with one of the highest (11th) population growth rates in the world, at 3.21 percent (Fransen and Kuschminder 2009). There is no doubt that a high population growth rate exerts pressure on the available resources and economic opportunities of the majority of the population, and this has implications for migration.

One of the most salient characteristics of current Ethiopian international migration is the flow of women migrating to the Middle East as domestic workers (Woldemichael 2013). The most popular destinations for Ethiopian female domestic workers are Saud Arabia, Lebanon, United Arab Emirates, and Yemen. From these destinations, some of them find their way to Europe. Trafficking of Ethiopian women both internally and internationally from rural areas to urban centres for prostitution and domestic labour, respectively, is a growing problem. The exact number of women trafficked remains unknown. Apart from the flow of irregular migrants, the recruitment made by the Ministry of Labour and Social Affairs (MoLSA) shows a massive increase in migrant workers. A Ministry of Labour report shows that between 2008 and 2011, 255,945 women and girls migrated to Saudi Arabia and Kuwait to work as domestic helps (Woldemichael 2013). By any standards, this is a large number of Ethiopian domestic workers in these two countries. Further, it is reported that, the MoLSA facilitated the migration of 104,131 girls during the first eight months in 2013. An approximate number of 1,500 trainees who follow the legal recruitment and travel process are said to receive 'orientation' from the MoLSA every day.

However, in spite of this large number of trainees that go through the MoLSA daily, it is important to note that partly because the process through the ministry is long and tedious (Wakgari 2014, 239), an even greater number of women seek to migrate with the 'help of business people', as those that we interviewed for this study put it. The business people are traffickers and human smugglers who work for a fee and promise not only to make the process less tedious, but also better jobs for the girls and more remittances to the families whose daughters migrate internationally. Thus they provide stronger incentives and are more likely to recruit a large number of women and girls mainly because they target individuals, families, and communities that are more vulnerable during recruitment. As I shall illustrate below, girls in the rural areas are vulnerable to trafficking first to the urban centres and then to international destinations. Woldemichael (2013, 13) observes that 'displacement is disguised as better employment opportunities; and the recruitment of potential victims is initiated by different parties including relatives, friends, local brokers, and private employment agents'.

The business of trafficking of Ethiopian women and girls has become well established, with a network of operators in neighbouring countries. Therefore, apart from those whose recruitment as domestic workers is facilitated by MoLSA, thousands of others are trafficked to the Middle East for involuntary domestic labour. It is reported that:

In 2013, NGOs observed a greater influx of workers from Ethiopia. Some migrant workers face forced labor after arriving in Bahrain, experiencing unlawful withholding of passports, restrictions on movement, contract substitution, nonpayment of wages, threats, and physical or sexual abuse. (USA Department of State 2014)

However, there are no statistical data on trafficked women and girls because the methods of recruitment and routes for trafficking are varied and clandestine. A number of studies have focused on trafficking of Ethiopian women and girls to the Middle East, for instance, Tekle and Belayneh (2000), Mesfin (2003), Beydoun (2006), Endeshaw, Gebeyehu, and Reta (2006), Wakgari (2014) and Reda (2012). But little attention has been given particularly to those who find their way into Europe: their individual and family background, process of recruitment, individual experiences and the challenges of being undocumented in a country such as Sweden where they are unlikely to gain access to welfare benefits and the implications of remaining excluded from the Swedish society and its system. It is not known what happens to these women on arrival in different European societies, yet their presence presents a completely different scenario from that of the domestic work in the Middle East. In this paper therefore, I shall endeavour to fill this lacuna, not least because it is urgent for the member countries of the European Union to find a viable solution to the current international trade in human beings that is otherwise known as human trafficking; and to prevent the horrific deaths of thousands in the North African desert and on the waters of the Mediterranean Sea that have become a regular item in international news; but also because the complexity of women trafficking warrants an examination both in the country of origin (Ethiopia) and countries of destination in Europe in order to generate data that can help us to understand the complexity of human trafficking and hence produce actionable results that can inform policy.

The data for this paper were generated in a large study – 'Captured in Flight: Experiences of violence among African women in Sweden' – funded by the Swedish crime prevention agency (Brottsoffermyndgheten). The research for the project has been carried out in Sweden, but the women whose case studies are presented in this paper have been in the Middle East, Turkey, Italy, Greece and France before coming to Sweden. Contact has also been established with a number of Ethiopian women who have been trafficked in these countries. During a recent (2015) visit to Ethiopia I gained important insights into the phenomenal migration of Ethiopian women to the Middle East. It was a spectacle for me to see hundreds of women on one side of the old part of the airport; and an impressive crowd of family and friends on the other side, waiting to meet them. Also because of the particularly close relationship between Sweden and Norway, which facilitates easy mobility of immigrants between the two countries, we had the opportunity to interview several Ethiopian women living in Norway.

Methods

The fieldwork for this study was rather difficult to carry out for a number of reasons. First, the population under scrutiny is what is usually referred to as 'hidden'. Many of these women do not have legal resident papers and therefore they are usually unwilling to give interviews to strangers for fear of being exposed to law enforcement agencies who would target them for deportation. Second, a number of others who were willing to be interviewed were too traumatized to talk about their experiences and yet some others were unwilling to give face-to-face interviews and preferred to be interviewed by telephone. Third, others were unwilling to give detailed descriptions of their experiences either because the experiences 'were too painful to recount', or as they put it, they did 'not want to dwell too much on the past'. It was difficult to find these women, and therefore I often depended on members of the Ethiopian community that I came to know through my previous research on African Churches and Christian communities in Sweden to be able to make contacts with potential research participants.

I also contacted a number of organizations that provide care and services to undocumented immigrants and visited a number of women's shelters for those who have been violated. In addition, I visited two refugee camps in the north of Sweden where there were hundreds of refugees who had arrived by boat via Italy and through other routes by air and across the desert. There, 12 women were interviewed and others participated in two focus group discussions. Intimate personal stories and detailed descriptions of experiences of violence during trafficking cannot be presented to a group discussion for important reasons. Therefore, the focus of the group discussions was the challenges of being an undocumented refugee in Sweden and the impact of the Swedish system on the individual women, who apparently 'fall through its cracks' and continue to endure untold suffering. It is important here to mention the connection with different church groups because our previous research (Kubai 2013, 2014a, 2014b shows that church networks play an important role in supporting immigrants, including those who have been trafficked. In many cases, the churches and church networks provided both material and psychosocial support to some of the women who made their needs known to pastors and community leaders. As a result of their roles, community leaders often helped to make contacts with potential research participants.

For this particular paper 17 women were interviewed in different places. Interviews were conducted in the form of conversations that took place in homes and restaurant, sitting quietly over a meal or coffee and at the refugee camps. Three of the women were interviewed on the phone: one was hiding from traffickers in the Emirates where she had been working for two years and another one was somewhere in Uppsala. The third interview was conducted with a woman who has lived in Sweden for 13 years without a resident permit and therefore she is 'hiding'. For this reason, she was willing only to speak on the phone without revealing her identity. The women in this study travelled through different countries and routes, including the 'Libya route' by boat across the Mediterranean Sea to reach Europe. Others came by air to different destinations but ended up in Sweden for different reasons. Their descriptions of the journeys and harrowing experiences on the way to Europe are analysed using an integrated framework of rational choice and rational action theory.

In spite of criticism directed at rational choice theory, Kroneberg and Kalter (2012), drawing upon Hedström and Stern (2008), Voss and Abraham (2000) and Wittek, Snijders, and Nee (2012) point out that this theoretical framework has found its way into many sociological fields, including social inequality, stratification, family crime and deviance, and sociology of religion. For our purpose, rational choice theory is useful for the analysis of the role of the individual women victims of trafficking. Its view of individual behaviour–that 'actors consider the costs and benefits of available alternatives, form expectations about the consequences and choose the alternative that best satisfies their preferences' (Kroneberg and Kalter 2012) – is relevant for our analysis of the choices that trafficked women have to make at every stage. This will be discussed in greater detail in the following section.

Human trafficking as a migratory response to current globalizing social economic trends

Migration is defined by UNESCO as 'the crossing of the boundary of a political or administrative unit for a certain period of time. It includes the movement of refuges, displaced persons, uprooted people as well as economic migrants ... International migration is a territorial relocation across nation states' (Appleton 2011, 6, citing Unesco.org). A trafficked person is an immigrant. Human trafficking is complex and generally recognized as a global phenomenon. It is estimated that globally 600,000–800,000 men, women and children are trafficked across international borders every year. Of these, approximately 80 percent are women and girls and up to 50 percent are children. In a review of research and data, Adepoju (2005, 92) aptly sums up human trafficking in Africa thus:

> Africa's human trafficking and smuggling map is complicated, involving diverse origins within and outside the region ... Parents are often forced by poverty and ignorance to enlist their children, hoping to benefit from their wages to sustain the family's deteriorating economic situation. Some of these children are indentured into slave labour ... In East Africa, young girls and women abducted from conflict zones are forced to become sex slaves to rebel commanders or affluent men in Sudan and the Gulf States. Ethiopia is a source of trafficked women to Lebanon and the Gulf States ... Traffickers have recently extended the destinations of children to the EU, especially the Netherlands, UK, and beyond. Women and children are trafficked to Europe (Italy, Germany, Spain, France, Sweden, UK, The Netherlands) ... Trafficking syndicates obtain travel documents and visas for women and link them up with brothels abroad.

According to the Trafficking in Persons Report 2014 tier placing, countries whose governments ensure full compliance with the Trafficking Victims Protection Act's minimum standards are placed in Tier 1. A cursory look reveals that there is no African country on the list of the 31 countries in Tier 1. In the East African region, Uganda, Kenya, and Ethiopia are placed in Tier 2, while Sudan and Eritrea are in Tier 3.

The bulk of the research on human trafficking from Africa suggests that poverty is the main push factor; lack of sustainable livelihood, economic, and social opportunities, and the pressure to provide for the family are the major driving forces that increase the vulnerability of specific groups (Beydoun 2006, Manion (n.d.); Cameroon and Newman 2008; Fernandez 2010). It is also important to test the claim that trafficking of women is clearly related to the gender question – perspectives about the nature and role of women vis-à-vis that of men in society.

Trafficking of women and children for sexual purposes is seen as a 'growing threat to Europe' (Manion n.d.). In our view, this sense of threat does not only give impetus to the development of policies and measures that are being put in place to combat human trafficking, but it also informs the attitudes of the various actors in the countries of destination. The questions are: What type of threat is it? Is it considered to be a threat to the European economies or social values? What about the societies that produce the victims in countries of origin – how does this form of slavery threaten their humanity? These important questions have been ignored in the bulk of current research on human trafficking, which has focused primarily on the organized crime dimension and the routes largely because human trafficking is seen as contemporary form of slavery and a crime against humanity (Obi 2008). In its 2009 *Global Report on Trafficking in Persons*, the UNODC 'advocated for the collection of more and better information on trafficking in persons in order to facilitate improved analysis at the international level'. Four years later not much research had been accomplished and therefore the 2012 report 'highlighted the knowledge crisis with respect to human trafficking' (UNODC 2012, 80). The UNODC further observes that 'the complex variety of the trafficking flows, the diversity of the forms of exploitation, which are sometimes not even coded or clearly defined ... show that assessing in terms of number and victims is not an easy task' (2012, 80). Therefore, the UNODC states unequivocally that 'There is a real need for field research in order to estimate the number of victims trafficked in specific trafficking flows or in specific forms of trafficking' (2012, 80). The project on which this paper is based is directed at a specific form of trafficking, that of African women who end up in Europe.

It is reported that through fraud, coercion, and violence, victims of human trafficking are stripped of human rights for purposes of sexual exploitation or forced labour. Modes of coercion differ, among other reasons, depending on the origin of the victims: coercion and deceit are more frequent among victims originating from Eastern Europe, while the use of magic and voodoo-like practices as well as debt bondage are more frequent among victims from Africa (ICMPD – International Centre for Migration Policy 2009). There is no doubt that even from a cursory look, culture beliefs and practices are implicated in the whole process of trafficking of African women. Yet, the role of social values in human trafficking has been underinvestigated, misunderstood, or ignored altogether. We argue that this is a gross omission in research if one wants to understand more fully the nature of and address the manifold challenges of this modern form of slavery.

In year 2000, the UN articulated an additional protocol concerning trafficking of persons. 'The Protocol to Prevent, Suppress and Punish Trafficking in Persons, especially Women and Children', became known as the 'Palermo protocol'. The Protocol supplements the United Nations Convention against Transnational Organized Crime and criminalizes human trafficking. According to Ollus's (n.d.) analysis, the definition of exploitation is one of the controversial aspects of the Palermo Protocol because different countries have different legislation and views regarding sex trade, abuse of power and vulnerability of trafficked individuals. Art. 3 of the Protocol defines trafficking as 'exploitation of the position of others or other forms of sexual exploitation, forced labour services, slavery or practices similar to slavery, servitude or removal of organs' (Ollus n.d., 22). This definition is rather vague. Therefore, such international instruments which are inherently weak also become ineffective in combating human trafficking. Their implementation is often curtailed by the different legislation and policies in different countries. Though there is a number of studies that focus on the legal implications and the challenges in the implementation of this and other international instruments; the Council of Europe GRETA report (2014) shows that various challenges need to be addressed.

Trafficking of Ethiopian women to Europe

Elsewhere, we (Kubai and Ahalberg forthcoming) have determined that trafficking of African women to Europe for purpose of prostitution is relatively more prevalent in west Africa. Other research has also shown that at least 60 percent of migrant women sex workers in Italy come from Africa, with the majority being west African and generally identified as Nigerian even though many of them are known to be nationals of other countries in the region. However, it is important for us to point out here that though traditional beliefs and practices are important factors in women trafficking in both Ethiopia and Nigeria, the methods of recruiting and the process of trafficking differ in important respects. For instance, early marriage which is linked to trafficking affects 27 percent of girls in east Africa and 40 percent in west Africa. Countries such as Niger have 15 years as the national average age of first marriage; Mali and Chad 16 years and Nigeria and Eritrea 17 years (UNICEF 2005). It is instructive therefore, to note that:

> each country presents specific factors or different combinations of multiple factors that are unique to each situation. Also any analysis of trafficking flows must take into account the rapidly changing environment that can alter the trafficking patterns at local and international levels. (UNICEF 2005)

UNICEF also affirms that human trafficking in Africa is driven by a demand that is complex and multifaceted, and in most cases not adequately analysed. In an attempt to examine some aspects of this complexity, I will focus on the experiences of individual women *en route* across the desert, and then on the perilous boat journey across the Mediterranean Sea, and finally in different countries in Europe.

In Ethiopia

> trafficking of women and children from the rural areas to urban areas is widespread. The psychological and social legacy of slave trade that was widely practiced in the country until the 1930s along with the institution of prostitution, which has a long history and a strong presence in Ethiopian society have created a psychosocial environment that tolerates and even promotes the practice of trafficking in women and children. (IOM n.d., 5)

Available evidence shows that methods of internal trafficking are similar to those of international trafficking of Ethiopian women and girls. It is reported that

> there are certain 'auction centres' in Addis Ababa where a number of women and children trafficked from different regions of the country are sold to brothel owners like commodities. These places which are the head offices of principal 'agents' receive victims from middlemen and carry out the human trade. (IOM n.d., 24)

A study conducted on in-country trafficking revealed that three-fifths of the victims of trafficking were made vulnerable by unemployment, poverty, violence within the family that targets women, death of parents, and particularly the contribution of HIV to a growing number of orphans in many communities. As suggested above, harmful cultural practices, particularly in the rural areas where girls in the Amhara region are married at 14, while the national level average marriage age for all women is 17 years, also contribute to trafficking in women and girls. Indeed, previous studies point to a direct link between early marriage and migration.

However, reliable data on trafficking of women and girls in Ethiopia are not available, The International Labour Organization (ILO) report (2011) shows that 53 percent of Ethiopian female migrants are between 19 and 25 years of age, 30 percent are between 25 and 30 years and 13.5 percent are older. In most cases girls are trafficked before they turn 18. Most of the trafficking is carried out through the use of service agencies and human smugglers who facilitate the process of migration through a number of routes. The ILO report further shows that though both educated and uneducated women and girls are potential victims, female students who are unsuccessful in passing the school examinations at the end of eighth grade, junior secondary at 10th grade, and sometimes at the preparatory 12th grade levels are most vulnerable to human trafficking. The report further shows that most of the girls are recruited by local brokers who go around in their communities recruiting migrants. These people are known by community members as key links in the migration process. 'They are also actively disseminating information about employment opportunities in Arab countries, routes that result in successful migration; returns as well as benefits of migration. They particularly target girls with economic, social, educational and family problems' (ILO 2011, 31). It should also be remembered that in many cases families are involved in trafficking either by contacting the brokers directly or urging by their daughters to make the necessary contact with traffickers.

Most Ethiopian women victims of trafficking are taken to the Middle East as domestic workers, for instance, in 2013, NGOs observed a greater influx of workers from Ethiopia to Bahrain. Some of these migrants were subjected to forced labour, restrictions on movement, non-payment of wages, threats, and physical or sexual abuse. Also, their passports were unlawfully withheld after their arrival in Bahrain. Many Ethiopians travel through the Sudan to reach Libya and then proceed across the Mediterranean to European countries, particularly Italy and Malta. It is estimated that 75,000–100,000 Ethiopians migrate to Libya annually. Some of these victims on this route were reported as saying that they had been sold to traffickers (ILO 2011, 48). Many of those who have used the 'desert route' often begin from Sudan to North Africa from where they cross to Europe. Some users of this route also travel to Turkey and from there to Greece and onward to other European countries. Also some of the women destined for the Gulf States end up in Europe where they join a large number of undocumented immigrants.

At the individual level, an important driving factor in the case of women being trafficked from Ethiopia is the stories of success that they hear from those who have migrated. Many women send money to their families and also when they return, they tell stories of their success and encourage others to migrate. The family is considered to be quite important in Ethiopian culture. For example, Abeba said that through all the years that she toiled 'like a slave' in the Middle East, Turkey, and Greece, she sent most of the money that she made to her family and helped one of her cousins to set up a hair dressing business in Addis Abeba and paid school fees for her siblings. When asked why she sent money home even when she was in such a difficult situations, she said that it was expected of her by the family. She reminded me that often whole families are involved in raising the money for the brokers and traffickers. When she returned home after 11 years with several boxes full of gifts, her family and the whole neigbourhood saw her as an example of a successful migrant. As she said to me on return, no one knew anything about the suffering she had endured for 11 years, and 'they would not believe it' even if she told them about it. This shows however powerful globalization is,

> At the macro level, economic and social changes are altering marketing traditions and labour requirement. Access to global markets and information resources can have the side effect of raising unrealistic or unattainable expectations about living standards. Young women exposed

to images of extravagant lifestyles may be tempted to seek their fortune abroad, and thus be susceptible to traffickers' fraudulent promises. (UNICEF 2005, 6)

Recently, human trafficking has become a political issue in Ethiopia, largely due to the pressure exerted by civil society groups that have brought the plight of women who are trafficked to the attention of the public and relevant authorities. As a result, the Ethiopian Government has responded by creating an Inter-Ministerial Committee on trafficking of women and children. Also an anti-trafficking ordinance, 'the Private Employment Agency Proclamation 104/1998, provides for aggravated penalties for the perpetration of human rights abuses, including those that occur in the context of trafficking' (UNICEF 2005, 22).

Willing victims, risk takers, or rational choice makers?

In October 2014, when the survivors of a boat that sank in the Mediterranean Sea were interviewed by the BBC in Lampedusa, a number of them said that they had paid as much as 4000 US dollars to traffickers and smugglers in order to 'try (their) chance' and that they believed that death in the sea or safe arrival in Europe depends on the individual's fate. The case studies for this paper also said that though they did not know how perilous the journeys through various countries would be; and how much violence they would be exposed to along the way and even on arrival, they had some idea that might it be difficult to get to Europe and they were unsure of the whole process because they were dealing with strangers. But then each of them wanted to try her chance nonetheless. However, the question that remains unanswered is who sells and who buys women and girls for labour and sexual exploitation? Who is behind this highly complex trade in human beings? No attempt will be made to answer these questions here.

Instead, the focus of this piece is the individual women victims of trafficking – the agency of these women in the whole trafficking process, that is the question of choice, 'trying a chance', or just taking a risk to get out of poverty or difficult social circumstances, in spite of the fact that they are lured, tricked, coerced, or even forced into the hands of traffickers by a wide range of circumstances and people, including family and friends. For this discussion, I will analyse excerpts of interviews with three women survivors of trafficking from Ethiopia using an integrated framework of rational choice and rational action theory. I will examine the decisions that they make at different stages and in different circumstances. Women trafficked to the Middle East are usually between 20 and 30 years of age, girls between 17 and 19 years are also trafficked. The age of the women in this study ranges from 18 to 38 and they come from different parts of Ethiopia. They travelled through different routes, including the Sinai Desert, through Libya to Italy and Spain. Others departed from different ports in Ethiopia's neigbours to Cairo, Turkey and other places and finally found their way into Europe.

As said earlier, some of them worked in the Middle East and saved money which was paid to smugglers and traffickers, while others obtained money from their families who often contacted the so-called agents or business people to help women and girls to leave the country. Even if some of them may have been vulnerable to trafficking, a few of them who could pay up to 10,000 dollars to traffickers (even if the money might have been borrowed) cannot be considered to be extremely poor. Four of the women come from families where one of the parents has a small government pension and six of the women had been to the Middle East and saved money for the trip to Europe. In two cases the families are described as 'relatively not poor', yet their daughters joined the growing numbers of trafficked women apparently seeking a better life in Europe. One general characteristic though, is that the girls and women in this study have low level of education ranging from four to eight years. More than half of them could not continue with education because their families could not afford; while the rest had been married off quite early for various reasons.

In the following section of this paper, I provide excerpts from interviews conducted and then comment on issues and patterns that emerge. To ensure anonymity and protect the identity the women whose stories are presented below, I have used pseudonyms, picked up from a list of common Ethiopian girls' names.

Case study one: Abeba

I have passed through a lot of challenges since childhood. My step father was not good to me. I was deprived of food and even sleep. I left home when I was 12 and started to live with my aunt ... When I was in grade 7 ... I was raped by my school principal. I cried and told him I will report him to police. He begged me no to and bought me lots of things: gold necklace and other expensive things. He took good care of me. We lived together for 2 years and we have a daughter together. After I gave birth, he started to be very controlling. He didn't want me to go out, he didn't want me to meet friends or family. I left him and went to my family taking my daughter with me. My step father was worse. He insulted me for being irresponsible and unable to take care of my husband and my house.

That is when I started to think of leaving the country to go to the Middle East ... The agency took us to Yemen and after a week's stay; we were sold for 2000 USD to Arabs who took us to Syria. Those people had the full right of doing whatever they wanted with us. Nobody would be accountable. The agency that sent us here, even if he was legal, our transportation was illegal. We didn't pass through the legal procedure of labour migration so no one would take the responsibility of our safety.

Case study two: Berhane

I was born and raised in Ethiopia but my father was from Eritrea. I have never been in Eritrea but when the conflict between Ethiopia and Eritrea began and Eritreans were expelled from Ethiopia, I left the country ... I don't remember much since I was a child. I and my siblings lived with my mother. My father was not with us after I was born and I didn't have any contact or information about him. But when the war began, we are considered Eritreans because of my father; therefore, my two elder brothers and I left for the Sudan.

In 2008 I went to Libya through smugglers who transported me and many others in cars through the Sahara desert. I asked different people for advice about travelling to Libya and all had different opinions. There were people who said it was good and there are others who said it was not and advised me not to try it. I tried it any way. When they said we would travel by car, I thought it was a bus and expected the trip to have a proper road. But it was totally different and scary. There were four trucks and they put as many people as possible in each truck where we sat on top of each other and suffocated in the desert weather to travel about 700 km. The smugglers used GPS to find their way ...

My brothers paid for me 800 Sudanese pounds and I had some money on hand in case we were asked to pay again. After few days' travel, our Sudanese smugglers passed us over to

Lebanese smugglers. We were from different countries – Ethiopia, Eritrea, Somalia, Sudan and so on. They finally moved us to two trucks and that made it almost impossible to breathe. But we were lucky, none died. So many migrants die in the desert for various reasons: lack of water, food, getting sick, or are killed by kidnappers for the purpose of selling their organs etc. But we survived all these. The smugglers shouted at us and they usually beat the men. At some point, the truck I was in failed to function and we spent 3 days waiting for replacement or repair. During the wait in the middle of the desert, we saw helicopters flying above us. The smugglers said it was Egyptians and they might arrest us. As it was feared, four military cars with soldiers came to us next day. They searched and interrogated us. One woman explained that we are going to Libya for work and they easily let us go. If we had told them we were heading to Israel, it would have been a problem as I heard it from our transporters.

Case study three: Sheba

In the beginning Sheba, came to Finland through the help of her aunt who 'hired' her as a house maid. She has an elder sister who came through the same aunt with the same means earlier on and is now living in Sweden, married with two kids. After her permit in Finland expired, she came to Sweden and sought asylum as an underage seventeen year old (though she was an adult) at the time. The process took a year and she turned 18–officially an adult – therefore, she was denied asylum and advised to leave the country. But she did not leave. She did not want to talk about her situation, but she allowed her sister to speak for her. She has two jobs and earns a decent salary, probably working 'black', otherwise earning 13,000 SEK per month should be enough to get her a work permit. Also, since she was told to leave the country, and she is still 'undocumented', it is not possible for her to be in the country's tax system ... She speaks the language fluently, she is apparently integrated in the society but she is illegally in the country.

These women's experiences represent different motivations, engagement with abuses, and mistreatment, as well as routes through which women from Ethiopia are trafficked to Europe. Nevertheless, there are several important common elements in their narratives: the first is their own individual agency in decision-making at every stage, regardless of the militating circumstances. The decisions are made in what the women believe are in their best self-interest and also in consideration of the prevailing circumstances. If a rational action theory approach is used, it is not necessary to claim that 'all actors at all times act in an entirely rational way' however this may be construed (Goldthorpe 1998, 168). Abeba, like many young girls, has experienced a history of abuse and violence, first from her step father, and then her teacher who took advantage of her vulnerability and raped her. She decides to leave the country, put her life in the hands of traffickers, and pay the money that they demand from their victims. Berhane was caught up in the Ethiopia–Eritrean war and fled to the Sudan when she was a young girl. She asked different people for advice about travelling to Libya and all had different opinions – some said it was good and others advised against it. But she decided to try anyway, regardless of the conflicting opinions from the different people that she asked for advice. Sheba came to Finland through her aunt to work as a house maid. But soon she decided to leave Finland when the visa expired and unsuccessfully sought asylum in Sweden. She is now stuck in Sweden as an undocumented immigrant and whatever decision she takes will have serious consequences after ten years of living in limbo.

It is evident that the decisions are not based on reliable information and knowledge about distant lands and what the process of being trafficked entails, but the women put their lives in the hands of the traffickers. This can be understood in the light of Goldthorpe's suggestion that

> even where limits of an actor's information are recognized in situations of risk or uncertainty, it is supposed that they have as much information and can calculate as accurately as such situations will allow in order to maximize their expected, or subjectively utility. (1998, 170)

But since people have reasons for what they do, their behaviour is predictable only if we know what motivates them.

From these individual narratives, we learn about the factors that contribute to Ethiopian women's vulnerability to trafficking. Abeba, like many other girls, has experienced violence as a child within her family. Being poor and vulnerable, she fell prey to the school principal who raped her and made her pregnant; and with no other alternative, she became his wife. But the violence did not stop there because her much older husband became more controlling and curtailed her freedom of movement and association even with family members. Berhane also grew up without knowing anything about who her father was and the conflict between Ethiopia and Eritrea shaped her life. Though she depended on her brothers when she was younger, she made the decision to go to Libya in order to cross to Europe. She does not say much about her boyfriend who facilitated her travel by boat. Sheba was trafficked with the help of her own aunt, but then without a valid visa first in Finland and then in Sweden. Life has been difficult. She lives in fear of being caught and deported. Yet, she works sends money home – giving the impression that, like many Ethiopians in Sweden, she is living well.

Also from these narratives, we learn much about the trips across the sea and the desert. We learn that women and girls are sold and bought by different people who are free to do whatever they want with them.

Abeba

> The employers that bought me from the brokers treated me like a slave ... I cried and complained. They returned me to the brokers' office. In the office, I saw a notice written in Amharic that says, 'if you are not comfortable with your employer and want to escape call this number'. Even the number was written in Amharic words so that the brokers will not know what it is. I called the number and talked to a girl and told her my problems. I told her I didnt have any money but I would pay back the money when I get a job. She told me to find other girls who also wanted to escape. I knew some Ethiopian girls ... We contacted them, they paid the money for the brokers. We escaped to Turkey ...
> Then the plan to cross to Greece came up. I heard from brokers that it was possible to go to Greece if I pay 2500 USD. The brokers took me and other girls to Izmir. They promised to transport ... But the boat was an air pumped plastic (an inflatable boat) and they put 26 people in it and no captain. They took our 2500 USD, lying to us ... Those of us who survived wondered around the island where we were left. We were starved ... We reached Athens and didn't know what to do or where to go. The paper we were given said we had to leave the country in a month ... I was trying to find a European man by paying money so that I could get a permanent permit to live in Europe. It costs 8000 Euro to marry a European–sham marriage. The man I was dealing was a drug addict Greek who lived on the street. If you pay such people, they will sign for you that you are the wife, and then you will get the permit. The intention was to go to another European country, not to stay in Greece.

Berhane

The smugglers in the beginning were saying our destination was so close. But it seemed to take forever. We were passed on from smugglers to smugglers. They even asked us to pay more money. We made an agreement with them that we would pay after we arrive. It took us 11 days to reach Libya. Some people were ill because of lack of water. Fortunately, there was no serious problem in our group of migrants. We reached Libya at night and they took us to a rural kind house in a forest. Since they are illegals, they make every movement during the night. The next step was to transport us to town. I had paid everything, so I was free to make the next move. But there were people who were held for being unable to make part of the payment.

After four days, they transported some of us because we didn't have any debt – we didn't owe them any money. They put us in a car which was used to transport sheep. I think they wanted us to look like sheep to the police. We could not be seen since it was covered. When we reached Tripoli, each one of us was taken to different places with different smugglers. I was taken to a house that a smuggler had rented to put people with cases like mine.

… I had paid 1500 Lebanese Pounds for crossing to Europe. After two months, I had to return to town again since the weather was getting worse and the sea was getting full. I had lost the money I had paid. Since there was a chain of smugglers, it was difficult to ask any of them to return my money. One can't find them. Some people who decided to try irrespective of the bad condition died or got lost in the sea.

Sheba

Her family advised her to get married (sham marriage) by paying money (could be 150–200 thousand SEK) to a citizen or someone with permanent residency. But she refused because of her strong Christian faith, saying 'I have waited for God for long. I will keep waiting for him rather than do something he doesn't like'. She has a good and well-to-do family in Ethiopia, she has a good amount of money that she has saved from a hard work of 10 years and she would be able to start her own business if she went back to her Ethiopia. But she doesn't want to go back. She says it is too late. She says her years have been wasted waiting in desperation and frustration. Nevertheless, she says she will keep waiting on God to respond to her prayers.

From these excerpts we get poignant descriptions of the women's experiences of human trafficking from Ethiopia. There is no doubt that the networks of the traffickers are complex. It seems that there are traffickers involved whenever the women and girls need to move from one place to another. Even on arrival in Europe, there are men who are involved with criminal gangs that arrange sham marriages for exorbitant amounts of money. The trafficked women do all sorts of work, including prostitution, to make the money to pay for these marriages in order to get valid residence papers. Available evidence shows that in these sham marriages women are often trapped in violence, where they are faced with a stark choice: leave the man, lose the money and the chance for getting the all-important papers; or tolerate the violence and if you survive, get the residence papers and live in Europe 'happily ever after'. The girls and young women make these choices without sufficient knowledge of what lies ahead of them. Therefore, contrary to Goldthorpe's assumption that an actor 'contemplates, in one comprehensive view, everything that lies before him' or her and 'understands the range of alternative choices open' to them, we can say that the women do not fully understand the consequences of any strategies, at least to the point of being able to assign some significant value to them. Most of them apparently did not fully understand what to expect, but they took the risks to attempt to better their lives. To use the words of Goldthorpe again, 'thus whether the complications of risk and uncertainty are acknowledged or not, the issue of realism would seem to arise' – the question is whether these women 'do in fact make choices according to rationality requirements'. How much of what happens to them can be attributed to their own choices and whether the choices were the most rational at the time they were made is difficult to determine. What one can however say is that the agency of the individual women and girls cannot be ignored in the trafficking process. It must also be borne in mind that a choice made when one is vulnerable is hardly a choice; and that 'the reality of human trafficking is much more subtle' (USA Department of State 2014, 35).

Conclusion

In their own words the women in this study describe their experiences of being trafficked from Ethiopia to Europe. From these narratives, we can identify a number of things. Trafficking in Ethiopia is carried out by dense networks of brokers, smugglers, and traffickers. Trade in human beings is well organized from the rural areas to the city where the middlemen pick up the women and girls and hand them over to the intricate chains of agencies and sponsors. At the local community level there are brokers who hand over women and girls to brokers responsible for transportation and smuggling across regional borders. Then they are handed over to other traffickers who receive them in groups and hand them over to other traffickers somewhere along the way before reaching the destination. These traffickers operate as agencies and they have links with traffickers in countries of destination who sell the women to local 'buyers' and also trade in visas. Some of them are registered as employment agencies, presenting themselves as well-established businesses. However, as said above, in spite of the fact that Ethiopian government has enacted laws regulating employment agencies, trafficking women flourishes and many women continue to fall victim to labour trafficking networks. Also there is no direct assistance from the government to victims of trafficking.

The journey across the desert and the sea is fraught with danger and women are exposed to all forms of violence, including sexual assault by the traffickers. They are transported in inhuman conditions and denied food and water, and many of them die on the way. The traffickers charge exorbitant amounts of money for this type of transportation and often they take the money and abandon the victims in dangerous situations. Because the women and girls are often invisible and afraid to go to the authorities, no one is held responsible for their suffering and abuse. Also suffering does not end on arrival in the country of destination if the women cannot get the necessary residence permits. For example, Abeba describes her life in Greece for two years as 'sleep on the tree' – she lived in fear of being caught and she took the risk of paying a drug addict in order to get 'papers'.

In conclusion, the journeys that these women make are plagued with individual experiences of violence, conflict in decision-making, poverty, and slavery, all intersecting to keep the women 'captured in flight' as this research project is called. The ways in which trafficked women negotiate the hazardous process of trafficking; and how they resist abuse are understood in terms of individual women's agency, which is the subject of this paper. Here, I use the concept of rational choice in an attempt to understand the decisions and the risks that women take in different circumstances. The extracts of the narratives that are presented above allude to some of the ways in which the women 'rationalize' and negotiate difficult situations in order to be able to move on. For instance, Berhane says that, when they were caught in the desert by Egyptian military and interrogated, they told them that they were going to Libya for work because the women knew that if they said that they were going to Israel, 'there would be a problem'. But there was no guarantee that the soldiers would believe that women caught in the middle of North African desert were going to Israel, yet a woman quickly figured out an explanation for why they were in the place where they were found. In this particular instance, they were able to negotiate and take themselves out of a potentially dangerous situation. Apparently, the Egyptian soldiers let them go.

In this study, I came to the conclusion that, in spite of its weaknesses, the rational choice conceptual framework is helpful in the analysis of both voluntary and involuntary cases of women trafficking as well as forced prostitution. For instance, though the choices made under vulnerable conditions in reality are not choices, at the same time people seek to migrate in conditions of uncertainty, they hope or rationalize that elsewhere is better than what they are leaving behind. The concept of rational choice is also helpful for the in-depth analysis of coercion and consent of victims of trafficking, particularly the important question of where to draw the line between these two in migratory circumstances. This is also important because of the unclear distinction made between human smuggling and trafficking (Hamood 2006); and the definition of trafficking as articulated in the Protocol to Prevent, Suppress and Punish Trafficking in Persons, especially Women and Children' – the 'Palermo Protocol'.

Finally, the 'culture of migration is another factor underlying high levels of trafficking. Cross-border migration is considered personal, social and material success in most communities, creating wrong role models for younger generation' (ILO 2011, 23). The culture of migration has emerged in such areas as Kombolcha, Kemisse, Dessie and its environs because migration is associated with personal, social, and material success. Hence migration becomes the norm rather than the exception and remaining at home is considered as failure. Returnees contribute to this by exaggerating migration opportunities and splendour of life abroad.

Also in terms of family obligations, daughters are expected to support their families, and therefore they are expected to make personal sacrifice, to bear the pain, and not fail to meet these expectations. That is why all the women described in this study continued to send money home even when they were in dire circumstances. This is also reflected in the way Abeba was treated by her step father at first and later when she left her school teacher husband: she was abused for failing to take care of her house, in other words for failing to be a dutiful wife at 17 years of age. That is the way this society treats its women by engaging in perpetuating cultural practices that encourage early marriage of young girls, many of whom escape to city brothels or put their lives in the hands of traffickers to get away or find a better life elsewhere.

In this paper, using examples from rural Ethiopia, case studies and individual narratives, I argue that trafficking of women in Ethiopia is not only due to poverty; there are other key factors that are of a social dimension, for instance women's low status, which in turn generates low self-esteem; structural vulnerability and marginalization related to lack of education and remoteness of rural areas related to the process of social development or lack of it. This intersectionality of key factors links my conclusion to Chong's observation that:

> the global flows and polarizations among the national state centres of power that reinforce neoliberal economic policies and the developing regions, which are battered by factors such as impoverishment as well as civil and political instability are all elements that facilitate trafficking and labour exploitation. (2014, 203)

Hence the factors that intersect and sustain modern-day slavery and trade in human beings are concomitantly local and global.

Disclosure statement

No potential conflict of interest was reported by the author.

References

Adepoju, A. 2005. "Review of Research and Data on Human Trafficking in Sub-Saharan Africa". *International Migration* 43 (1/2): 76–98.

Agnarson, L. 2006. *The Integration of Ethiopian Immigrants in Sweden, 1990–2000.*

Ali, M. 2013. "Socio-Economic Status of Tigrean Ethnic Immigrants. The Case of North Ethiopia." *Journal of Settlements and Spatial Planning*, 4 (2): 239–247.

Andersson, L. 2014. *Migration, Remittances and Household Welfare in Ethiopia*. United Nations University Working Paper Series 2004–004.

Appleton, J. 2011. *Assimilation or Integration: Migrants in Europe*. Gloucester: Redcliffe College. https://encountersmissionjournal.files.wordpress.com/2011/08/appleton_-2011-03_integration_and_migration.pdf

Beydoun, K. A. 2006. "The Trafficking of Ethiopian Domestic Workers into Lebanon." *Berkeley Journal of International Law* 24 (3): 250–286.

Cameron, S., and E. Edward Newman, eds. 2008. *Trafficking in Humans: Social Cultural, Political Dimensions*. New York: United Nations University Press.

Council of Europe. 2014. *Group of Experts on Action against Trafficking in Human Beings*. GRETA report.

Endeshaw, Y., Gebeyehu, M., and B. Reta. 2006. *Assessment of Trafficking in Women and Children in and from Ethiopia*. Addis Ababa: IOM.

Fernandez, B. 2010. "Cheap and Disposable? The Impact of the Global Economic Crisis on the Migration of Ethiopian Women Domestic Workers to the Gulf." *Gender & Development*, 18 (2): 249–262.

Fransen, S., and K. Kuschminder. 2009. "Migration in Ethiopia: History, Current Trends and Future Prospects". Paper Series: Migration and Development Country Profiles. Maastricht Graduate School of Governance.

Goldthorpe, J. H. 1998. "Rational Action Theory for Sociology." *The British Journal of Sociology*, 49 (2): 167–192.

Hamood, S. 2006. *African Transit Migration through Libya to Europe: The Human Cost*. The American University.

Hedström, Peter, and Stern. Charlotta. 2008. "Rational Choice and Sociology." In *The New Palgrave Dictionary of Economics*, edited by Steven N. Durlauf and Lawrence E. Blume. Palgrave Macmillan. http://www.nuffield.ox.ac.uk/users/hedstrom/rct.pdf

ICMP (International Centre for Migration and Development). 2009. "Legislation and the Situation Concerning Trafficking in Human Beings for the Purpose of Sexual Exploitation in EU Member States." http://ec.europa.eu/dgs/home-affairs/doc_centre/crime/docs/evaluation_eu_ms_thb_legislation_en.pdf

International Labour Office (ILO). 2011. *Global Employment Trends for Youth: 2011 Update*. Geneva: ILO.

Kroneberg, C., and F. Kalter. 2012. "Rational Choice Theory and Empirical Research: Methodological and Theoretical Contributions in Europe." *Annual Review of Sociology* 38: 73–92. doi:10.1146/annurev-soc-071811-145441.

Kubai, A. 2013. "'Singing the Lord's Song in a Strange Land': Challenges and New Frontiers for African Churches in Sweden." In *Babel is Everywhere! Migrant Readings from Africa, Europe and Asia*, edited by K. Asamoah-Gyadu, D. Fröchtling and A. Kunz-Lübcke, 251–266. New York, NY: Peter Lang.

Kubai, A. 2014a. "Accommodation and Tension: African Christian Communities and their Swedish Hosts." In *The Changing Soul of Europe: Religions and Migration in Northern and Southern Europe*, edited by H. Vilaça, E. Pace, I. Furseth, and P. Pettersson, 149–172. London: Ashgate.

Kubai, A. 2014b. "Living by the Spirit. African Christian Communities in Sweden". In *The Public Face of African New Religious Movements in Diaspora: Imagining the Religious 'Other'*, edited by A. Adogame, 163–189. London: Ashgate Inform Series on Minority Religions and Spiritual Movements.

Kubai, A., and Ahlberg. forthcoming. "Spiritually Bound: 'Folk Religion', Human Trafficking and Sexual Exploitation of African Women in Sweden." *Nordic Journal of Migration Research*.

Manion, K. n.d. "Trafficking in Women and Children for Sexual Purposes: A Growing Threat in Europe." *Social Work in Europe* 9 (2). Accessed May 17, 2013. http://www.scie-socialcareonline.org.uk/repository/fulltext/81042.pdf.

Mesfin, E. 2003. *Women and Children Trafficking within and from Ethiopia*. Faculty of Law, Addis Ababa University.

Obi, N.I. 2008. *Global Trafficking in Women and Children: An Overview of Trafficking in Women and Children*. Boca Raton, FL: Taylor & Francis Group, LLC.

Reda, A. 2012. *An Investigation into the Experiences of Female Victims of Trafficking in Ethiopia*. Pretoria: University of South Africa.

Tekle, A. & Belayneh, T. 2000. *Trafficking of Women from Ethiopia*. Report, Women Affairs Sub-sector, Office of Prime Minister and IOM.

Terrazas, A. M. 2007. *Beyond Regional Circularity: The Emergence of an Ethiopian Diaspora*. Washington, DC.: Migration Policy Institute.

UNICEF. 2005. Trafficking in Human Beings, Especially Women and Children in Africa. *Innocenti Research Centre*. http://www.unicef-irc.org/publications/pdf/trafficking-gb2ed-2005.pdf

UNDOC (United Nations Office on Drugs and Crime). 2012. *Global Report on Trafficking in Persons*. New York: United Nations.

USA Department of State. 2014. *Trafficking in Persons Report*. June 2014.

Voss, T., and M. Abraham. 2000. "Rational Choice Theory in Sociology: A Survey." In *The International Handbook of Sociology*, edited by Stella R. Quah and Sales Arnaud, 50–83. London: SAGE.

Wakgari, G. 2014. "Causes and Consequences of Human Trafficking in Ethiopia: The Case of Women in the Middle East." *International Journal of Gender and Women's Studies* 2 (2): 233–246.

Wittek, R., T. Snijders, and V. Nee, eds. 2012. *Handbook of Rational Choice Social Research*. Stanford: Stanford University Press.

Woldemichael, S. 2013. *The Vulnerability of Ethiopian Rural Women and Girls – The Case of Domestic Workers in Saudi Arabia and Kuwait*. Saarbrücken: Lambert Academic.

World Bank. 2011a. *Leveraging Migration for Africa: Remittances, Skills, and Investments*. Washington, DC: World Bank Publication.

World Migration Report. 2011. *International Migration Trends*. Geneva: International Organization for Migration.

Determinants of diaspora policy engagement of Ethiopians in the Netherlands

Katie Kuschminder and Melissa Siegel

Maastricht Graduate School of Governance, United Nations University, Maastricht, The Netherlands

ABSTRACT
State-diaspora relations is an emerging area of inquiry as we seek to deepen our understandings of state-diaspora policies. Few studies have yet to examine how the diaspora reacts to state-led policies for engagement. This paper examines Ethiopian migrants in the Netherlands awareness of and participation in five different diaspora policies implemented by the Government of Ethiopia. We explore the factors that contribute to having knowledge of these diaspora policies from a sample of 350 Ethiopians in the Netherlands. Five categories of factors are investigated including: socio-demographic characteristics, transnational ties, integration, migration experience, and trust. We find that trust and migration experience are the most significant variables in determining knowledge of the Ethiopian diaspora policies.

Introduction

The relationship between migrants and their countries of origin has been transformed in the era of globalization where migrants can send money, vote globally, and engage regularly in their country of origin with the ease of temporary visits and regular communications (Bauböck 2003). Originally negative attitudes toward migrants that persisted in many nation-states/countries in the 1970s have shifted to positive orientations from nation-states/countries toward their migrants, particularly in light of remittances (Bauböck 2003; Itzigsohn 2000). A dramatic example of this transformation has been India wherein migrants went from being 'non-required Indians' to 'angels of development' through the critical role migrants have played in moving India forward over the past two decades (Hercog and Siegel 2013). A second example would be the case of Mexico where Jorge (2004) termed this transition from 'traitors to heros'. The forms of diaspora engagement utilized by states and the rhetoric regarding diaspora and engagement vary depending on particular nation-states capacities and needs.

Globalization has enabled new forms of relationships to develop between migrants and their countries of origin that can now be facilitated through origin country governments' diaspora policies. States have become actively engaged in seeking participation from their diaspora, and in effect 'globalizing' their policies. New technologies and the ease of travel within globalization have helped enable this process.

Recently, more research has been conducted on the policies and approaches taken by states to incorporate and create relationships of belonging with their emigrants (Ragazzi 2014). This has included increasing understandings of how and why states engage their diaspora (Levitt and de la Dehesa 2003), diaspora institutions and diaspora governance (Gamlen 2014); diaspora policies (Gamlen 2006) extra-territorial voting (Bauböck 2003); the notion of wider 'stakeholder' views of citizenship and extra- territorial citizenship (Bauböck 2007; Fitzgerald 2000; Smith 2003); directly elected 'special representation' of emigrants in national legislatures (Collyer 2014); and an increase in the number of country case studies on this topic (see Collyer 2013). However, there is less research on the response of migrants to these specific policies. To what extent do migrants have knowledge of these policies and under what conditions do migrants chose to partake or not in these diaspora policies? Although there is a wide-body of literature on how migrants engage in their countries of origin, this literature is not specific in examining migrants' responses to their origin countries diaspora policies and these questions have remained largely unanswered with a dearth of literature on diffusion policies. One of the possible reasons for this is that diaspora policies from origin countries are not only recent in their development, but also they are not static and continually change and evolve, therefore being difficult to clearly define and assess at one point in time.

This paper contributes to this research area by examining Ethiopian migrants living in the Netherlands knowledge of and participation in the Government of Ethiopia's diaspora engagement policies. Since 2000, the Ethiopian government has been actively implementing new policies to engage the Ethiopian diaspora in development and investment activities in Ethiopia, which has been made possible through globalization. This culminated with the implementation of the new diaspora policy in 2013. Yet, prior to 2013, several new policies were introduced such as the 'Yellow Card', foreign currency bank accounts, and the diaspora bond. A key challenge for the government was spreading awareness of these policies and ensuring take-up rates.

The Netherlands is home to the fifth largest Ethiopian migrant population in the Organisation for Economic Cooperation and Development states. As of 2014, there were 12,596 people of Ethiopian origin residing in the Netherlands. These statistics are based on people registered at a Dutch municipality, meaning that all legal migrants, including temporary migrants such as students, are included in this figure. The number of Ethiopians in the Netherlands has been steadily increasing over the past two decades and this increase can largely be attributed to the growth in the second generation. Although the population of Ethiopians in the Netherlands is not representative of the globalized Ethiopian diaspora, we will use it as a case study to examine diaspora awareness and participation in government diaspora policies and state-sponsored activities.

In 2011, Maastricht University conducted a household survey with 351 Ethiopians in the Netherlands. Ethiopians in the Netherlands are primarily from two groups: those who received refugee status prior to 1991 and current students. The survey conducted with the Ethiopian diaspora included information on the Ethiopian diaspora's awareness and participation in the following five government diaspora policies and state-sponsored activities: Yellow Card, diaspora bond, foreign currency bank account, Ethiopia diaspora day in Addis Ababa, and government investment incentives.

Why do states engage the diaspora? A brief overview of state-diaspora relations

Although still considered relatively scant, the literature on state-diaspora relations is growing and can be characterized by three threads of inquiry (Collyer 2013; Delano and Gamlen 2014). The first is the migration and development approach, which takes an optimistic perspective that migrants contribute to the development of their origin country. The focus of this approach is on remittances and the role of the state to facilitate remittance flows. In addition, the 'brain gain' discourse requires states to 'harness brain drains' (Brinkerhoff 2005) through policies to attract highly skilled engagement and returnees. A third strand of the literature considers the role that states play a key role in attracting philanthropy and investments for national development projects.

The assumed connections are understandable because through attracting finances, knowledge, and skills from the diaspora, development processes will increase in the country of origin. One key challenge with this approach is that it presumes a harmony between the state and diaspora, which is clearly not always the case given that states and diaspora can be in opposition, as in the case of Sri Lanka (Orjuela 2008) and many other conflict countries. A second key challenge cited by Delano and Gamlen (2014) is that this perspective represents states as rational actors; however, this is not always the case because competing internal and external interests can drive national agendas.

This leads to the second approach to state-diaspora relations which is the theory of transnationalism. Migrant transnationalism can be defined as 'the multiple ties and interactions linking people or institutions across the borders of nation-states' (Vertovec 1999, 447). Transnationalism depicts migrants with a dual sense of identity, belonging, and often citizenship. Clearly, not all migrants are transnational and the ways in which migrants engage in their countries of origin differ (Levitt 2009). It is evident that within the space of transnationalism, diaspora engagement policies are 'reinventing the role of states outside of territorial boundaries and in this way reconfiguring traditional understandings of sovereignty, nation and citizenship' (Levitt and de la Dehesa 2003, 606). Transnationalism allows for dual notions of belonging that states can tap into and create allegiances with their migrants.

Another view of state-diaspora relations regards notions of citizenship. States differ on approaches to citizenship, but there has been an increasing trend of states from the south to allow for dual citizenship and expand rights of non-resident citizens. In some cases countries have gone as far as to install directly elected special representatives in national legislatures for extra-territorial citizens (Collyer 2014). These expanding notions of citizenship reflect the ability of states to govern their diaspora, that is, their citizens beyond their borders. Through this 'transnational governmentality' states seek to mobilize national identities, create linkages, and develop relationships with their diaspora beyond their borders (Delano and Gamlen 2014).

The three approaches described above while overlapping in some characteristics, represent three different theoretical bases for understanding state-diaspora relations. This paper draws upon elements of all three theories, for the case of Ethiopia's diaspora policies, the most relevant approach focuses on migration and development issues.

Finally, it is important to note that state-led diaspora engagement policies have become 'en vogue'. This is evidenced by the increase in practical publications such as the International Organization for Migration (IOM) 'Diaspora Handbook' which provides a hands-on guide for states about how to engage their diasporas (2012). Organizations such as the IOM, World Bank, and Migration Policy Institute promote and support states to engage their diaspora for development of their countries. In this regard, the success of countries such as India provides incentives to states because of positive results that could occur from such engagement.

Ethiopia's diaspora engagement policies

This section will provide a short overview of the specific policies that are of relevance for this paper, noting that this list is not exhaustive of all of Ethiopia's diaspora engagement policies.[1] In 2013 the Government of Ethiopia launched its first diaspora policy. The objective of the policy is clearly stated as building the relationship with the diaspora and improving engagement of the diaspora in several areas in Ethiopia. Prior to the implementation of a cohesive diaspora policy, the Government of Ethiopia had been active in implementing specific policies aimed at attracting engagement from its diaspora.

The most prominent policy implemented by the Government of Ethiopia is the Ethiopian Origin Identity Card, which is most commonly referred to as the 'Yellow Card'. Ethiopia does not allow for dual citizenship, but the Yellow Card makes travel more accessible to people of Ethiopian origin by giving right of entry and permission to work to Ethiopians that have foreign citizenship (thus having renounced their Ethiopian citizenship). The Yellow Card has been described as providing all the rights of citizenship, except the right to vote and hold public office (Kuschminder and Siegel 2013). Clearly, the Yellow Card is of more interest in this paper to Ethiopian migrants in the Netherlands that have naturalized, as compared to students or temporary migrants.

The second policy of relevance is the diaspora bond. Ethiopia has issued two diaspora bonds: the first being the Millennium Corporate Bond which was intended to raise funds for Ethiopian Electric Power Corporation (EEPCO), and the second being the Renaissance Dam Bond which was intended to raise funds for the construction of the Grand Ethiopian Renaissance Dam (Plaza 2011). The first bond was launched in 2008 and did not meet expectations, and the second bond was launched in mid-2011 with new features to make it more attractive (Plaza 2011). As stated later in the methodology section of this paper, the interviews were conducted for this study from July 2010–July 2011, meaning that the diaspora bond referred to in this paper is the Millennium Corporate Bond.

The third policy refers to foreign currency bank accounts that were introduced in 2004. The purpose of these accounts is to encourage investment from the diaspora and assist in supporting international foreign exchange and balance of payments in Ethiopia. In 2009, only one thousand accounts had been opened, which was considered a disappointment to the Ministry of Foreign Affairs (Kuschminder and Siegel 2013; Teshome 2009).

Fourth, an Ethiopian Diaspora Day was first held in Addis Ababa in 2009. Diaspora days are viewed as an opportunity to celebrate the achievements of the diaspora and to create connections with the government. Gamlen (2006) defines these forms of events as 'symbolic nation building' to build diaspora members 'sense of belonging' to the country of origin. Since the launch of the new diaspora policy in 2013, discussions have been in progress to have an annual week-long celebration of the diaspora in Addis Ababa.

The final policy included in this study regards government investment incentives. Primarily, this refers to the 2002 policy Investment Proclamation which allowed an Ethiopian by birth to be considered a domestic investor, versus a foreign investor. This has significant implications in the ability of Ethiopian non-citizens to invest in Ethiopia because foreigners must invest a minimum of US $100,000 in a single project, whereas there is no minimum investment requirement for domestic investors (Kuschminder and Siegel 2013). Furthermore, as from 2003, domestic investors are able to import construction materials and capital goods for the development of their enterprise duty-free (Kuschminder and Siegel 2013). These investment incentives make starting a business in Ethiopia far more accessible to the diaspora.

Methodology

This study is based on data collected on data collected for the *IS Academy on Migration and Development project*. For this project, household level survey data were collected in the Netherlands with several immigrant groups including Ethiopians. The data were collected by face-to-face interviews in the Netherlands in July 2010–July 2011 and includes information on 351 Ethiopian households. For this study, we focus on the first-generation migrant respondents born in Ethiopia. Consequently, the subsample used in this paper consists of 350 individuals (however, the sample can be smaller for some of our analyses depending on which questions were answered by particular individuals).

Dependent variables

There are six dependent variables that we investigate in this study. The main dependent variable of interest is if Ethiopians in the Netherlands are aware of any of the main diaspora policies and activities offered by the Ethiopian government. Respondents were asked if they knew about the Ethiopian Origin Identity card (Yellow Card), Diaspora Bond, Ethiopian Foreign Currency Bank Account, Ethiopia Diaspora Day in Addis Ababa, and government investment incentives. For the main analysis, we use knowledge of at least one policy as the main dependent variable. We also analyze each type of policy individually. Descriptively, we also look at taking up of these policies, but the number who actually take up the policies is too small for conducting more sophisticated analysis.

Independent variables

The independent variables used in our study can be grouped into five groups: (1) socio-demographic characteristics, (2) transnational social ties, (3) integration in the Netherlands, (4) migration experience, and (5) trust. First, we consider socio-demographic characteristics, which include age, sex, household size, ethnicity, and number of years of education completed. We do not expect to see any differences on most of these variables in terms of knowledge of diaspora policies, with the exception of education. *We would expect the more educated to have more knowledge regarding diaspora policies (Hypothesis 1)*.

Second, we consider transnational social ties. Building on the literature review, *we would expect that individuals who are more engaged in Ethiopia are more likely to have knowledge of the diaspora policies (Hypothesis 2)*. We analyze transnational social ties with three variables: frequency of contact with family/friends in Ethiopia, return to Ethiopia, and sending of remittances. These variables represent different ways that migrants can engage in the country and connections to Ethiopia that could build awareness regarding the diaspora policies.

The third set of variables we consider is integration in the Netherlands. Based on the concept of 'simultaneity' (Bilgili 2014) *we expect that migrants who are more integrated in the Netherlands would also have higher knowledge of diaspora policies (Hypothesis 3)*, as one reflection of a dual engagement. We operationalize integration in the Netherlands with five variables. First, we look at primary activity in the past 30 days to consider economic integration and employment status of the migrant. Employment status is one of the most common proxies for economic integration; however, because integration is multifaceted we also consider net income in the Netherlands to gain insight into the wealth of the migrant. Turning to sociocultural integration, we examine the migrants' level of understanding of Dutch, speaking Dutch poorly, or speaking Dutch well. Language is an important indication of sociocultural integration that has been demonstrated to have a positive effect on integration processes (Van Tubergen, Maas, and Flap 2004). For sociocultural integration we also explore the amount of time spent with Dutch people during leisure time. Leisure time preferences are a strong indicator for sociocultural reintegration because it reflects migrants' preferences and social networks (Sigelman et al. 1996). This variable is assessed as a dichotomy of 'spends more time with Dutch people or spends less time with Dutch people'. Finally, within integration we consider having Dutch citizenship. Here, *we expect that migrants that have Dutch citizenship would be more likely to have knowledge of Ethiopian diaspora policies, in particular the Yellow Card because they would be the target population for the Yellow card (Hypothesis 4)*.

Next we examine migration experience, which we operationalize with two variables: reason for initial migration (e.g. family, education, or security/political reasons) and time spent in the Netherlands. We *expect that individuals whose reason for initial migration was not for security purposes would be more likely to have knowledge of the diaspora policies (Hypothesis 5)*. It is possible that this is not the case as ample research suggests that refugees are just as transitionally engaged as economic migrants but this is a specific type of transnational engagement with the government which may be less likely among forced migrant populations (Koser 2007).

The final category that we examine is trust, which is considered using two variables: trust in Ethiopian economy and trust in the Ethiopian government. Trust is a central component in state-diaspora relations that must flow both ways. *We expect that individuals with higher levels of trust in either the Ethiopian economy or government would be more likely to have knowledge of the diaspora policies (Hypothesis 6)*. The variables described in this section are all used descriptively as well as for our regression analysis.

Modeling knowledge of diaspora policies

We use probit regressions to examine the predicted probability of having knowledge of first, any of the diaspora policies, and second, each separate diaspora policy. Probit analysis allows for the model to estimate the probability that an observation with particular characteristics will fall into a specific one of the categories. The model takes the form as follows:

Results

The results are presented in two sections: the first provides a descriptive overview of knowledge of diaspora policies and the second section examines the probit regression analysis on the knowledge of diaspora policies. Due to the small number of respondents who have participated in a policy as illustrated in Table 1, it is not possible to do more sophisticated statistical analysis;

$$Pr(Y = 1|X) = \Phi(X'\beta),$$

therefore, we will only focus on knowledge of diaspora policies for the elaborated results.

Descriptive overview

Table 1 shows responses for the questions of knowing about specific diaspora policies offered by the Ethiopian government and actual participation in these policies. It is clear that knowledge of a policy is much higher than actual participation. Still, only 41 percent of respondents had knowledge of any policy. The Yellow Card and investment incentives were the most known policies but these were still relatively low percentages with 31 percent and 29 percent, respectively. Only 7 percent of our sample had participated in any policy, with the Yellow Card having the largest number of participants at 6 percent, followed by the diaspora bond at 2 percent.

Based on the independent variables listed in the previous section we compare first-generation migrants with knowledge of at least one policy compared to those without knowledge of any policies in the areas of socio-demographic characteristics, transnational social ties, integration, migration experience, and trust as shown in Table 2. Variables with statistically significant differences between the groups are noted by stars (* .10, **.05, ***.01 significance level).

First, we examine socio-demographic characteristics. The average age of those with knowledge of at least one policy and those without knowledge of any policies is similar at 39 percent and 37 percent. The self-reported ethnic identification of respondents was primarily stated as Ethiopian (meaning no specific ethnicity was identified), followed by Amhara. There is a significant difference among individuals with Amhara ethnicity in

Table 1. Knowledge of diaspora policies and participation in policies.

	Knowledge of the policy						Participate in the policy					
	Yes		No		Total		Yes		No		Total	
Policy	Freq	%	Freq	%	Freq	%	Freq	%	Freq	%	Freq.	%
Yellow Card	103	30.93	230	69.07	333	Ā	21	6.31	312	93.69	333	100
Diaspora bond	54	16.22	279	83.78	333	100	8	2.40	325	97.60	333	100
Foreign currency bank account	80	24.17	251	75.83	331	100	6	1.81	325	98.19	331	100
Ethiopia diaspora day	48	14.55	282	85.45	330	100	2	0.61	328	99.39	330	100
Government investment incentives	94	28.57	235	71.43	329	100	6	1.82	323	98.18	329	100
At least one policy	144	41.14	206	58.86	350	100	26	7.43	324	92.57	350	100

regards to their knowledge or not of the diaspora policies and the difference is not significant among the other ethnic groups. In regards to years of education completed, both groups are similar at between 15 and 16 years.

Turning to transnational social ties, two of the variables were statistically significant: frequency of return to Ethiopia and the sending of remittances. Frequency of return to Ethiopia is significantly different between the two groups because those without knowledge of any policies have less frequency of return visits to Ethiopia than do individuals with knowledge of at least one policy. Those respondents with knowledge of policies send remittances significantly more than those without knowledge (67–57 percent). There was no significant difference between the two groups of respondents with regard to their frequency of contact with family and friends in Ethiopia. From this first look, it is clear that those who have knowledge of at least one policy are also more engaged in the country, specifically with regard to remittance sending and return visits.

In regards to integration in the Netherlands, two variables were statistically significant. Primary activity in the Netherlands shows that those who are employed are more likely to have knowledge of diaspora policies. Similarly, respondents who had a higher income of over €1000 per month were 18 percent more likely to have knowledge of diaspora policies. This is in line with the literature that individuals with more resources are more likely to be aware of policies because they are more likely to have the capacity to utilize the policies. We also see that migrants with Dutch citizenship are more likely to be aware of diaspora policies at 46percent than migrants without Dutch citizenship at 33 percent.

In terms of migration experience, first, the reason for leaving Ethiopia is not significantly different between the two groups with most leaving for education (42 percent) or security or political reasons (37 percent). A smaller percentage left for reasons of family reunification or family formation (11 percent). Migrants who have policy knowledge have more years spent in the Netherlands: ten years in the Netherlands compared to eight years for those without knowledge. Those with knowledge of policies are slightly less likely to have plans for permanent stay in the Netherlands at 35 percent compared to 41 percent.

Finally, trust in the Ethiopian economy is also significantly different. Those with knowledge of at least one policy have more trust in the economy, but there is no significant difference with trust in the government. In general, both groups have low trust in the government.

The descriptive overview provided above suggests that Ethiopians in the Netherlands who have knowledge regarding Ethiopia's diaspora policies are transnationally engaged in Ethiopia, economically integrated in the Netherlands, and have Dutch citizenship. This fits with the profile expected from the literature review and will be further tested in the regression analysis.

Regression analysis of policy knowledge

As described in the methodology section, we use a probit analysis to investigate the predicted probability that an individual respondent is aware of first, any diaspora policy and second, each individual diaspora policy. Six different regressions models have been estimated below using six different dependent variables (first, one aggregated variable for knowledge of any policy and second five separate variables for each policy uniquely). Marginal effects, standard errors, and significance levels are shown in Table 3.

Table 2. Knowledge of diaspora programs.

Socio-demographic variables	Knowledge of at least one policy Freq.	%	No knowledge of any policies Freq.	%	Total sample Freq.	%
Sex*						
Male	97	67.36	120	58.25	217	62.00
Female	47	32.64	86	41.75	133	38.00
Age***						
Average	39		37		38	
Range	25–74		22–69		22–74	
Ethnicity						
Amhara***	50	34.97	37	18.50	87	25.36
Ethiopian	50	34.97	86	43.00	136	39.65
Other	43	30.07	77	38.50	120	34.99
Years of education completed						
Average	16		15		16	
Range	0–24		0–22		0–24	
Household size						
Average	2		2		2	
Range	1–9		1–8		1–9	
Transnational social ties: frequency of contact with family/friends in Ethiopia						
Every month or less	66	46.15	91	44.61	157	45.24
Every week or more	77	53.85	113	55.39	190	54.76
Frequency of return to Ethiopia***						
Never returns to Ethiopia	40	28.99	99	52.38	139	42.51
Returns to Ethiopia	98	71.01	90	47.62	188	57.49
Sending of remittances*						
Does not send remittances	48	33.33	89	43.20	137	39.14
Sends remittances	96	66.67	117	56.80	213	60.86
Integration in the Netherlands: primary activity in the past 30 days*						
In paid work	75	52.08	92	44.88	167	47.85
Education	40	27.78	67	32.68	107	30.66
Unemployed	9	6.25	25	12.20	34	9.74
Other	20	13.89	21	10.24	41	11.75
Net income in the Netherlands from all sources***						
Income < 1000 Euro per month	55	40.74	103	55.98	158	49.53
Income > 1000 Euro per month	80	59.26	81	44.02	161	50.47
Level of understanding of Dutch						
Speaks Dutch poorly	63	43.75	91	44.17	154	44.00
Speaks Dutch well	81	56.25	115	55.83	196	56.00
Frequency of spending time with Dutch people during leisure time						
A few times a month or less	87	60.42	110	54.19	197	56.77
Several times a week or more	57	39.58	93	45.18	150	43.23
Dutch citizenship is held***						
No	No	No	No	No	No	No
Yes	Yes	Yes	Yes	Yes	Yes	Yes
Migration experience: reason for leaving Ethiopia						
Family reunification or formation	20	14.39	17	8.76	37	11.11
Security/political or other	61	43.88	95	48.97	156	46.85
Education	58	41.73	82	42.27	140	42.04
Years spent in the Netherlands***						
Average	11		8		9	
Range	0–44		0–38		044	
Trust						
Trust in the Ethiopian economy*						
No trust	14	10.22	33	17.65	47	14.51
Some level of trust	123	89.78	155	82.35	277	85.49
Trust in the Ethiopian Government						
None or very little trust	79	58.09	120	64.52	199	61.80
Some or a great deal of trust	57	41.91	66	35.48	123	38.20

Note: Significance levels are
*0.1.
***0.01.

Table 3. Probit regression results.

	Knowledge of at least one policy dy/dx (se)	Knowledge of Yellow Card dy/dx (se)	Knowledge of diaspora bond dy/dx (se)	Knowledge of foreign currency bank account dy/dx (se)	Knowledge of diaspora day dy/dx (se)	Knowledge of government investment incentives dy/dx (se)
In contact w/ family or friends in Ethiopia every week or more	−0.06 (0.09)	0.01 (0.08)	−0.10 (0.06)	−0.09 (0.08)	−0.07 (0.06)	−0.12 (0.08)
Returns to Ethiopia	0.21** (0.24)	0.17** (0.09)	0.08 (0.06)	0.14* (0.08)	0.06 (0.06)	0.11 (0.09)
Trusts Ethiopian Econ.	0.21*** (0.09)	0.09 (0.10)	0.18** (0.08)	0.25** (0.11)	0.22** (0.09)	0.26** (0.11)
Trusts Ethiopian Gov. some or a lot	−0.01 (0.09)	0.14* (0.08)	0.08 (0.05)	0.08 (0.07)	0.08* (0.05)	0.09 (0.07)
Sends remittances	0.12 (0.08)	0.11 (0.08)	0.13** (0.06)	−0.02 (0.07)	0.02 (0.05)	−0.00 (0.07)
Employed	−0.09 (0.13)	0.24** (0.11)	−0.12 (0.08)	0.04 (0.11)	0.07 (0.09)	−0.14 (0.11)
High-Earner (1 = 1,000euro p/m or more)	0.15 (0.14)	−0.07 (0.12)	0.17** (0.08)	0.07 (0.11)	−0.00 (0.09)	0.18 (0.19)
Speaks Dutch well	−0.24 (0.15)	−0.01 (0.13)	0.07 (0.09)	−0.05 (0.12)	−0.05 (0.09)	0.08 (0.14)
Spends leisure time with Dutch people a few times a month or more	−0.09 (0.08)	0.08 (0.07)	0.04 (0.05)	0.01 (0.07)	0.04 (0.05)	−0.10 (0.07)
Left Ethiopia for family reasons (compared to security)	0.59*** (0.21)	0.24 (0.15)	.25*** (0.09)	0.20 (0.12)	0.01 (0.10)	0.32** (0.14)
Left Ethiopia for education reasons (compared to security)	−0.08 (0.13)	0.07 (0.12)	0.06 (0.08)	0.07 (0.11)	−0.01 (0.08)	0.16 (0.12)
Dutch citizen	−0.05 (0.14)	−0.05 (0.12)	0.13 (0.09)	−0.05 (0.12)	0.03 (0.09)	−0.08 (0.13)
Years spent in the Netherlands	0.01 (0.01)	0.01 (0.01)	−0.01* (0.01)	−0.00 (0.01)	−0.01 (0.01)	−0.01 (0.01)
Female	−0.10 (0.09)	0.00 (0.08)	−0.08 (0.06)	−0.02 (0.07)	−0.09 (0.06)	0.00 (0.08)
Age	0.00 (0.01)	0.00 (0.01)	0.00 (0.00)	−0.00 (0.01)	0.00 (0.00)	0.00 (0.01)
Amhara ethnicity (Ethiopian base)	0.25** (0.10)	0.11 (0.09)	−0.10 (0.06)	−0.06 (0.08)	−0.03 (0.06)	0.00 (0.09)
Other ethnicity (Ethiopian base)	0.01 (0.09)	−0.09 (0.08)	−0.12** (0.06)	−0.01 (0.07)	−0.10* (0.06)	−0.03 (0.08)
Years of education completed	0.01 (0.01)	−0.00 (0.01)	−0.00 (0.01)	0.00 (0.01)	0.00 (0.01)	0.01 (0.01)
Household size	−0.01 (0.04)	−0.01 (0.03)	−0.02 (0.02)	−0.03 (0.03)	−0.01 (0.02)	0.01 (0.03)
_cons	−1.79**	−2.38***	−2.00**	−1.18	−1.79	−2.44***
N	216	216	216	216	216	216
LRch2(20)	57.79	62.13	42.38	24.42	25.10	35.50
Prob > Chi^2	0.00	0.00	0.00	0.18	0.16	0.01

(Continued)

Table 3. Continued.

	Knowledge of at least one policy dy/dx (se)	Knowledge of Yellow Card dy/dx (se)	Knowledge of diaspora bond dy/dx (se)	Knowledge of foreign currency bank account dy/dx (se)	Knowledge of diaspora day dy/dx (se)	Knowledge of government investment incentives dy/dx (se)
Pseudo R^2	0.19	0.23	0.20	0.1	0.13	0.13

Note: Significance levels are
*0.1.
**0.05.
***0.01.

Column 1 shows knowledge of at least one policy. First, we see that an individual who has returned to Ethiopia for a visit (i.e. not permanent return) is 21 percent more likely to know about at least one policy. Second, individuals with trust in the Ethiopian economy are 21 percent more likely to have knowledge of at least one policy. Third, individuals who left Ethiopia for family reunification or family formation (compared to security or political reasons) are 59 percent more likely to have knowledge of at least one policy. Finally, we also see that people of Amhara ethnicity are 25 percent more likely to have policy awareness.

Column 2 refers to knowledge of the Yellow Card policy. As with the results of the knowledge of any policy, return is an important predictor of policy knowledge, with individuals who have engaged in return visits being 17 percent more likely to have knowledge of the Yellow Card policy. This is intuitive as the purpose of the Yellow Card is to ease temporary return visits for non-citizens. Trust in the Ethiopian government and being employed in the Netherlands are also significantly positively correlated with Yellow Card knowledge. Those with trust in the Ethiopian government are 14 percent more likely to know about the Yellow Card policy and respondents who are employed in the Netherlands are 24 percent more likely to know about the Yellow Card.

Column 3 investigates knowledge of the diaspora bond noting that only 16 percent of our sample had knowledge of the diaspora bond. Trust in the Ethiopian economy, being a remittance sender, having a higher income, and having left Ethiopia for family reunification or formation (as compared to security reasons) are all significantly positively associated with knowledge of the diaspora bond. Years spent in the Netherlands and reported ethnicity other than Amhara and Ethiopian are negative predictors of policy awareness. Those with trust in the Ethiopian economy are 18 percent more likely to be aware of the diaspora bond policy, while remittance senders are 13 percent more likely to be aware of the diaspora bond policy, high earners are 17 percent more likely to be aware of the diaspora bond, and family reasons for migration are 25 percent more likely to be aware of the diaspora bond policy. Years spent in the Netherlands are slightly negative with one more year spent in the Netherlands corresponding to being 1 percent less likely to know about the diaspora bond policy. Other reported ethnicities than Amhara and Ethiopia are also 12 percent less likely to be aware of the diaspora bond policy.

Column 4 shows the knowledge of a foreign currency bank account, which was the third highest reported after the Yellow Card and government investment incentives. Return visits and trust in the economy is the only significant predictor in this regression and is positive. Those with trust in the economy are 25 percent more likely to be aware of the foreign currency bank account policy and those who have participated in return visits are 14 percent more likely to be aware of the foreign currency bank account policy.

Column 5 examines knowledge of the diaspora day in Addis Ababa, which was the least known policy with only 15 percent of respondents being aware of the diaspora day in Addis Ababa. Again, we see that trust in the Ethiopian economy is significant, as is trust in the Ethiopian government and ethnicities other than Amhara or Ethiopia. The effect of trust in the economy is higher than trust in the Ethiopian government with an effect of 22 percent compared to 8 percent higher likelihood of being aware of the diaspora day in Addis Ababa for trust in the Ethiopian government. Other ethnicities than Amhara or Ethiopian were 10 percent less likely to be aware of the diaspora day in Addis Ababa.

Finally, column 6 considers knowledge of Ethiopian government investment incentives, which was the second most known policy with 29 percent of respondents having knowledge of this policy. Only two variables were significant in this regression: first, trust in the economy is associated with 26 percent higher awareness of this policy; second, family reasons for migration are associated with 32 percent higher awareness of this policy.

It is clear that trust in the Ethiopian economy is the most significant variable across the regressions, followed by return visits to Ethiopia and reason for migration. This suggests that both transnational ties and migration experience are important predictors of diaspora policy awareness.

Discussion

Returning to our first hypothesis that *Individuals with higher levels of education would be more likely to have knowledge of diaspora policies*, we find that education proved to not be significant. Level of education was not associated with knowledge of any of the policies. This was surprising because as the highly skilled are often assumed to have a greater potential to affect development both in terms of resources and to contribute and for knowledge transfer purposes (Sturge, Bilgili and Siegel, forthcoming).

Moving to the second hypothesis that *Individuals who exhibit more transnational engagement in Ethiopia are more likely to have knowledge of diaspora policies*, we find that this is correct. Different transnational social ties variables were significant for different iterations of the regression analysis. Return visits are only significant in the individual policy regressions for the Yellow Card and Foreign Currency Bank Accounts. This is sensible for the Yellow Card because the policy is meant to facilitate the ease of return visits. Furthermore, it is interesting that remittance sending is only significant for the diaspora bond. A potential reason for this is that remittance senders are more likely to have disposable income that they can contribute to the diaspora bond and they have already demonstrated willingness to send more back more generally.

The third hypothesis, *Individuals who are more integrated in the Netherlands would also have higher knowledge of diaspora policies*, proved to be slightly upheld. Employment was significant in the Yellow Card policy and income was significant in knowledge of the Diaspora Bond. Thus, economic integration proved to be important; however social integration was insignificant. This is quite understandable as most of the Ethiopian government diaspora policies require some level of income to participate, especially the diaspora bond.

Fourth, we expected that *Migrants with Dutch citizenship would be more likely to have knowledge of diaspora policies, in particular the Yellow Card*, and were surprised to see that this is not the case. Although showing significance in the descriptive results, Dutch citizenship was insignificant in the regression analysis for all of the policies, including the Yellow Card.

Our fifth hypothesis that *Individuals whose reason for initial migration was not for security purposes would be more likely to have knowledge of the diaspora policies* did prove to be partially correct. Individuals who migrated for family reunification or formation (as compared to security reasons) were more likely to have knowledge of both the diaspora bond and the government investment incentives. However, for the remaining policies the reason for migration was not a determinant of awareness.

The final hypothesis, w*e expect that individuals with higher levels of trust in either the Ethiopian economy or government would be more likely to have knowledge of the diaspora policies,* can also be deemed correct. Trust in the Ethiopian economy was significant in all of the regressions, except for the Yellow Card policy. Conversely, trust in the Ethiopian government was significant for the Yellow Card, but none of the other policies. This is coherent because the Yellow Card is an investment in the government, whereas the other policies require investments of capital. On the whole, trust is the only variable that is significant across all of the regressions.

Conclusion

In returning to the beginning of this paper, state-diaspora relations are a growing field of inquiry with little empirical studies that highlight the relationships between diaspora and the governments of their countries of origin in an increasingly globalized world. The government of Ethiopia has worked to implement policies aimed at engaging its diaspora over the past decade. In this paper, we have sought to understand what determines if Ethiopians abroad have knowledge of these policies and participate in these policies through a case study of Ethiopians in the Netherlands, keeping in mind that we have only been able to capture knowledge and engagement at one point in time.

First, it is striking that less than half (41 percent) of the respondents in this study has knowledge of any of the diaspora policies examined in this paper. On the one hand, this could be interpreted as a high level of awareness of policies; on the other hand, it could be interpreted as a low level of awareness. Unfortunately, it is not possible to bench-mark to other studies to make accurate claims in this regard. However, it does seem that 41 percent can be interpreted as quite low for knowledge, especially considering the majority who are aware of the policies chose not to participate in any of the diaspora policies. It would be logical to assume that the government would aspire for higher awareness of the policies.

Furthermore, only 7 percent of the sample had participated in any of the policies. As mentioned at the beginning of the paper, the Government of Ethiopia was not satisfied with the uptake of several of these policies. The majority of respondents who had knowledge of the policies, but chose not to participate cited their main reason as being that they were not interested.

The regression results suggest that both transnational ties and migration experience are important predictors for having knowledge of diaspora policies. In this case, the most consistently significant variable was trust in the Ethiopian economy. However, participating in return visits, trust in the Ethiopian government and sending remittances were also significant in some of the models. This supports the theory of state-diaspora relations that transnationalism is a key part of state-diaspora engagement: States can draw on migrants' dual notions of belonging through their polices to engage them in the country of origin. In the case of Ethiopia, having more transnational ties does suggest higher knowledge of state-diaspora engagement policies.

In regards to the other two notions of state-diaspora relations, we are unable to test the relationship with development through knowledge of policies. It is clear that the government would like to make use of migration for development but seems to be challenged in realising this goal as policies have very low uptake. In addition, it unclear to what extent these policies would impact development if they did have a higher uptake.

In terms of citizenship policies, it was interesting to see that citizenship was not a predictor for knowledge of the diaspora policies. At the same time, the policy with the highest level of participation was the Yellow Card, which provides a form of partial citizenship. This is a step in the right direction for the Ethiopian government by giving easier access to engagement, especially in ways that would directly contribute to development such as investment, for which the Yellow Card gives easier access.

In conclusion, the results of our study suggest that much further work is required to understand the response of the diaspora to policies implemented by their origin country governments. As we improve our understandings of states' actions in the context of globalization, we need to understand how the diaspora responds and reacts. In this small case of the Ethiopian diaspora in the Netherlands, we find that trust in the economy of Ethiopia is the most critical variable in determining if Ethiopians in the Netherlands have knowledge of the government of Ethiopia's diaspora policies. Future work comparing different countries and diaspora could be far more informative regarding the determinants of awareness and participation in state-sponsored diaspora policies.

Acknowledgements

The authors would like to express their gratitude to Sarah Langley for valuable research assistance and to the Dutch Ministry of Foreign Affairs for funding this study.

Disclosure statement

No potential conflict of interest was reported by the authors.

Funding

This work was supported by the Dutch Ministry of Foreign Affairs under the IS Academy: Migration and Development *A World in Motion* project.

Notes

1. For an in-depth account of Ethiopia's diaspora policies see Kuschminder and Siegel (2013).

References

Bauböck, R. 2003. "Towards a Political Theory of Migrant Transnationalism." *International Migration Review* 37 (3): 700–723.

Bauböck, R. 2007. "Stakeholder Citizenship and Transnational Political Participation: A Normative Evaluation of External Voting." *Fordham Law Review* 75 (5): 2393–2447.

Bilgili, O. 2014. *Simultaneity in Transnational Migration Research: Links Between Migrants' Host and Home Country Orientation*. Maastricht: Boekenplan.

Brinkerhoff, J. 2005. "Diaspora, Skills Transfer, and Remittances: Perceptions and Potential." In *Converting Brain Drains into Gains*, edited by Clay Wescott and Jennifer Brinkerhoff, 1–32. Asian Development Bank.

Collyer, M. 2013. "Introduction: Locating and Narrating Emigration Nations." In *Emigration Nations*, edited by Micheal Collyer, 1–24. London: Palgrave Macmillan.

Collyer, M. 2014. "Inside out? Directly Elected 'Special Representation' of Emigrants in National Legislatures and the Role of Popular Sovereignty." *Political Geography* 41: 64–73. doi:10.1016/j.polgeo.2014.01.002.

Delano, A., and A. Gamlen. 2014. "Comparing and Theorizing State Diaspora Relations." *Political Geography* 41: 43–53. doi:10.1016/j.polgeo.2014.05.005.

Fitzgerald, D. 2000. *Negotiating Extra-territorial Citizenship: Mexican Migration and the Transnational Politics of Community*. CCIS Monograph 2. San Diego: University of California.

Gamlen, A. 2006. *Diaspora Engagement Policies: What are They, and What Kinds of States Use Them?* Working Paper 32, Centre on Migration, Policy and Society, University of Oxford.

Gamlen, A. 2014. "Diaspora Institutions and Diaspora Governance". *International Migration Review* 48 (S1): S180–S217.

Hercog, M., and M. Siegel. 2013. "Diaspora Engagement in India: From Non-Required Indians to Angels of Development." In *Emigration Nations*, edited by Micheal Collyer, 75–99. London: Palgrave Macmillan.

IOM and MPI. 2012. *Developing a Roadmap for Engaging Diaspora in Development*. Geneva: IOM.

Itzigsohn, J. 2000. "'Immigration and the Boundaries of Citizenship: The Institutions of Immigrants' Political Transnationalism." *International Migration Review* 34 (4): 1126–1154.

Jorge, D. (2004). *From Traitors to Heroes: 100 Years of Mexican migration policies*. Accessed December 22, 2014. http://www.migrationpolicy.org/article/traitors-heroes-100-years-mexican-migration-policies.

Koser, K. 2007. "Refugees, Transnationalism and the State." *Journal of Ethnic and Migration Studies* 33 (2): 233–254.

Kuschminder, K., and M. Siegel. 2013. "Diaspora Engagement and Policy in Ethiopia." In *Emigration Nations*, edited by Micheal Collyer, 50–74. London: Palgrave Macmillan.

Levitt, P. 2009. "Routes and Roots: Understanding the Lives of the Second Generation Transnationally". *Journal of Ethnic and Migration Studies* 35(7): 1225–1242.

Levitt, P., and de la Dehesa, R. (2003). "Transnational Migration and the Redefinition of the State: Variations and Explanations." Ethnic and Racial Studies 26 (4): 587–611.

Orjuela, C. 2008. *The Identity Politics of Peacebuilding: Civil society in War-torn Sri Lanka*. New Delhi, London: Sage.

Plaza, S. 2011. "Ethiopia's New Diaspora Bond: Will it be Successful This Time?" People Move Accessed on: 10 December 2014 http://blogs.worldbank.org/peoplemove

Ragazzi, F. 2014. "A Comparative Analysis of Diaspora Policies." *Political Geography* 41: 74–89.

Sigelman, L., T. Bledsoe, S. Welch, and M. Combs. 1996. "Making Contact? Black-white Social Interaction in an Urban Setting." *American Journal of Sociology* 101: 1306–1332.

Smith, M. P. 2003. "Transnationalism, the State and the Extra-territorial Citizen." *Politics and Society* 31 (4): 467–502.

Sturge, G., Ö. Bilgili, and M. Siegel. Forthcoming. "Migrant Skills and Development Potential: A Study on Economic and Social Remittances". *Global Networks*.

Teshome, M. 2009. "Low Remittance Spurs Ministry On." Addis Fortune. Accessed online at: www.addisfortune.com/LowRemittanceSpursMinistryOn.htm Retrieved: 25 June 2010.

Van Tubergen, F., I. Maas, and H. Flap. 2004. "The Economic Incorporation of Immigrants in 18 Western Societies: Origin, destination and Community Effects." *American Sociological Review* 69: 704–727.

Vertovec, S. 1999. "Conceiving and Researching Transnationalism." *Ethnic and Racial Studies* 22 (2): 447–462.

Ethiopian taxicab drivers: forming an occupational niche in the US Capital

Elizabeth Chacko

Department of Geography & International Affairs, The George Washington University, Washington, DC, USA

ABSTRACT
This paper analyzes the relative roles of cultural and structural factors in the emergence and solidification of taxi driving as an ethnic occupational niche among Ethiopian immigrants in the Washington DC metropolitan area within the wider context of globalization and immigrant integration. An ethnic occupational niche is the concentration and specialization of members of an ethnic group in a particular occupational activity. Using data from the US Census Bureau and in-depth interviews with 25 (male) Ethiopian cab drivers and three Ethiopian cab company owners, it examines the factors that affected the entrance of first-generation Ethiopian immigrants in this occupation since the 1980s. This research demonstrates that mixed embeddedness or the interplay of structural factors such as blocked mobility as well as cultural factors such as the strong social networks that exist among Ethiopian immigrants were important in the induction of new immigrants into taxicab driving. The demographic composition of the Washington metropolitan area and policies of the DC Taxicab Commission that allow for fairly easy entry of new drivers in the taxicab business also facilitated the emergence of this occupational niche.

Introduction

The intensification of the movement of people across international boundaries is an integral part of globalization, a process that is also characterized by the increasing global flows of capital, goods, services, cultures, and ideas (Livi-Bacci 2012). Refugees and immigrants, estimated at 232 million (IOM 2014), form a part of these population movements and engage in the ongoing task of social, cultural, economic, and political adjustment in a new country. Most critical among these imperatives for the newcomers is the need to support themselves and their families in the receiving country by finding employment or creating a job for themselves through entrepreneurship.

Immigrants are known to engage in entrepreneurship in higher proportions than the native-born in the USA (Borjas 1986). Although some governments court immigrants who have financial capital to invest in existing business ventures or establish new ones (Ley 2010), such immigrant entrepreneurs are in the minority. Most first-generation immigrants who turn to entrepreneurship do so as a means to upward mobility and socio-economic integration in the receiving country. The higher rate of self-employment of immigrants and the kinds of enterprises that they engage in have been attributed to factors that range from structural inequalities and disadvantages, to the use of and reliance on co-ethnic resources and more recently, the recognition of the interplay between structural and cultural factors in the emergence of ethnic enterprises. The immigrants' ability to make a living as self-employed entrepreneurs is affected by legal-institutional factors, national and local economies as well as their individual and group characteristics (Kloosterman and Rath 2003; Wang and Li 2007).

The Washington DC metropolitan area is the second largest urban area of settlement of African-born immigrants after New York City, and has a population of approximately 41,450 persons of Ethiopian ancestry. Part of the diaspora that began leaving Ethiopia in large numbers in the 1970s in the wake of a brutal Marxist revolution, Ethiopian immigrants have continued to migrate to the Washington area. As these immigrants settled in the Washington area, they added to the multicultural demographic makeup of the metropolis while their presence could be readily observed in the cultural landscape in the form of ethnic stores, restaurants, and institutions. Although employed in a wide range of occupations, over time Ethiopian immigrants in the city developed occupational niches (the concentration and specialization of members of an ethnic group in a particular occupation) in activities such as taxi driving and working as parking garage attendants.

This paper analyzes the relative roles of cultural and structural factors and their interactions in the emergence and solidification of taxi driving as an ethnic occupational niche among Ethiopian immigrants in the Washington metropolitan area within the wider context of globalization and immigrant integration. It offers an understanding of taxi driving as a viable and relatively well-paid occupation for immigrants in an era of transnationalism, and a pathway for their children to acquire the skills that would equip them to participate in the lucrative knowledge-intensive sectors of the global economy. The paper also examines how Washington as a place has facilitated the development of the niche through its large Ethiopian diasporic population with its ethnic institutions and local policies that offer relatively easy entry into taxi driving for immigrants from Ethiopia.

Ethnic economies and entrepreneurship – the role of immigrants

The scholarship on ethnic economies and ethnic entrepreneurship is extensive. Several explanations have been proposed for the higher prevalence of entrepreneurship among immigrants and ethnic groups. The 'disadvantage theory' (Min and Bozorgmehr 2000) suggests that structural inequalities that minority ethnic groups face are catalysts for ethnic entrepreneurship. It posits that immigrants may have to resort to creating their own jobs when they have limited options because of the employment structure or prejudices in the receiving society's labor market (Light 1979; Volery 2007). Limited receiving-country language skills, lack of recognition of credentials, and degrees earned in the sending country as well as racial and ethnic prejudices could therefore steer immigrants toward entrepreneurship. According to Bonacich (1973) who proposed the 'middleman minority' thesis, immigrant/ethnic entrepreneurs are likely to establish small businesses and to engage in occupations that do not place them in direct competition with the native majority. Ethnic entrepreneurship is thus a strategy for overcoming immigrants' marginal status as newcomers in the receiving country and often hinges on intra-group solidarity and cooperation, which facilitate critical inputs such as the raising of needed capital and labor.

The blocked mobility hypothesis is a variation of the disadvantage theory that argues that self-employment stems from immigrants' blocked opportunities in the US labor market. According to Raijman and Tienda (2000), highly educated immigrants whose degrees do not transfer in the American context and who lack English proficiency face the most intensely blocked mobility. A more culture-based hypothesis emphasizes the creation of ethnic economies that depend on co-ethnics. Also known as the enclave thesis, this view stresses that immigrant entrepreneurship often arises from the demand for goods and services within the ethnic or immigrant community itself, especially when it is spatially concentrated. The spatial clustering of employees, customers and entrepreneurs in an ethnic enclave can greatly assist in the solidification of ethnic economies that primarily serve co-ethnics (Wilson and Portes 1980; Zhou 2004). Spatial concentration in this context thus helps immigrant entrepreneurship (Wilson and Portes 1980; Hiebert 2002; Zhou 2004; Kaplan and Li 2006). Traditionally, immigrant entrepreneurs set up businesses in inner-city ethnic enclaves that offer the necessary ethnic financial, social, and human capital. Concentrations of people belonging to a particular ethnic community could provide business owners with a ready and protected market, a steady stream of co-ethnic workers and, just as importantly, a sense of familiarity and trust.

Immigrant communities are often characterized by extensive social networks based on strong ties between and among individual members that tend to be close and stable (Zhou 2004). Ethnic social networks with strong ties provide immigrant entrepreneurs with opportunities to interact with and obtain help from co-ethnics and find employment in co-ethnic businesses. The immigrant entrepreneur's social network can also be critical in garnering sufficient capital or credit for in a successful business start-up as well as its subsequent growth. Raijman and Tienda (2003) in their comparative study of Korean and Mexican immigrant entrepreneurs in a Chicago neighborhood note that ethnic vertical integration of producer, supplier and consumer services and resource mobilization through ethnic ties are critical for the creation and sustenance of a self-sustaining entrepreneurial class. However, weak ties, those that tend to be more superficial and lacking in emotional investment such as those forged with the wider community, may be equally critical in the continued success of a business enterprise, particularly if entrepreneurs wished to expand their business and include larger numbers of non-ethnics within their clientele.

Aldrich and Waldinger (1990) attempted a more comprehensive study which suggests that an ethnic/immigrant group's access to economic opportunities, its characteristics (particularly in terms of stores of different types of capital), and evolving strategies in response to the prevailing structures and group traits can help explain ethnic entrepreneurship. The concept of 'mixed embeddedness' offers a newer approach to understanding ethnic and immigrant entrepreneurship, underscoring the interaction rather than separation of structural and cultural factors. According to this explanation, social, political, and economic structures and market demands provide frameworks within which immigrants can mobilize ethnic resources to create entrepreneurial ventures (Kloosterman 1999; Kloosterman and Rath 2001, 2003).

Ethnic occupational niches

Certain ethnic minorities and immigrant groups are known to cluster in distinct lines of work to form ethnic occupational niches (Waldinger 1994; Light and Gold 2000). These niches may be defined as the over-representation of an ethnic group in occupations and activities related to the production of a good or service (Wilson 2003). According to Waldinger and Bozorgmehr (1996) and Waldinger and Der-Martirosian (2001), occupational niches form when an ethnic group accounts for a greater percentage of those employed in a particular job than their share in the general work force. Specifically, they characterize such niches as employing at least 1,000 persons, with the group's share in the niche being at least 150 percent of its share of the overall labor market. Brettell and Alstatt (2007) further distinguish between ethnic-niche businesses (that cater to co-immigrants or co-ethnics) and occupational niches, describing the latter as industries and services in which a particular immigrant group is over-represented.

Immigrant entrepreneurs may take advantage of ethnic market niches, forming commercial ethnic enclaves that provide needed goods and services to co-ethnics (Kaplan and Li 2006). New immigrants in particular use these niches to enter the local labor market and as a potential path for upward socio-economic mobility (Zhou 1992). The spatial concentration of ethnic businesses in the ethnic enclave can be beneficial to business development by creating conditions akin to agglomeration economies (Kaplan 1998). The advantages of such agglomeration can sometimes lead to a broader clientele beyond the ethnic community, as seen in the 'Balti Quarter' in Birmingham, England. Here, the localized agglomeration of well-regarded South Asian restaurants exerted 'spatial magnetism' on non-ethnic customers who were drawn to and patronized the restaurants in the neighborhood (Ram et al. 2002). This kind of pull is beneficial for the long-term business prospects of the ethnic economy, since overdependence on a highly limited co-ethnic or local neighborhood market can retard business development.

Ethnic/immigrant niches are often found in occupations such as construction, manufacturing, and some service occupations that are not attractive to the native-born because they involve long hours, low pay, dangerous conditions, few or no benefits and limited opportunity for socio-economic advancement. However, some niches such as the over-representation of Asian Indians in the IT sector do not fit this framework. In the USA, ethnic niching is more than twice as likely to occur among non-European groups such as Latinos and Asians, according to a study using 1990 data across 216 metropolitan areas (Wilson 2003). Among the niches filled by new immigrants in the USA are the grocery business by Koreans, domestic work by Hispanics (Hondagneu-Sotelo 2001), motel ownership and management by Asian Indians (Dhingra 2012), nail salons by Vietnamese (Eckstein and Nguyen 2011), and nursing by Filipinos (Ong and Azores 1994; Parrenas 2005). In all of these cases in order to be successful and to grow, the niche cannot rely solely on the ethnic community, but needs to draw on non-ethnic populations as customers and clients.

Taxi driving has become an ethnic-niche occupation among immigrants in many cities in the USA. It is a profession that has relatively low barriers to entry: basic requirements are the ability to drive, the possession of a valid driver's license and the ability to speak English. Although taxi driving can be insecure and exploitative work (Mathew 2005), in the face of high rates of unemployment, labor market discrimination and inadequate human capital, immigrants and refugees often turn to it as a viable occupation (Kalra 2000; Colic-Peisker and Tilbury 2006; Abraham, Sundar and Whitmore 2008; Swanton 2010). In the 1960s, New York City's taxi drivers were generally second-generation immigrants from central and southern Europe, Ireland and Puerto Rico, as well as native African Americans. But by the mid-1980s, the majority of taxi drivers in the city were first-generation immigrants, and the region of origin of the majority of the drivers had shifted to the Indian subcontinent (Del Valle 1995). More recent studies conducted in New York City also note that immigrants form a majority among taxi drivers in the city (Mathew 2005; Mitra 2008).

Methods used

Using data from the US Census Bureau and in-depth interviews with 25 Ethiopian (male) cab drivers and three Ethiopian cab company owners, I examine the factors that affected the entrance of first-generation Ethiopian immigrants in taxi driving since the 1980s. I assess the roles of human and social capital and discrimination in the niche's formation and the impacts of cultural, economic and political factors in its solidification. I also investigate aspirations of the immigrant taxicab drivers for themselves and the next generation within the context of an increasingly globalized economy, and the role of cab driving in realizing these goals.

Because no database of Ethiopian cab drivers was available, I relied on nonrandom opportunity sampling, making initial contact with the 25 first-generation immigrant drivers in locales such as eateries (where they had lunch) and taxi stands (where they congregated on a regular basis). Given that taxi drivers do not have fixed schedules, plans were usually made to speak with each driver at his convenience at a later time or date. The all-male sample varied in age from 32 to 77 years. Persons interviewed had been in the USA from 8 to 41 years and had an average of 15.2 years of formal education. Of the taxi drivers interviewed, 4 had completed high school, 3 had Associate's degrees, 3 had Master's degrees, and the remaining 15 had Bachelor's degrees. Most of the taxi drivers in my sample came from middle-class backgrounds and had either held or expected to hold white-collar jobs. A few were trained in fields such as urban planning, economics, and journalism and had worked as professionals in Ethiopia. On arriving in the USA, they could not get jobs in their preferred professions, although manual and low-wage service jobs were available to them.

The first jobs of this sample of immigrant drivers were often in parking lots, hotels, convenience stores, and security services. Almost all had worked as an attendant or manager in parking lots while a few had joined the taxi driving business after spending time accompanying co-ethnic cab drivers on their rounds in the Washington metropolitan area. When they were interviewed, the vast majority (18) stated that they owned their taxis. The Ethiopian cab company owners were identified through personal networks and interviewed in person or over the phone, with each interview lasting 45 minutes–1 hour.

Ethiopian immigration and taxi driving in Washington, DC

Immigration reform in USA in 1965 eliminated national quotas, thereby allowing the globalization of its immigrant streams and growing numbers of immigrants from developing countries of Asia, Latin America, and Africa. However, it was only after the 1974 Ethiopian revolution led by the Derg, a military junta, that Ethiopian immigrants began arriving in the USA in large numbers. In their brutal campaign known as the Red Terror, the Derg targeted students, elites and educated urbanites, killing more than 30,000 Ethiopians during the first four years of the Red Terror. Civil unrest, political strife, and heightened insecurity in Ethiopia were compounded by famine during 1973–1974, providing a strong impetus for out-migration (Getahun 2007). Today, the Ethiopian diaspora is widespread, and found in all traditional immigrant-receiving countries as well as newer destinations. The USA has the largest number of persons of Ethiopian ancestry of any immigrant-receiving country, and the Washington metropolitan area reportedly has the largest Ethiopian population of any city outside of Africa.

Although early migrants from Ethiopia initially intended to return once political conditions improved, most of them stayed on in the USA. Over the years, they were joined by refugees and asylum seekers (particularly after the Refugee Act of 1980), and those who came on diversity visas and as part of family reunification programs. Today, approximately 210,000 persons of Ethiopian ancestry live in the USA. Predominantly urban, nearly a fifth (19.8 percent) of the group lives in the Washington Metropolitan Area (US Census Bureau, ACS 2010–2012). The metropolis has always been the primary area of settlement of this population and Ethiopian immigrants have become integrated socially, culturally, economically, and politically. They formed ethnic institutions to help ease adjustment to a new place and to keep cultural traditions alive (Chacko 2009), but also have been more actively involved in forging relationships with local economic and political entities and associations (Chacko 2011). Some 22 percent of Ethiopians in the metropolitan area are employed in production, transportation, and material moving occupations; taxi drivers are likely to make a significant contribution to this category of work (US Census Bureau, ACS 2010–2012).

The self-employment rate for Ethiopians at 9 percent in the Washington metropolitan area is about 1.5 times higher than that for both Ethiopians nationally (6.1 percent) and for the entire US population (6.2 percent) (US Census Bureau, ACS 2010–2012). Although merchants and tradesmen had a low social status in pre-Derg Ethiopia (Korten 1972), a significant proportion of Ethiopian immigrants evidently overcame the alleged cultural stigma of being engaged in a business and embarked on careers as self-employed entrepreneurs. Among the entrepreneurial activities undertaken by immigrants from Ethiopia in the Washington area is the driving of taxicabs.

Taxi driving in twentieth century Washington, DC had been dominated by the African American community until the 1970s, when the nativity and country of origin of taxi drivers shifted to a more mixed and first-generation immigrant pool. The basic criteria for driving taxis in Washington – namely, having a valid driver's license and the ability to speak English, taking and passing the taxicab operator's license examination offered through the District of Columbia Taxicab Commission, proof of authorization to work in the USA and of having lived in the Washington Metropolitan Area for at least a year – were not difficult to meet for most Ethiopian immigrants. All taxi drivers had driven cars while in Ethiopia and on passing the test were able to obtain drivers' licenses. Because Ethiopia's language education policy involves a transition from instruction in the mother tongue to English during the fifth, seventh, or ninth grades, most educated Ethiopians speak English (Bogale 2009). The immigrants' ability to speak English is a valuable skill in the USA and a critical one for taxi driving because it allows them to join the ranks of taxi drivers without the significant lag time usually required to learn basic conversational skills in the language of the receiving country.

All the immigrant drivers interviewed began by driving rented taxis, saving money to buy their own vehicles once they decided to take up taxi driving as a long-term occupation. During the period when the sample was interviewed, drivers who did not own their cabs usually spent between $250 and $300 a week in rental fees and an additional $100 for insurance. For all taxi drivers, 10–12 hour workdays were not uncommon, although many noted that cabbies driving rented taxis usually worked longer hours and on weekends because they had to pay the owner of the taxi a set fee regardless of the money made from fares. Unlike South Asian taxi drivers in New York City, most of whom reported that they turned to taxi driving because they lacked the human capital and English language skills required to work in white-collar jobs (Mitra 2008), Ethiopian cab drivers interviewed for this study on average had 15.2 years of formal schooling and over 75 percent reported that they were college graduates. The immigrants in the sample had turned to taxi driving as a strategy for overcoming labor market disadvantages and their inability to find jobs in keeping with their educational status. However, within these structural constraints, they wished to be engaged in an occupation that would allow them to earn a good living and enjoy a coveted middle-class lifestyle.

Taxi driving as an occupational niche: motivations and limitations

In 2006, taxi drivers in the District of Columbia generally came from over 70 countries and numbered nearly 5,000. At the time, Ethiopian immigrants accounted for over a quarter of all taxi drivers in the city (Kelly 2006), clearly forming an occupational niche in the city. Although difficult to determine because the DC Taxicab Commission does not collect information on the immigrant status or ethnic background of the city's taxi drivers, Ethiopians comprise a significant proportion (reported variously as between 20 and 40 percent) of cab drivers in Washington, DC according to cab companies.

The community's involvement in the taxicab business can also be gauged from the existence of many Ethiopian-owned and Ethiopian-managed cab companies, such as Grand Cab, Travelers' Cab, Allied Cab Company, and Rapid Cab, most of which employ co-ethnic drivers. Ethiopians have also formed ethnic taxi owner associations such as the Ethio-American United Cab Owner Association with almost 1,000 members. Foreign-born Ethiopians are also represented in the leadership of non-ethnic organizations such as the DC Professional Taxi Drivers' Association and the Washington DC Taxi Operators Association, which represent the interests of all taxi drivers in the city.

A network built around social ties of religion, ethnicity, and place of origin formed the foundation for the development of taxicab driving as an ethnic niche among Ethiopian immigrants. Community-based linkages were critical in the rising numbers of Ethiopian immigrants involved in the taxicab business. More established first-generation immigrants recruited drivers from among newly arrived emigres, introducing taxi driving as an option that allowed part-time work, provided income, and could be a stepping stone to another job. Several of the owner-drivers who were interviewed for this study reported having co-ethnic partners who shared ownership of the taxi and also drove it. Ethiopian immigrants expressed several reasons for turning to taxi driving as a feasible occupation, among which the most salient ones were that it provided avenues for upward socio-economic mobility for first and second generations, and that the occupation offered autonomy and flexibility that worked well with the lifestyles and aspirations of the group. In the following section I will discuss some of these factors in greater detail.

A strategy for upward socio-economical mobility

Ethiopian immigrants entered the USA through different visa categories and followed diverse paths in the hopes of realizing the American Dream of economic success and social mobility. Clark (2003) noted that immigrant flows to the USA are bifurcated. Low-skilled, poor migrants, and refugees with few resources start at the bottom of the economic ladder, working in low-paying service jobs, while high-skilled, highly educated, and resource-rich immigrants are channeled into high-level jobs in fields such as finance, engineering, information technology, science, and medicine. Like other immigrants, Ethiopians seek avenues of upward mobility that will bring them closer to achieving their desired goals of economic success and social and institutional integration.

Ethiopian taxi drivers in the sample did not fully belong to either of the flows mentioned above. Rather, on average they had some college education but were unable to put their skills sets and education to use as professionals in the receiving country. While many of those interviewed had worked in white-collar professions in Ethiopia and would have preferred to continue to do so in the USA, given their constraints in the labor market due to blocked mobility, they viewed taxi driving as an occupation that offered the surest and swiftest path for upward economic mobility. Although the hours were long and a few cab drivers mentioned that driving in certain neighborhoods in the District of Columbia could be dangerous, all agreed that if an individual was willing to work hard, he could earn enough to enjoy a middle-class lifestyle. Although reluctant to put a figure on weekly or monthly earnings, Getachew (age 49) admitted that taxi drivers could make a 'decent living' but also that they were likely to significantly under-disclose their earnings:

> There is good money in driving cabs. You can make a decent living. It is hard work all right, but the money is good. Ask a taxi driver how much he makes driving a cab and no one will tell you how much he really makes. And then there are the tips. Nobody, not even Uncle Sam can keep track of you!

Home ownership is another central dimension of a middle-class lifestyle and achieving the American Dream (Clark 2003). Like other immigrants in the metropolis, Ethiopians reside overwhelmingly in suburban Washington, where they are more likely to find an affordable home in a safe neighborhood with amenities such as good public schools. Approximately 36 percent of all Ethiopians living in the Washington metropolitan area own their home, while 40 percent of taxi drivers interviewed for this study reported being home owners. Homeownership was perceived as a symbol of upward mobility and evoked a greater sense of belonging and integration into the social fabric of the city and country. Although homeownership in the sample was achieved largely through combined earnings of married couples, taxi driving was considered by those interviewed as a critical pathway in being able to fulfill this aspect of the American Dream.

Even though they considered themselves to be somewhat financially comfortable and several were on the path of social integration through the purchase of a home, the

Ethiopian immigrants also regretted the loss of social status and respect that attended their new jobs as cab drivers. According to Dawit (age 77)

> Even though the money is good, you don't get respect. Do people care that I have a college degree? Not at all! What they see is a black man, an immigrant with an accent driving a cab. They don't treat you with consideration. Or politeness. Not everyone is like that, but mostly, that's it – no respect. I have grown old. America has made me old, but old without respect.

A route for second-generation progress

Having obtained a foothold in the USA and hopeful of potential economic and social gains, first-generation immigrants also look to trajectories for advancement that will benefit succeeding generations. Taxi driving was perceived by first-generation immigrants in the sample as not only a way to earn a living but also as an intergenerational pathway for their children to regain the social standing that the family had lost along with their white-collar jobs. Unlike some other ethnic occupational niches, Ethiopian cab drivers did not wish for the next generation to continue in the taxi business, in part because of its working-class connotations. The taxi drivers wished for jobs that conferred a high social status, an assured and sufficiently high income and good work environments for their children. 'That's why we drive, we never got to go to college here', said Yonas, aged 45 years, underscoring the importance placed on tertiary education by these immigrants, who viewed obtaining a degree from an American institution of higher learning as the most efficient pathway to economic and social success. Having themselves been locked out of high-paying tertiary-sector jobs, the immigrants recognized that access to higher education and degrees, skill sets, and social and professional networks gained through university education improved their children's opportunities in a globalized and highly competitive economy.

Immigrants stated that their long workdays were a necessary sacrifice so that the next generation could get American college degrees and pursue professional careers as doctors, lawyers, teachers, and accountants. That the hope for upward socio-economic mobility from working-class to white collar within a generation was not just aspirational is borne out by evidence from the interviews. All drivers aged 50 years and above with children reported that their offspring were in the process of getting a college degree or had already earned one. Among the success stories that proud fathers relayed were of sons and daughters who had careers as a medical doctor, nurse, interior designer, public health professional, chartered accountant, and investment banker.

But along with stories of accomplishment and triumph were those of college-educated children finding it difficult to find jobs in the slowing economy. Some immigrant cab drivers were concerned about diminishing opportunities and the lack of a 'burning desire, like us' among the second generation. Amanuel (age 51) says of his son,

> He is lazy. He is smart all right, but he is lazy. He could do much, much better at school, but he does not try.... The kids are American. They already live the good life. That is the life they know. They did not have to struggle like us. Yes, the kids are American.

The perceived loss among the second generation of alleged Ethiopian and immigrant traits such as hard work and a yearning to succeed was keenly felt by first-generation fathers. They worried about deepening economic inequality in the USA and the destabilization wrought by globalization, the weakening American economy, outsourcing and the competition for jobs that their children were likely to face, but also noted that without college degrees their offspring were less likely to be among the 'winners'.

Autonomy and self-sufficiency

Most taxis in the District of Columbia are independent owner-operated and function like small businesses. Greater independence in the work environment and the opportunity to be the proprietor of their business was attractive to Ethiopian immigrant taxi drivers, who were also usually affiliated with driver associations or driver-run companies. Washington, DC is considered one of the few cities in the USA where there are over a hundred taxi companies, but none dominates the market. The majority of the drivers are independent owners because licenses are relatively inexpensive and the ability to enter the business is not limited through the purchase of costly medallions as they are in cities such as New York City, Boston, and Chicago.

In 2010, several driver-owned companies, two driver associations, as well as individual drivers founded the Small Business Association of DC Taxicab Drivers. One of the objectives of this association is to 'Protect individual ownership and entrepreneurship' and it has successfully opposed the DC Council's plan to impose a system that would require drivers to purchase a medallion (which could run to thousands of dollars) in order to drive a taxicab in the city. Among the key points made by the association was that having a medallion system in place would impose a financial penalty on individual taxi drivers, in particular immigrants and older native drivers, who were less likely to be able to afford a medallion. Instead, these potential entrepreneurs would have to work for a large taxicab company if they wished to be in the business of driving cabs. Ethiopian and other Washington taxi drivers were in opposition to national and global trends of the loss of small owner-operated enterprises and the concomitant rise of corporatized employment, a development that they fought.

Not having to wait until the end of the month or the week to be paid was added incentive. As Tesfaye noted,

> If you need extra money for something, you just work longer hours to make that money. You decide what to do. No one tells you which days to work, how long to work, when to start work, when to stop work. Nothing! You are the master of your life, not some boss or manager.

The theme of autonomy was brought up several times during conversations by drivers who also appreciated that they could set their own hours and take time off when needed to spend time with family, take a break or visit Ethiopia.

Flexibility

Flexibility of schedules and workdays went along with autonomy as an important and attractive aspect of taxi driving for the immigrants. The occupation was seen to offer immigrants more work–life balance and more time to spend with family. Worried that his children would neglect their studies and waste time 'Fooling around playing video games and not realizing how critical it is to focus, focus, focus on school', Desta (age 53) said that he decided to do a 4:00 a.m.–2:00 p.m. shift on week days so that he was home when his four sons returned from school. He not only enforced regular hours for homework, but also checked that the completed homework was correctly done. His strategy appears to have paid off. Desta's eldest son is studying to be an engineer at a university in Washington, DC and even got a basketball scholarship, while the other sons are reportedly also doing well in school.

Some drivers drove cabs part-time, combining driving with studying or working concurrently at another job. A couple of drivers were students who were working toward college degrees that they hoped would help them get steady, salaried employment that paid well. These drivers carried their books and laptops with them and used the time waiting for customers at taxi stands to catch up on reading for their courses. Still others combined taxi driving with another job that offered medical and other benefits that were not available to those who were employed full-time as cabbies.

In today's globalized world, it is more likely for people to belong simultaneously to multiple communities, embrace a plethora of identities and loyalties, and in the case of immigrants, lead transnational lives that span countries and continents. Most (73 percent) of Ethiopians in the USA are foreign-born (U.S. Census Bureau, ACS 2010–2012), and have attachments to the sending country as well as to family, friends, institutions, and places within it. They are the source of transnational capital flows in the form of remittances and investments in the home country, a process that has been facilitated by the globalization of economies and societies (Chacko and Gebre 2013). The improved capability, falling costs, and ease of use of global telecommunications in the form of the mobile phones, Fax, and the Internet and its applications have made it possible for the diaspora to easily exchange information and engage in collaborations with family and friends in Ethiopia.

Nearly a fifth of the taxi drivers interviewed lived a transnational existence, spending several weeks to a few months each year in Ethiopia for business or personal reasons. Several had made business investments in Ethiopia and returned periodically to check on their businesses, which were often co-owned or run by relatives who lived in the sending country. This enabled the immigrants to straddle countries and societies and literally operate in multiple worlds. One taxi driver in the sample spent almost half of the year in Ethiopia, where he is co-proprietor of an Internet café and a guesthouse in Addis Ababa. The increased frequency of direct flights between Washington, DC and Addis Ababa has also helped Ethiopian entrepreneurs in their business ventures in their home country.

All persons interviewed for this study stated that unlike taxi driving, working in a 'regular' job with limited vacation time would not have allowed them to be transnational entrepreneurs. The flexibility of driving was offset by the fact that time off, as for all self-employed persons, was unpaid. However, drivers who owned their cabs usually made up some of the loss of earnings when they were away by renting their taxis to fellow Ethiopians drivers who did not own cabs.

Conclusion

This study underscores the usefulness of the concept of mixed embeddedness in understanding the rise of taxi driving as a niche occupation among first-generation immigrants from Ethiopia, but also the impact of the opportunities that the Washington metropolitan area as a specific milieu offered these entrepreneurs and the role that globalization plays in their presence in the area and their current and aspirational social and economic trajectories. Ethiopian immigrants overcame institutional and financial constraints while making effective use of ethnic networks and cultural affinities to become taxi drivers, because they perceived taxi driving as both an individual and a group strategy, geared toward maximizing income and the promise of upward mobility for individuals, families, and across generations.

Structural factors such as blocked mobility related to a lack of recognition of their educational qualifications, as well as cultural factors such as the strong social networks and social capital that exist among Ethiopian immigrants were important in the induction of new arrivals into taxicab driving and the creation of taxicab driving as an ethnic occupational niche. The flexibility of cab driving (which allows taxi drivers to work part-time, combine driving with studying for a degree, work simultaneously at another job that offers medical and other benefits, and take time to spend several weeks or months in Ethiopia for business or personal reasons), and the potential of earning a relatively good living were additional factors that attracted Ethiopian immigrants to this occupation. Besides providing an avenue for upward socio-economic mobility, driving cabs also allowed these immigrants greater autonomy and flexibility. They could determine their work hours and also take time off if necessary. Being home when their children returned from school and being able to monitor and supervise their studies were also critical factors for these immigrants, most of who had college degrees, and who wished for their children to earn degrees from American universities and obtain well-paying white-collar jobs.

The criteria set by the DC Taxicab Commission for the entry of new drivers in the taxicab business, the existence of a large community of Ethiopian immigrants with strong ethnic networks in the Washington metropolitan and the fact that potential cabbies did not have to be residents of the District of Columbia to obtain DC taxi operators' licenses also played an important role in the formation and solidification of the niche. Provided the taxicab commission's policies with regard to the costs of joining the ranks of DC taxi drivers do not change dramatically and in the event of likely continued flow of Ethiopian immigrants to the Washington area from the home country and through secondary migration within the USA , taxicab driving as an Ethiopian occupational niche is likely to persist and even grow.

Disclosure statement

No potential conflict of interest was reported by the author.

References

Abraham, S., A. Sundar, and D. Whitmore. 2008. "Toronto Taxi Drivers: Ambassadors of the City." A Report on Working Conditions. Toronto: Ryerson University and University of Toronto.
Aldrich, H., and R. Waldinger. 1990. "Ethnicity and Entrepreneurship." *Annual Review of Sociology* 16 (1): 111–135.
Bogale, B. 2009. "Language Determination in Ethiopia: What Medium of Instruction?" In *Proceedings of the 16th International Conference of Ethiopian Studies*, edited by S. Ege, H. Aspen, B. Teferra, and S. Bekele. Vol. 4, 1089–1101. Trondheim: Norwegian University of Science and Technology.
Bonacich, E. 1973. "A Theory of Middleman Minorities." *American Sociological Review* 38 (5): 583–594.

Borjas, G. J. 1986. "The Self-Employment Experience of Immigrants." NBER Working Paper Series, No. W1942.

Brettell, C. B., and K. E. Alstatt. 2007. "The Agency of Immigrant Entrepreneurs: Biographies of the Self-Employed in Ethnic and Occupational Niches of the Urban Labor Market." *Journal of Anthropological Research* 63: 383–397.

Chacko, E. 2009. "Africans in Washington, D.C: Ethiopian Ethnic Institutions and Immigrant Adjustment." In *The Neo-African Diaspora in the United States and Canada at the Dawn of the 21st Century*, edited by J. W. Frazier, J. T. Darden, and N. F. Henry, 243–256. Binghamton, NY: Global Academic Publishing.

Chacko, E. 2011. "Translocality in Washington, D.C. and Addis Ababa: Spaces and Linkages of the Ethiopian Diaspora in Two Capital Cities". In *Translocal Geographies: Space, Places, Connections*, edited by A. Datta and K. Brickell. 163–178. Surrey: Ashgate.

Chacko, E., and P. Gebre. 2013. "Leveraging the Diaspora: Lessons from Ethiopia." *GeoJournal* 78 (3): 495–505.

Clark, W. A. V. 2003. *Immigrants and the American Dream: Remaking the Middle Class*. New York: The Guilford Press.

Colic-Peisker, V., and F. Tilbury. 2006. "Employment Niches for Recent Refugees: Segmented Labour Market in Twenty-First Century Australia." *Journal of Refugee Studies* 19 (2): 203–229.

Del Valle, F. F. 1995. "Who's Driving New York? A Profile of Taxi Driver Applicants". *Migration World Magazine* 23 (4): 12.

Dhingra, P. 2012. *Life Behind the Lobby: Indian American Motel Owners and the American Dream*. Palo Alto, CA: Stanford University Press.

Eckstein, S., and T. N. Nguyen. 2011. "The Making and Transnationalization of an Ethnic Niche: Vietnamese Manicurists." *International Migration Review* 45 (3): 639–674.

Getahun, S. A. 2007. *The History of Ethiopian Immigrants and Refugees in America, 1900–2000: Patterns of Migration, Survival and Adjustment*. New York: LFB Scholarly Publishing.

Hiebert, D. 2002. "The Spatial Limits to Entrepreneurship: Immigrant Entrepreneurs in Canada." *Tijdschrift voor Economische en Sociale Geografie* 93 (2): 173–190.

Hondagneu-Sotelo, P. 2001. *Domestica: Immigrant Workers Cleaning and Caring in the Shadows of Affluence*. Berkeley: University California Press.

IOM (International Organization of Migration). 2014. "Global Migration Trends: An Overview." http://www.iomvienna.at/sites/default/files/Global_Migration_Trends_PDF_FinalVH_with%20References.pdf.

Kalra, V. S. 2000 *From Textile Mills to Taxi Ranks: Experiences of Migration, Labour, and Social Change*. Aldershot: Ashgate.

Kaplan, D. H. 1998. "The Spatial Structure of Urban Ethnic Economies." *Urban Geography* 19 (6): 489–501.

Kaplan, D., and W. Li. 2006. *The Landscapes of Ethnic Economy*. Lanham, MD: Rowman and Littlefield.

Kelly, J. 2006. "Driving Around the World in D.C." *The Washington Post*, March 10.

Kloosterman, R. 1999. "Mixed Embeddedness: (In)formal Economic Activities and Immigrant Businesses in the Netherlands." *International Journal of Urban and Regional Research* 23 (2): 252–266.

Kloosterman, R., and J. Rath. 2001. "Immigrant Entrepreneurs in Advanced Economies: Mixed Embeddedness Further Explored." *Journal of Ethnic and Migration Studies* 27 (2): 189–201.

Kloosterman, R., and J. Rath. 2003. *Immigrant Entrepreneurs: Venturing Abroad in the Age of Globalization*. Oxford: Berg.

Korten, D. C. 1972. *Planned Change in a Transitional Society: Psychological Problems of Modernization in Ethiopia*. New York: Praeger Publishers.

Ley, D. 2010. *Millionaire Migrants: Trans-Pacific Life Lines*. Oxford: Blackwell-Wiley.

Light, I. 1979. "Disadvantaged Minorities in Self-employment." *International Journal of Comparative Sociology*, 20 (1–2): 30–45.

Light, I., and S. Gold. 2000. *Ethnic Economies*. Bingley: Emerald Group.

Livi-Bacci, M. 2012. *A Short History of Migration*. Cambridge: Polity.

Mathew, B. 2005. *Taxi! Cabs and Capitalism in New York City*. New York: The New Press.

Min, P. G., and M. Bozorgmehr. 2000. "Immigrant Entrepreneurship and Business Patterns: A Comparison of Koreans and Iranians in Los Angeles." *International Migration Review* 34: 707–38.

Mitra, D. 2008. "Punjabi American Taxi Drivers the New White Working Class?" *Journal of Asian American Studies* 11 (3): 303–336.

Ong, P., and T. Azores. 1994. "The Migration and Incorporation of Filipino Nurses". In *The New Asian Immigration in Los Angeles and Global Restructuring*, edited by Paul, Edna Bonacich, and Lucie Cheng, 164–195. Philadelphia, PA: Temple University Press.

Parrenas, R. S. 2005. "The Gender Paradox in the Transnational Families of Filipino Migrant Women." *Asian and Pacific Migration Journal* 14 (3): 243–268.

Raijman, R., and M. Tienda. 2000. "Immigrants' Pathways to Business Ownership: A Comparative Ethnic Perspective." *The International Migration Review* 34 (3): 682–706.

Raijman, R., and M. Tienda. 2003. "Ethnic Foundations of Economic Transactions: Mexican and Korean Immigrant Entrepreneurs in Chicago." *Ethnic and Racial Studies* 26 (5): 783–801.

Ram, M., T. Jones, T. Abbas, and B. Sanghera. 2002. "Ethnic Minority Enterprise in its Urban Context: South Asian Restaurants in Birmingham." *International Journal of Urban and Regional Research* 26 (1): 24–40.

Swanton, D. 2010. "Flesh, Metal, Road: Tracing the Machinic Geographies of Race." *Environment and Planning D: Society and Space* 28: 447–466.

US Bureau of the Census, American Community Survey. 2010–2012. "American Fact Finder." Washington DC.

Volery, T. 2007. "Ethnic Entrepreneurship: A Theoretical Framework." In *Handbook of Research on Ethnic Minority Entrepreneurship: A Co-Evolutionary View on Resource Management*, edited by L. P. Dana, 30–41. Cheltenham: Edward Elgar.

Waldinger, R. 1994. "The Making of an Immigrant Niche." *International Migration Review* 28 (1): 3–30.

Waldinger, R., and M. Bozorgmehr. 1996 "The Making of a Multicultural Metropolis." In *Ethnic Los Angeles*, edited by R. Waldinger, and M. Bozorgmehr, 3–38. New York: Russell Sage Foundation.

Waldinger, R., and C. Der-Martirosian. 2001 "The Immigrant Niche: Pervasive, Persistent, Diverse." In *Strangers at the Gates: New Immigrants in Urban America*, edited by R. Waldinger, 228–271. Berkeley: University of California Press.

Wang, Q., and W. Li. 2007. "Entrepreneurship, Ethnicity and Local Contexts: Hispanic Entrepreneurs in Three U.S. Southern Metropolitan Areas." *GeoJournal* 68: 167–182.

Wilson, F. D. 2003. "Ethnic Niching and Metropolitan Labour Markets." *Social Science Research* 32 (3): 429–466.

Wilson, K. L., and A. Portes. 1980. "Immigrant Enclaves: An Analysis of Labor Market Experiences of Cubans in Miami." *American Journal of Sociology* 86 (2): 295–319.

Zhou, M. 1992. *Chinatown: The Socioeconomic Potential of an Urban Enclave*. Philadelphia, PA: Temple University Press.

Zhou, M. 2004. "Revisiting Ethnic Entrepreneurship: Convergences, Controversies, and Conceptual Advancements." *International Migration Review* 38 (3): 1040–1074.

Ethiopian female labor migration to the Gulf states: the case of Kuwait

Faiz Omar Mohammad Jamie and Anwar Hassan Tsega

Center for Peace and Development Studies, University of Bahri, Khartoum, Sudan

ABSTRACT
International labor migration is one of the most salient features of the modern globalized world. However, the phenomenon has its roots in some earlier periods in human history. Africa is traditionally a sending continent of all types of migrations, voluntary or forced. This study examines the above-mentioned issues through the mounting phenomenon of migration of single independent women in search for better economic, social, or political conditions across the boundaries of their home countries. In the past, African women migrants were only spouses or dependent family members. But as modernity swept most African societies, with rising unemployment rates, there is evidence everywhere in Africa that women labor migration is a growing phenomenon that deserves to be understood in the context of current gender-related research. This work explores these issues further, focusing on the experience of Ethiopian women labor migrants to Kuwait, within Gulf Cooperation Council, an area with a shared socio-economic background. In addition to numerous difficulties already facing labor migrants, Ethiopian women suffered greater degrees of gender-based violence, underpayment, and trafficking, to mention only few aspects of human rights violations. This situation could be attributed to the fact that most of these women fall under the category of unskilled and/or illiterate migrants, as irregular migrants who are employed within the private sector, outside the purview any legal or labor regulatory authorities.

Introduction

International migration has come to be one of the central themes of debate and concern among different academic, political, and economic domains. Like any other human activity, migration is a multi-dimensional phenomenon, having a lot to do with security, development, health, culture, etc.

Before we engage further in the analysis of migration, female migration in particular, it is necessary that we review some of the current theories that explain the dynamics of the process. This should help deepen our understanding about how different scholars have examined the phenomenon, and sheds light on the principles from which they depart building and synthesizing empirical information. This is particularly necessary because this area of study (migration) belongs to a relatively new discipline (population studies) where theoretical foundation should inform empirical research work.

Ethiopia, one of the most populous countries in Africa, has been experiencing an ever-growing rate of labor migration of skilled and unskilled workers since the 1970s, after the collapse of the Haile Selassie regime. This work is primarily concerned with a specific type of migration (female labor migration), as an issue having to do with culture, social norms, immigration policies of the sending country, population structure, fertility rate, population size, population policies, and other indices. The paper will examine the push factors within Ethiopian societies that stimulate this type of migration, drawing upon Neoclassical economic theory mainly relating the causes of migration to sheer economic factors, which shape personal decisions concerning one's livelihood on rational grounds. The vast majority of Ethiopian women live in rural areas, working in the low-income, labor-intensive informal agricultural sector. Therefore, because of limited access to formal sector of economy, coupled with inability to make tangible progress in small-scale private projects, it is understandable that women leave their home country, Ethiopia, as migrant workers to the Gulf States. In this regard, the paper will examine the extent to which large numbers of these women became victims of trafficking and related abuses.

Migration is one salient feature of economic life in the whole area of the Gulf as a receiving-area mostly attracting labor migrants. The enormous demand for foreign labor in the oil-producing countries was remarkable in the post-1970s. The current economic development in the area owes a lot to this type of migration as a main provider of labor. For that to be researched, authentic and reliable data have to be collected from various sources, including receiving countries' immigration policies, socio-cultural aspects (including religion), and value systems. The significance of this work rests on the understanding of the extent to which female migrants could influence all these aspects among others. However, up-dated empirical evidence is advisable, in this context, to provide proof-based knowledge on this dynamic phenomenon. For our study, we focus on Kuwait as an example of women's migration within the Gulf States.

Future trends of female migration in the context of a globalized world affect cultural dynamics in the Gulf, taking into consideration wider repercussion of Arab Spring Movements in the area.

Theoretical framework

The growing phenomenon of international migration is leading individual states to become more diverse and multi-ethnic societies. So far the theoretical bases for understanding these dynamics are still in the making (Massey et al. 1993, 432). However a full understanding of the migratory process will hardly be achieved without an interdisciplinary approach, considering more than one level of analysis, grounded on a sophisticated theory encompassing a variety of perspectives, and assumptions.

Neoclassical macro-economic theory was developed as far back as the 1950s, by the second generation of European classical economists (Lewis 1954; Harris and Todaro 1970; Todaro 1976). This particular theory follows the most obvious economic motivations for migration, making comparisons between countries with large labor supply where wages tend to be low, and countries with large capital supply where wages tend to be relatively higher. The resulting differential according to this theory is behind the movement of laborers who move from low-wage countries to high-wage countries. This movement has a twofold impact. On the one hand, the movement decreases the volume/supply of labor in the poor countries, leading to a consequent rise in wages. On the other, it increases the volume/supply of labor in the destination countries, leading to a subsequent decrease in wages. At the macro-economic level, this leads to an international equilibrium of wages where other factors matter; cost of movement and other opportunities forgone.

Another corresponding dynamic also follows this in terms of what we can call human-capital flow, which includes the movement of highly qualified professionals, mangers, and entrepreneurs from capital-rich countries to capital-scarce countries, in search for better opportunities and high returns of capital and skill investment. This type of movement should be separately approached from the conventional movement of ordinary labor because the dynamics involved are slightly different.

The school of thought based on this theory has influenced much of the literature on international migration and policies. The most characteristic feature of this school is the assumption that labor market is mostly the sole mechanism of labor-related human movement.

Neoclassical micro-economic theory was developed sometime later than the preceding one, starting from late 1960s, by economists and population scholars (Todaro 1969; Todaro and Maruszko 1987). This theory focuses on the individual migrant as a rational actor who possesses tools enabling him/her to take decisions based on informed calculations about the positive and negative implications of decision made; in case he/she found out that migration returns outweigh negative impacts, he or she is deemed to decide to migrate. Therefore this theory considers this as the most important motivating factor, rather than any other macro-economic considerations.

This theory has been challenged by many scholars (Stark and Bloom 1985), pointing to the fact that individual migrant decisions are not as individual as they seem; in fact, they are influenced by other associated co-actors: families, friends, ex-/current migrants, etc. Decisions are not necessarily targeting maximizing earnings; they could include diversifying sources of income to avoid local production failures, consequently minimizing household income risks.

This model suggests that households and families are appropriate units for migration research rather than independent individuals. Apart from the basic fact taken for granted in neoclassical theories that wage differentials and employment are the driving forces for migration, this model considers household expectation to engage in both local labor and international market even in the absence of wage differentials. According to this perspective, governments seeking to control migration could obviously employ policies providing insurance opportunities against different economic failures.

Other scholars developed their own approaches independent of the influences of these macro–micro analyses; one noteworthy among them is Piore (1979), who argued that international migration is stimulated by a permanent demand for immigrant labor because of structural built-in factors related to developed economies. Therefore, according to Piore, immigration is initiated by the pull factors in rich societies as an original need for foreign labor, more than by push factors in terms of low-wages or unemployment rates, in developing countries.

Another approach (World Systems approach) was developed by sociological theorists who related the origins of international migration to the structure of market economy that emerged after the colonization era of sixteenth century (Wallerstien 1974; Sassen 1988; Morawska 1990). According to this approach, the experience of the colonial period in poor societies gave rise to a class of people with expectations emulating the ex-colonial societies, consequently developing an ever-growing aptitude to migrate abroad. Therefore, international migration is a function of penetration of capitalist market economy relations into less-developed societies and settlements.

International migration in this framework is more likely to take place between colonies and their ex-colonial powers, more often than not due to cultural, linguistic and familiarity factors; over and above communication links were already established during the colonial period. People from Chad, for example, because of their familiarity with French language, aspire to pursue their studies in France; therefore they most likely tend to migrate because of this linguistic tie, which is why, according to this approach, international migration has little to do with wage differentials and employment opportunities.

As current globalization process is reinforcing democratization trends in world peripheral areas, ever-growing parts of the globe are becoming more and more assimilated into international free-market economic system. Many aspects of original/traditional livelihood systems were subject to transformation processes, making them complementary to the core areas in Western Europe, North America, and Japan. In the case of agricultural subsistence, production styles were replaced by modern mechanized farming systems producing high crop yields at relatively low unit prices, driving small producers out of local markets (Chayanov 1966), leading to the emergence of labor force with weak ties to land, ready to migrate. Introduction of foreign-owned industries in peripheries related to capitalist centers benefiting from low-wage local labor force, mostly attractive to women, limiting opportunities for male labor force indirectly tempting them to seek opportunities abroad. All this is being reinforced by mass communications and media campaigns transmitting propaganda about life styles and living standards, by specialized foreign advertising agencies.

The so-called global cities in Europe, America, and the Pacific, where most of the international wealth is concentrated, is generating a great demand for unskilled labor, which has to be imported from the peripheries, in the light of the resistance of poorly educated natives taking jobs at the bottom of the occupational hierarchy (Castells 1989).

Network theory: The idea behind this theory is to seek explanation of international migration in terms of pioneer migrants ability and aptitude to make it easier for those who want to migrate to do so with minimal costs and risk. Because most of those pioneers have relatives, friends, and acquaintances in their home countries, having the same motivations for migration, but lack the know-how; therefore, to meet these demands, networks as interpersonal ties that connect migrants with sending countries were established.

International migration expands over time so long as those pioneer migrants provide tempting information to their fellow would-be migrants to follow them, a fact that would reduce the risk of moving to another country, a totally new culture. In this way, every wave of migrants follows the same trajectory, and the number becomes ever-growing. This line of reasoning is in total divergence with the wage differential/employment analyses. It would very difficult for governments to control flows of migration, because network formations fall beyond their control, and they (networks) would remain active regardless of policies governments adopt. In this manner, migratory behavior/attitude spreads outward to encompass broader segments of peripheral areas (Hugo 1981; Taylor 1986).

In relation to this, many other details may be of concern, according to Piore, Massey and others: somebody with prior experience of migration is more likely to repeat that than another without that experience; the closer the relative who is abroad to a potential migrant raises the possibility/probability of migration for him. If networks are important, they are so because they assist new migrants in documentation, acquiring legal papers, and avoiding arrest and deportation. This is why networks reduce risks and costs of international movement.

International migration of Ethiopians

Ethiopia is one of the most populous countries in Africa (83 million in 2009), and also among the poorest countries in Africa, and the world over (Fransen 2009). The population is predominantly rural traditional farmers. It is an established fact in migration studies that the poorest of the poor do not migrate. Sub-Saharan region is the poorest region in the world. Ethiopia, which belongs to this region, has an emigration rate of 0.06 percent, considered to be low in comparison to Africa as a whole. However, in the post-1980 period, Ethiopia became internationally known for its refugee crisis. This has of course changed drastically as Ethiopians seeking refuge in other countries decreased over the last decades. The Ethiopian Diaspora is one of the largest of all African countries, concentrated mainly in North America and UK notably because of the inclusion of the right for free movement in the constitution of the post-1991 Ethiopia, among other less important factors.

Most of the developing countries have high population growth rates, including Ethiopia, which is estimated to be around 3.21 percent in 2008, considered to be the 11th highest worldwide (CIA World Fact Book). This high population growth rate exceeds the economic growth rate, leading to an increased phenomenon of unemployment as high as 48 percent for urban males (Fransen 2009).

It is quite understandable that because of the above-mentioned factors, Ethiopian regime encourages migration because it enables the government to avoid the negative social and political impacts of the growing urban unemployed Ethiopian citizens. In fact the World Bank estimates that unemployment in Ethiopia is approximately 20.5 percent. Emigration is also an opportunity for the government to benefit from the anticipated remittances and their significant contribution in the national economy.

Another dimension stimulating migration in Ethiopia is related to the state of food insecurity most rural population has faced for decades. The Food and Agriculture Organization estimated that up to 44 percent of rural Ethiopians were undernourished in 2009. Food insecurity is primarily related to successive droughts, degradation of natural resources, and rapid population growth. The resulting famines Ethiopia experienced were in 1973, 1977–1978, 1983–1984, 1987–1988, and 1993. The most severe one being in 1983–1984 as part of the famine that hit the whole African Sahel, which left over one million deaths among Ethiopians.

The country is a regular recipient of food aid; some sources have estimated up to five million Ethiopians would require food aid, however well the rain and the harvest (Hammond 2008). Therefore, food insecurity is persistently a challenge for Ethiopia and is presumably the key driver for the out-migration flows for Ethiopians, who are up to 80 percent rural dwellers. Apart from that, Ethiopia has suffered substantially from 'brain drain' or the out-migration of highly skilled Ethiopians over years (Elkawas 2004).

All of this is coupled with the rising demand for foreign labor in many parts of the world, including Middle Eastern and Arab countries, where an enormous growth in the demand for skilled and unskilled labor was more real than apparent. Due to mechanisms of a globalizing world, where everybody is well aware of the opportunities and better life conditions around the globe, young Ethiopians like any other youth dream of a brighter future and leave their country in pursuit of this dream. However this particular type of migration (brain drain) has profound negative effects in the rural areas, where medical staff is badly needed, along with other highly skilled government service providers.

Ethiopian government policies and legislations on labor migration

It is worth noting here that migration for employment is part of the concerns of the International Labour Organization (ILO) particularly the decent work agenda. The ILO has an obligation to help governments develop principles and guidelines in this respect. Conventions Nos 97 and 143 are important instruments for protection of the rights of international migrant workers, providing measures against exploitation and discrimination against workers. Unlike what we have discussed earlier in the Gulf area, the ILO considers all international labor standards, unless otherwise stated as applicable to migrant workers. This could be interpreted to indicate that no worker is to be excluded from labor laws, or at least there has to be some sort of legal provisions stating the rights and obligations of alien and national workers; however, in practice at least in the Gulf area foreign domestic workers are excluded from national labor laws.

In Ethiopia, the Ministry of Labor and Social Affairs (MOLSA) is the legal government body responsible for regularizing migration, according to Ethiopian Labor Proclamation No. 42/1993. To protect rights, safety and dignity of Ethiopians employed outside the country, MOLSA issued the Private Employment Agency Proclamation No. 104/1998, to facilitate migration of workers. Furthermore MOLSA stipulated conditions under which an Ethiopian national can be employed abroad, including the fact that his/her employment should not adversely affect federal manpower requirement or needs, and the fact that worker's contract should be in the context of bilateral or multilateral agreements. The laws and policies are all meant to combat the rising phenomena of human trafficking, where possibilities of exploitation of workers are extremely high. The challenge before Ethiopia is how to enforce these laws and how best to control private employment agencies. Another limitation facing government policies is the limited number of labor attachées in destination countries to provide support services and ensure application of policies regarding employment issues and affairs, involving many political and legal frameworks in terms of bilateral agreements or protocols, assuring fair and just work conditions for migrant workers.

In fact, some African countries have taken good steps to improve work situations for their nationals. For example, Kenya was one country where repeated cases of abuse against domestic workers in the Middle Eastern countries were reported, prompting establishment of Ministerial task force to develop an action plan and guidelines on labor migration. Kenya went as far as banning employment of nationals as domestic workers in the Middle East (ILO 2013). Another way of doing that – ensuring good work situations for nationals of sending countries – could be including agreements and memoranda of understanding between sending and receiving countries.

Ministry of Labor and Social Affairs, in collaboration with International Organization of Migration, organizes pre-departure orientation sessions for prospective women labor migrants, to help them better understand destination countries, culture, religion, expectations of conduct and also provide some knowledge about procedures in airports, banks, etc. The overall rationale is to construct the prototype of an ideal worker.

Labour migration in Kuwait

Kuwait as a constitutional monarchy is an oil-rich state possessing 8 percent of world oil reserve. Migrants constitute up to 68 percent of the total population, of which 30 percent constitute female labor migrants (World Bank 2011) mostly from South East Asia. An important factor in feminization of migration is the growing demand for paid domestic labor in Kuwait as in other Gulf Cooperation Council (GCC) countries. In fact, non-nationals outnumber nationals in both population and labor force. Whereas the number of nationals is 32 percent of the total population in Kuwait, they make only 17 percent of the labor force, most of them are recruited in the public sector. A Noted increase in inflow of migrants to Kuwait was reported after the 1990 Kuwait–Iraqi war, coupled with illegal trade in visas. Contrary to the declared policies, most non-nationals occupy unskilled jobs.

Therefore, Kuwait considers labor immigration rates to be high, consequently pursuing policies aiming to reduce these levels. These policies were threefold:

(1) Regulatory policies: this package includes ways to determine duration of stay for each, plus restricting opportunities for employment for non-nationals only for jobs that require high skills.
(2) Restrictive policies: this package aims to reduce recruitment of non-nationals in public employment, reactivate illegal migration procedures and controls, raising fees for renewal of visas, insurance certificates, etc.
(3) Protective policies: are those policies aiming at safeguarding rights of workers, minimum wages, work conditions, etc.

All these policies were meant to restore some measure of balance between the relatively small national population sizes and non-nationals. This situation is more serious in Kuwait than in other GCC states. That is why in the Kafala system there is more conservative than elsewhere. Under this system, as indicated earlier, migrants' legal and economic situation is closely connected with his/her employer/Kafeel, where he has to sign a document to declare that a certain employee works for him and is ready to inform immigration authorities of any change in the labor contract (validity, renewal, cancellation), or workers' residence.

This system is in need of reform to be consistent with modern international conventions on the rights of migrant workers whether domestic or else. However in Kuwait theoretically it seems to be consistent with declared migration policies, but in practice, one of the side effects is the emergence of visas trade, which is an illegal practice according to normal immigration principles. The Kafal system in Bahrain and Oman (where the native population is relatively higher) is more liberal than in Kuwait, Qatar, and United Arab Emirates, where native population is a minority. In both cases, the system is meant to protect the privileges of the local population, who perceive themselves besieged by migrant workers. Consequently the system severely compromises fundamental rights and freedoms, exploiting their dependency and vulnerabilities.

Migration of Ethiopian women

For many women migrant workers, migration can represent a positive and empowering experience because they become the principal breadwinners of their families, giving them more important roles in their family affairs, where both benefit from migration. The ILO estimates that 47 percent of international migrants in Africa are women, many of whom are engaged in the domestic sector (ILO 2013). However migration of women in Ethiopia or elsewhere is not a new phenomenon because they used to migrate before as members of their families; the current wave of international migration of women is characterized by increasing number of women migrating independent of men, married or not, and the point is that they travel without the company of their husbands or fathers.

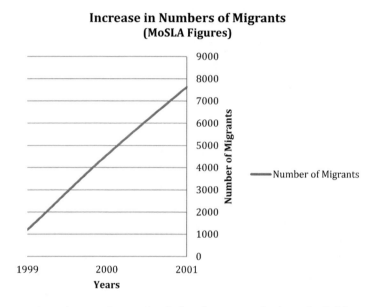

Ethiopian society is mostly patriarchal, where gender-based division of labor is observed. This is particularly so in rural areas where most Ethiopians live. Women and children make up to 75 percent of the population size, with a high birth rate and prevalent poverty countrywide. Also because of patriarchal culture, women have little access to education and training opportunities, and as a consequence employment chances are limited. Other culture-related factors also contribute to the phenomenon: early marriage, habitual abduction for marriage, sexual harassment, etc. All these factors lead to the phenomena of school drop-out of girls as they move up to higher grades. Therefore with limited access to formal economy employment opportunities, coupled with inability to achieve success in informal economy, it is commonsense that many able-bodied women consider leaving their country as migrant workers abroad. This trend has been supported by the current gender-sensitive culture towards enabling women to achieve equal participation in all public spheres of life, economic, social, or cultural.

Another culture-related issue concerns Moslem women among whom unemployment is relatively higher than their non-Moslem counterparts. One can understand that young Muslim women in traditional societies are not encouraged to take up paid work in public domains, where they necessarily mix with 'foreign' unrelated men. For Ethiopian Muslim women employment as domestic workers may be seen as more acceptable, particularly if the household is Muslim. This is more obvious in the Sudan, where most Ethiopian girls who work with Sudanese families as domestic helpers are Muslims (Jamie 2012).

> Women who migrate because of the mentioned circumstances are necessarily unskilled, and poorly educated; therefore the available opportunity for them is to take domestic workers jobs which are at the bottom of the occupational hierarchy. For one reason or another Destinations of these women include oil-rich Gulf Arab and Middle Eastern countries. Although data or figures for these migrant women are scarce (Emebet n.d.), the first official wave of emigration of Ethiopian domestic workers was to Lebanon in 1999–2000. Later on Saudia Arabia and Kuwait followed as top destination countries. Migration of domestic workers is closely related to human trafficking because most of the migrants belong to the least educated classes of Ethiopian society. They can easily fall victims for professional brokers and illegal agents or even gangs. Still making it difficult for authorities to trace irregularities, some Muslim or non-Muslim women claim to be going for the 'Omra' or 'Hajj' as religious rituals as a pretext to go to Saudia Arabia and from there to other destinations (Ibid). Although Saudia Arabia is the largest destination for foreign workers, dependence on migrants is greatest in smaller Gulf States; however both places have become common destinations for Ethiopian domestic labor migrants. from 2008 onwards an estimated 35,000 women have been annually reported as migrating through official documented channels, and an equal number is believed to have been migrating through irregular channels. Domestic jobs are offered on short-term contract basis, with salaries ranging from 100–150 US Dollars (a month).

After 1990, neighboring Sudan attracted substantial number of Ethiopian migrant women as domestic workers; this happened after the exploration of petroleum and the economic boom that followed (Jamie 2012). The long border (exceeding 800 miles) between the two countries encourages cross-border movement of people and goods. One can understand that between these neighboring countries, this movement is reciprocal for many political, economic, and even social factors. Nonetheless the current wave of migration involves the movement of exclusively young women seeking domestic jobs with Sudanese families, whose demand for foreign labor was stimulated by the success of Sudanese women securing jobs in public sector, and their ability to pay for domestic care-takers (Tsega 2010). This migration of young Ethiopian women is still ongoing (2014) even after secession of South Sudan and the loss of substantial petroleum resources.

Migrant workers situation in the Gulf states

The six countries of GCC; (Bahrain, Kuwait, Oman, Qatar, Saudia Arabia, and the United Arab Emirates) became the most attractive receiving countries for international labor migration, from Asia, Africa, and other sending areas. It goes without saying that the modern pattern of international migration in these Gulf Arab States followed the discovery of oil resources there. ILO estimates world population of migrant workers to be between 53 and 100 million in the GCC, where the total population is 35 million, half of them are migrant workers who clean, cook, and care for the children and the elderly.

Most of the migrant women population in the Gulf is primarily employed as domestic helpers. The majority of them are from Asia (Philippines, Indonesia, and Sri Lanka), and a growing number is coming from Ethiopia, Eritrea, Sudan, and Egypt. Migrants in Gulf

States were granted an entry visa and a residence permit if and only if they were employed by a GCC citizen or institution. That is done according to the Kafala/sponsorship system, where the sponsor assumes full economic and legal responsibility of the employee during the contract period.

Current labor laws in most Arab League States exclude women employed as domestic workers from any sort of protection, since their work is in households (not considered workplace) of individuals (not considered employers), not easily accessible for supervision by labor inspectors (Esim and Smith 2004). Therefore, their work situation is hardly protected by national labor laws. This explains the large and growing number of complaints presented to Governments in recent years. In Saudia Arabia alone, 19,000 domestic workers fled their employers for mistreatment or non-payment; in 1998 the Sri Lankan authorities received 5,518 complaints of harassment by migrant workers from Kuwait. This is further understood in the context within which domestic workers affairs is dealt with, through ministries of Interior, rather than ministries of social affairs and labor.

> because migrant women are hardly aware of the difference between trafficking and regular migration most of them arrive at destinations without having signed clear work contract with an identifiable employer/sponsor, which is obviously the moral/legal responsibility of the recruiting agency. More surprisingly some migrants could have signed contracts in Arabic without prior knowledge of the language. In the absence of legal protection the value of a contract is nominal, depending on the credibility of the recruiters who are professional brokers. Within these severe circumstances migrant workers are necessarily helpless victims of the 'Kafala' system, designed to ensure that an entry visa is issued upon request of a sponsor/employer, and once the employment is terminated the sponsor is responsible for the repatriation of the worker. Therefore there is no way that any problem arises between a migrant and her sponsor who keeps her passport with him, a weapon to be used against her, in case she thinks of leaving him, or feel that working circumstances not favorable, she will definitely end up in jail and face humiliating deportation. This is because domestic jobs are not legally given regular employment status within labor laws and legislations. Migrants who are deported their home countries most often experience difficulties later in attempting to reintegrate within their societies; hence they may reconsider to migrate again.

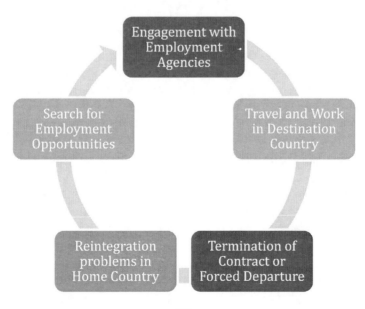

Ethiopian domestic workers migrants in Kuwait

The Ethiopian Embassy in Kuwait estimates that the number of Ethiopian migrant women has drastically increased from 6,000 to 40,000 between 2006 and 2010, respectively (Fernandez 2011). Ethiopia is the major country of origin of African migrant domestic workers in the GCC. Asian domestic workers receive preferential treatment, Pilipino women at the top with the highest salaries, followed by Indonesian and other South Eastern women, with African women at the bottom (Fernandez 2011, 451). Challenges related to decent working conditions and abuse of rights mostly start at the recruitment stage, more often than not, undertaken by irregular agencies, exploiting the gaps in recruitment procedures in many sending countries, including Ethiopia. The ILO (2013) itself admits that in many countries domestic employment is not recognized as part of the regular employment sector, nor is it covered by labor legislation. This applies to Kuwait as well as elsewhere in the GCC. In fact labor Laws in Kuwait were enacted in 1974 before the occurrence of this large-scale influx of domestic workers. Some new attempts were made in 2000 to pass new laws related to migrant domestic workers, detailing on minimum wages, work hours, rest times, etc. However progress in this regard was so slow that no laws were actually passed so far.

Once an Ethiopian woman reaches Kuwait, led by the recruiting agency, she goes directly to the house of her Kafeel/Sponsor – who will take her passport. She disappears there, left entirely to the mercy of her Kafeel, without legal or moral support from a reliable entity, embassy, or labor attaché exposing her to the maximum degree of vulnerability one can think of. Some of the returnee women reported that they were made to work for their employers and the friends of their employers without extra pay. Overtime pay is virtually non-existent. Others reported that their employers had the right to return them to the agency within three months if they are not happy with their work, in the meantime they were not given salary, many were returned back without pay for the first, the second three months of work with provisional employers. Some may stay for a year within this process.

Hours of work for domestic workers are generally long, interviewed workers report them to be ranging from 78 to 100 hours per week, whereas surveyed employers report them to be 60–66 hours per week for males and females, respectively. The contract for migrant foreign worker can be written or verbal, but both are of very limited value in the light of the current Kafala/Sponsorship system, which is a law by itself over any other law. In Kuwait where foreign labor accounts for more than half the total population, the Kafal system is stricter than in Bahrain and Oman. Those helpless workers – as has been earlier indicated – have no reliable and effective institution to report their complaints to, other than their sponsor, who may be the source of their problems. They seldom report these complaints to the Embassy or Police. In fact, conflicts between domestic workers and their employers are considered as private family disputes under the jurisdiction of the security or police, rather than as labor conflicts to be resolved in courts of law. Therefore in the case of conflict with their employers, domestic workers can only hope that their Kafeel/sponsor terminates their contract and sends them home.

As far as clauses of contracts are concerned, as Ethiopian women are non-Arabic speakers, they are never part of the bargaining with employers. They are made to sign on contracts stating penalties as much as 3,000 USD if they decided to return to their home countries, irrespective of the reasons for that. In a published focus group discussion (Kebede n.d.), one migrant woman who was seriously ill wanted to get back home. Her employer insisted to be paid the sum of 3,000 USD, she had only 300, she had to devise another strategy advised by a fellow worker; she pretend to have mental illness. That is how she managed to leave. In some other instances, some employers let visa of employed/migrant expire and sell it to another employer, as an evidence of occurrence of visa trading, which will necessarily lead to existence of surplus of foreign workers.

However, regarding problems related to work, the most frequently cited concern by majority of migrant women in Kuwait was the existence of physical, sexual and psychological abuses by their employers/sponsors, their sons and other visitors (Kebede n.d., 20). This type of compliant needs to be reported to a legally reliable institution to take necessary actions against perpetrator/s; however, such last-resort asylum does not exist for domestic migrants. In fact, domestic workers are not allowed free movement without the company of their employers. Sometimes that is stated in their contracts; not only that, sometimes when the family leaves the house, the domestic worker will be locked in for extended periods of time. Such workers' greatest worry is fear of fire breaking out while they are inside.

As far as remuneration is concerned, most domestics earn 100–125 USD a month. When they arrive to the destination they are already indebted to the recruitment agencies for fees against these services. If a woman is lucky, she will be able to repay that debt on a monthly basis. Otherwise, if she has encountered problems with employers, she will need more time to start repaying; how long will that take depends very much on the working circumstances. Wages are relatively lower than in the private sector, with preference for men. Nationality also matters here. Pilipino women (who are mostly educated) earn the best wages; those from Bangladesh earn less than other nationalities.

Overall, Kuwait is far better than other GCC in many respects. The Kuwaiti constitution allows the formation of unions to represent domestic workers as long as the organization is peaceful and abides by the law. Not only that but although the Constitution states clearly that Islam and Sharia Law are main sources of legislation, freedom of religion is secured by law, opening the door wide for other believers to maintain their beliefs and faith. Kuwait also ratified 18 ILO conventions, and became a signatory of the Convention on the Elimination of All Forms of Discrimination Against Women in 1994.

Migration-related Ethio-Kuwaiti relations

Following an incident of a death of a Kuwaiti lady believed to be killed by an Ethiopian domestic worker, in 2014, widespread concern arose in Kuwait about Ethiopian workers. As several lawyers expressed protest, the Kuwaiti authorities declared that it had stopped 'recruiting domestic helpers' from Ethiopia; in fact the ban also included drivers and gardeners. The decision was made by Immigration authorities of the Kuwaiti Ministry of Interior. The ban applies to male and female Ethiopian workers. That will definitely have far-reaching impacts on the Ethiopian community that was estimated to be around 74,000 persons, particularly that protestors against the incidence called for the deportation of all Ethiopians currently working in the country.

From the Ethiopian side, domestic workers were also banned from traveling to Kuwait. The ban is enforced until recruitment procedures as well as regulations that organize the work of recruitment offices and medical tests in Kuwait are reviewed, Annahar reported, quoting Ministry of Social Affairs and Labor insiders.

These are of course actions and reactions towards what happens in each country.

Conclusion

This paper has examined different aspects on female labor migration focusing on the case of Ethiopian domestic workers in Kuwait. After reviewing some theoretical dimensions, the paper discussed migration in the GCC states which share some of the same socio-cultural and economic backgrounds. As one of the biggest workers-attracting areas worldwide, the oil-rich Gulf enjoys the pull factors for most African labor migrants. Ethiopia, as one of the most populous among African countries suffering from food insecurity and successive droughts, is a country where out-migration is a solution for the government's mounting social economic problems. Therefore the Ethiopian government encourages migration and has issued legislations to regularize the process.

Because there is no bilateral agreement between Ethiopia and Kuwait on labor migration affairs, most migrant women in Kuwait suffer adverse work conditions; unclear work contracts up to Kafala system where a domestic worker stays with her employer at home, out of protective umbrella of labor laws, instead; they fall under the jurisdiction of the Ministry of Interior. Non-existence of labor bilateral agreement between Ethiopia and Kuwait caused adverse work conditions for women labor migrants. ILO and UN conventions provide plenty of clauses protecting workers' rights, but all of these international documents remain non-binding for even member states.

Kuwait among other Gulf States may become more concerned about the mounting phenomena of foreign labor migration, because foreigners in most cases outnumber nationals, both among the workforce as well as the indigenous population.

Further research on this topic can provide insights into the experiences of Ethiopian women who migrate to work as domestic workers in the Gulf States. Comprehensive studies could provide the bases for developing effective policies to protect women's rights, which could result in just and fair coexistence between nationals and non-nationals in the Gulf area, in general, and Kuwait, in particular.

Disclosure statement

No potential conflict of interest was reported by the authors.

References

Castells, Manual. 1989. *The Information City: Information Technology, Economic Restructuring and the Urban-Regional Process*. Oxford: Basil Blackwood.

Chayanov, Alexander V. 1966. *Theory of Peasant Economy*, Vol. 4. Homewood: Richard D. Irwin.

Elkawas, M. A. 2004. "Brain Drain: Putting Africa Between a Rock and a Hard Place." *Mediterranean Quarterly* 15 (4): 36–56.

Esim, Simel, and Monica Smith. 2004. Gender and Migration in Arab States: The Case of Domestic Workers. Beruit: International Labor Organization, Regional Office for Arab States.

Fernandez, Bina. 2011. "Household Help? Ethiopian Women Domestic Workers Labor Migration to the Gulf Coutries." *Asian and Pacific Migration Journal* 20 (3–4): 433–457.

Fransen, Sonja. 2009. "Migration in Ethiopia: History, Current Trends and Future Prospectus." Paper Series Migration and Development Country Profiles, Maastricht Grduate School of Governance.

Hammond, L. 2008. "Strategies of Invisibization: Hoe Ethiopia's Resettlement Programme Hides the Poorest of the Poor." *Journal of Refugee Studies* 21 (4): 517–536.

Harris, J. R., and Micheal P. Todaro. 1970. "Migration Unemployment, and Development: A Two-Sector Analysis." *American Economic Review* 60: 126–142.

Hugo, Graeme J. 1981. "Village-Community Ties, Village Norms, Ethnic and Social Networks: A Review of Evidence from the Third World." In *Migration Decision-Making: Multidisciplinary Approaches to Micro Level Studies in Developed and Developing Countries*, edited by Gordon F. DeJong and Robert W. Gardner, 186–225. New York: Pergamon Press.

ILO. 2013. Protecting the Rights of Migrant Domestic Workers, Briefing Note No. 4, Regional Knowledge Sharing Forum, Dar es Salam, Tanzania.

Jamie, Faiz Omar. 2012. "Gender and Migration in Africa: The Case of Ethiopian Women Labor Migrants in the Sudan." *Law and Politics Journal* 6 (1): 186–192.

Kebede, Embede. n.d. "Ethiopia: An Assessment of the International Labour Migration Situation; The Case of Female Labor Migrants." Gender Promotion Program Working Paper No. 3, International Labor Office, Geneva.

Lewis, W. Arthur. 1954. "Economic Development with Unlimited Supplies of Labor." The Manchester School of Economic and Socila Studies 22: 139–191.

Massey, Douglas S., Joaquin Arango, Graeme Hugo, Ali Kouaouci, Adela Pellegrino., and J. Edward Taylor 1993. "Theories of International Migration: A Review and Appraisal." *Population and Development Review*, 19 (3): 431–466.

Morawska, Ewa. 1990. "The Sociology and Historiography of immigration." In *Immigration Reconsidered: History, Sociology, and Politics*, edited by Virginia YansMaclaughlin, 187–240. New York: Oxford University Press.

Piore, Michael J. 1979. *Birds of Passage: Migrant labour in Industrial Societies*. Cambridge: Cambridge University Press.

Sassen, Saskia. 1988. *The Mobility of Labor and Capital: A Study in International Investment and Labour Flow*. Cambridge: Cambridge University Press.

Stark, Oded and David E. Bloom. 1985. "The New Economics of Labour Migration." *American Economic Review* 75: 173–178.

Taylor, J. Edward. 1986. "Differential Migration, Networks, Information and Risk." In *Research in Human Capital and Development*, edited by Oded Stark, Vol. 4, 147–171. Migration, Human Capital, and Development. Greenwich, CT: JAI Press.

Todaro, Michael P. 1969. "A Model of Labor Migration and Urban Unemployment in Less Developed Countries." The American Economic Review 59: 138–148.

Todaro, Michael P. 1976. Internal Migration in Developing Countries. Geneva: International Labor Office.

Todaro, Michael P., and Lidya Maruszko. 1987. "Illegal Migration and US Immigration Reform: A Conceptual Framework." *Population and Development Review* 13: 101–114.

Tsega, Anwar Hassan. 2010. "Ethio-Sudan Migration; the Case of Women Labor Migrants." MSc thesis, University of Juba, Sudan.

Wallerstien, Immanuel. 1974. The Modern World System, Capitalist Agriculture and the Origins of European Economy in the Sixteenth Century. New York: Academic Press.

World Bank. 2011. Migration and Remittances Factbook 2011. 2nd ed. Washington, DC: World Bank. http://siteresources.worldbank.org/INTLAC/Resources/Factbook2011-Ebook.pdf.

'Deported before experiencing the good sides of migration': Ethiopians returning from Saudi Arabia

Marina de Regt[a] and Medareshaw Tafesse[b]*

[a]Department of Social and Cultural Anthropology, VU University Amsterdam, Amsterdam, The Netherlands; [b]Independent scholar, Ethiopia

ABSTRACT
In the period November 2013–April 2014 more than 160,000 Ethiopians were deported from Saudi Arabia after a seven months amnesty period for undocumented migrants came to an end. This large-scale regularization campaign of the Saudi government must be seen in light of the 'Arab Spring', when popular uprisings in the Middle East were threatening dictatorial regimes. The effect of the Arab Spring was felt globally; the uprisings impacted upon migrants living in countries in the Middle East and on their countries of origin. This paper looks into the experiences of Ethiopian deportees prior, during and after their forced return. We argue that the fact that the migrants were not prepared for their sudden return affected their economic, social network and psychosocial embeddedness back in Ethiopia. In addition, the Ethiopian government has not been able to improve the returnees' economic embeddedness, which has affected their social and psychological status negatively.

Introduction

Salam had worked five years as a domestic worker in Saudi Arabia when she was deported to Ethiopia in the beginning of 2014. Hoping to help her parents and siblings back home she returned empty-handed. 'We were deported before we could experience the good sides of migration', she said in an interview. Salam is one of the 163,000 Ethiopian migrants that were forced to return from Saudi Arabia to Ethiopia after an amnesty period for undocumented migrants came to an end in November 2013. Saudi Arabia's large-scale campaign to regularize the migrant population was an indirect result of the 'Arab Spring' and underlines the global dimension of a seemingly regional migration issue. The popular protests in Tunisia and Egypt were mainly about high unemployment rates and widespread corruption practices. Afraid of similar protests, the Saudi government proactively addressed these issues. The two main reforms implemented were the 'Saudization' of the workforce and a multi-dimensional campaign against undocumented migrants (De Bel-Air 2014, 4).[1] In April 2013, the Saudi government announced a seven months period in which undocumented migrants could regularize their residence and employment status or

---
*Current affiliation: Crime Investigation and Forensic Science Institute, Ethiopian Police University College, Addis Ababa, Ethiopia.

leave the country without having to pay a penalty for the time they had been undocumented. In the period April–November 2013, 4.7 million undocumented migrants were regularized, and 1 million migrants left the country (De Bel-Air 2014, 10).

After the expiration of the amnesty period, the Saudi Ministry of Labor carried out raids on labor sites and the police arrested undocumented migrants in their homes and on the street. The crackdown was accompanied by severe human rights abuses, including arbitrary detention, theft of migrants' belongings, rape, beatings, and killings (see HRW 2013). In November 2013, the Ethiopian government decided to repatriate all undocumented migrants from Saudi Arabia, facilitated by international organizations such as the International Organization for Migration, UNICEF, and the Red Cross. Within a period of four months Ethiopia received more than 160,000 returnees, many traumatized by the experiences during their arrest and deportation. The forced return of Ethiopians from Saudi Arabia was an indirect result of the Arab uprisings and shows that the uprisings also impacted upon migrants living in countries in the Middle East, and on their countries of origin. The effect of the 'Arab Spring' was felt globally.

This paper discusses the experiences and expectations of Ethiopian migrants during and after their repatriation in the context of globalization. Most of the literature on forced return migration and deportation is based on South–North migration. Very few studies have looked at deportation in the Global South. The case of Ethiopians who were forced to return from Saudi Arabia can shed new light on the debate about deportation and its consequences. We focus in particular on the discussion about the relationship between migrant's preparedness to return home and their resulting embeddedness in their home societies.

The paper is structured as follows. We first introduce our theoretical framework, and then briefly describe the history of Ethiopian migration to the Middle East and to Saudi Arabia in particular. After the methodology we present some data on the backgrounds of the respondents. We then move on to discuss the preparedness and embeddedness of Ethiopian return migrants. The paper is based on material collected during a two months fieldwork period in Addis Ababa in April–May 2014 as part of the Master research of Tafesse (2014).

Forced return migration: theoretical perspectives

For a long time, migration studies focused on the experiences of migrants in the countries of migration. Since the 1980s more attention is being paid to return migration. In the beginning the focus was largely on voluntary return migration; forced return migration and deportation were often neglected (see, for example, Gmelch 1980; Cassarino 2004). In his theoretical overview of perspectives on return migration, Cassarino (2004) also pays relatively little attention to forced return. However, his notion of preparedness is very useful when studying forced return migration. He argues that the ways in which migrants are able to mobilize resources for their return home and their preparedness are crucial for a successful return.

> Preparedness pertains not only to the willingness of migrants to return home, but also to their *readiness* to return. In other words, the returnee's preparedness refers to a voluntary act that must be supported by the gathering of sufficient resources and information about post-return conditions at home. (Cassarino 2004, 271)

Cassarino distinguishes three groups of returnees based on their preparedness to return, including those returnees whose level of preparedness is non-existent: 'These returnees neither contemplated return nor did they provide for the preparation of return. Circumstances in host countries prompted them to leave, for example as a result of a rejected application for asylum or following forced repatriation' (Cassarino 2004, 275).

In the past decade a body of scholarship has emerged about forced return migration and deportation (see, for example, De Genova 2002; Peutz 2006; Ellermann 2009; Ruben, van Houte, and Davids 2009; De Genova and Peutz 2010). Attention to the consequences of forced return migration has increased rapidly because of the tightening of borders worldwide. Governments of Western countries in particular, but also those in other parts of the world, are becoming more and more reluctant to accept refugees and asylum seekers. In addition, border controls have increased in order to prevent undocumented migrants from entering the country. The global war on terror has also contributed to the stricter border controls. These restrictive immigration and asylum policies have created a new interest in the most suitable conditions of return (Ruben, van Houte, and Davids 2009, 909). Governments and international organizations are concerned with the question how refugees, asylum seekers and migrants whose applications for residence permits were rejected can be assisted so that their return will become sustainable.[2]

Ruben, van Houte, and Davids (2009) developed a framework to understand the factors that influence the process of re-embeddedness of forced return migrants. 'Embeddedness refers to the ways how individuals find and define their position in society, feel a sense of belonging and possibilities for participation in society' (Ruben, van Houte, and Davids 2009, 910). They distinguish three dimensions of embeddedness: economic embeddedness, social network embeddedness, and psychosocial embeddedness (Ruben, van Houte, and Davids 2009, 910). Their study is based on surveys and interviews with 178 return migrants and stakeholders in 6 countries: Afghanistan, Armenia, Bosnia and Herzegovina, Sierra Leone, Togo, and Vietnam. While they focus on forced return migration from the North to the South, their framework is also very useful to understand similar processes in the South, such as the forced return of Ethiopians from Saudi Arabia.

According to Ruben, van Houte, and Davids (2009), a sustainable embeddedness of return migrants is affected by three factors. First, the individual characteristics of migrants, such as age, gender, education, and religion affect the ways in which migrants experiences their return. Second, the migration cycle the migrant went through affects his or her experiences, such as the reason for leaving the home country, the situation in the host country, the length of stay abroad and the conditions of return. Third, the pre-and post-return forms of assistance delivered by the state, private, or civic organizations are important for the ways in which forced return migrants will be re-embedded in their home societies (Ruben, van Houte, and Davids 2009, 914). On the basis of the collected data Ruben, van Houte, and Davids (2009) conclude that most returnees were economically still highly vulnerable and lacked future prospects. Socially, many returnees depended on family and close friends and had difficulties building up social networks that would increase their sense of belonging. The psychosocial status of the forced return migrants depended very much on personal and contextual factors (Ruben, van Houte, and Davids 2009, 931–932). Traumatic experiences before migration, feelings of unsafety upon return and frustrating migration experiences abroad affect the notion of belonging back home (Ruben, van Houte, and Davids 2009). The assistance returnees receive is often limited to temporary financial support (Ruben, van Houte, and Davids 2009). A considerable number of returnees mentioned that they would leave again if they had the chance to do so (Ruben, van Houte, and Davids 2009, 924).

Ruben, van Houte, and Davids' (2009) conclusions are based on the experiences of migrants who had been back in their home countries for a much longer time than the Ethiopian migrants that returned from Saudi Arabia. In addition, the return migrants they studied had not been forcefully expelled. Yet, the focus on economic, social network, and psychosocial embeddedness is in our opinion also relevant for our study. A number of conclusions were particularly relevant such as the fact that single return migrants and female migrants had more difficulties becoming socially embedded again. Also the fact that most return migrants had difficulties to embed themselves economically corresponds with our findings in Ethiopia. Ruben, van Houte, and Davids (2009) conclude that return migrants with children were more successful economically than single and female return migrants (Ruben, van Houte, and Davids 2009, 928). Migrants who had sent remittances were also able to mediate their economic situation upon return (Ruben, van Houte, and Davids 2009). With regard to psychosocial embeddedness, female migrants, especially those who were not married, had a lower psychosocial well-being. In addition, migrants who had been able to live in independent housing in the country of migration had maintained their self-esteem in contrast with those who had lived in shelters and reception centers.

In the following part of the paper, we will use the concept of preparedness from the literature on voluntary return (Cassarino 2004) and the concept of embeddedness from the literature on forced return (Ruben, van Houte, and Davids 2009) to analyze the experiences of Ethiopian return migrants. Our main argument is that migrants who are forcefully expelled have no possibilities to prepare themselves for their return, which greatly affects their embeddedness in their home societies. We first give more background information about Ethiopian migration to the Middle East and present the methodology of the study.

Ethiopian migration to the Middle East

Historically, Ethiopia and the Middle East have been closely related for centuries (see Erlich 1994, 2007). The movements of slaves, soldiers, merchants, traders, laborers, tourists, pilgrims, priests, and scholars have been accompanied by the circulations of commodities, money, language, ideas, and religion. More recently, labor migration has become one of the most prominent features of the relationship between Ethiopia and the Middle East, and the Arabian Peninsula in particular. While labor migration was restricted under the military regime of Mengistu, the government that came to power in 1991 made the freedom of movement a constitutional right. Despite economic liberalization policies and Ethiopia's integration in the global economy, many Ethiopians consider out-migration as the only way to achieve better living standards. Educated people in urban areas have difficulties finding paid jobs in both the public and the private sector. In rural areas poverty prevails despite the government's efforts to develop the countryside economically. As a result numerous Ethiopians are trying to reach Saudi Arabia via Djibouti and Yemen. They migrate over land to South Africa, or cross the border with Sudan in order to travel on to Libya, Egypt, Israel, Turkey and countries in Europe.

The large majority of regular migrants to the Middle East are women. In the past two decades particularly young women have migrated to the Middle East (see, for example, Kebede 2001; Fernandez 2010; de Regt 2010; Minaye 2012). They respond to the demand for paid domestic labor among middle and upper middle class families in Lebanon, Kuwait, the United Arab Emirates, and Saudi Arabia where African women have increasingly replaced Asian domestic workers (Fernandez 2010, 251). In an interview, a representative of the Ministry of Labor and Social Affairs (MOLSA) reported that licensed Ethiopian overseas recruitment agencies received 182,000 applications for work in 2012–2013, a small decrease from the number received in 2011. The Ministry estimated that this represents only 30 to 40 percent of all Ethiopians migrating to the Middle East. The remaining 60 to 70 percent are either trafficked or smuggled with the facilitation of illegal brokers (see Fernandez 2013). On 19 October 2013, the Ethiopian government installed a ban on labor migration from Ethiopia to the Middle East as a response to the human rights violations against Ethiopian migrants, which was still in place at the time of writing (May 2015). Such bans had been installed before, but this time they apply to every country in the Middle East.

In most countries in the Middle East, the *kafala* system of sponsorship binds migrant workers' residence permits to 'sponsoring' employers, whose written consent is required for workers to change employers or leave the country. A migrant cannot change his or her sponsor or job unless a release from the sponsor is issued, along with a new sponsorship from a new employer and an approval from the concerned authorities. Those who do so without permission are considered undocumented or illegal and liable for imprisonment and deportation. According to a representative of the Bureau of Labor and Social Affair of Addis Ababa most of the migrants that were arrested during the Saudi government's crackdown and deportation of undocumented migrants were women who had ran away from their sponsors. Widespread migration irregularity and deportation can be seen as a direct result of the kafala system.

Saudi Arabia is one of the main destination countries for Ethiopian migrants. According to a report by the Regional Mixed Migration Secretariat in Nairobi, around 100,000 regular Ethiopian labor migrants moved to Saudi Arabia in 2011 (RMMS 2014, 17). In the first half of 2012 over 160,000 domestic workers migrated to Saudi Arabia, which was ten times more than the year before. The large majority (96 percent) were women. Most Ethiopian women who migrate to Saudi Arabia are unmarried Muslim women who have finished at least some years of secondary education (Fernandez 2010, 253). They are often coming from rural areas and intend to help their families back home. Those who migrated via regular channels sometimes attended a short pre-departure training at the MOLSA in Addis Ababa. These trainings cover legal rights, the content and terms of employment contracts and information on whom to contact in case of problems (RMMS 2014, 24). Yet, in most cases they are unprepared for the work they have to do, they are unfamiliar with modern household equipment, and they do not speak Arabic. Upon arrival they are often confronted with a heavy workload and no day off, they face emotional, physical, and sexual abuse, their passports are withheld as part of the kafala system and sometimes they are denied their salaries (see Kebede 2001; Fernandez 2010; Dessiye 2011; ILO 2011). Irregular migration to Saudi Arabia, via Djibouti and Yemen, consists mainly of men (RMMS 2014, 17), which explains why a considerable part of the returnees were male. Male migrants were mainly employed as guards, as daily laborers and on farms.

Methodology

The data on which this paper is based was collected during two months fieldwork in Addis Ababa (April–May 2014). Of the 163,000 deportees 2 percent (around 3,000) originated from Addis Ababa; the large majority came from areas outside Addis Ababa and returned to their home communities (IOM 2014, 1). The study was based on quantitative and qualitative methods. First, a survey was carried out among 168 returnees who had registered at the city administration. The sample population comprised of deportees who were formerly residents of Addis Ababa and who arrived between 4 November 2013 and 24 March 2014. In contrast with the national number of male deportees (62 percent according to the IOM) (IOM 2014), in Addis Ababa almost 75 percent are female returnees. From the 3,000 returnees from Addis Ababa, 2,748 returnees asked for assistance from the city administration. According to the key informant from the Addis Ababa Bureau of Labor and Social Affairs some returnees were not included in the support program, either because they were not in need of support or for other reasons. Provision of assistance was conducted in two phases. In the first phase 1,999 returnees were included in the program and in the second phase 749 returnees. At the time of the survey only the first group was known to the city administration; therefore 1,999 deportees were taken as the survey population.

Despite the availability of a list of registered returnees, conducting random sampling was found challenging and very costly. Thus, we decided to conduct stratified sampling. Five areas in the city where returnees came together for various reasons[3] were selected randomly.[4] Three of them were meeting halls, the fourth was a vocational training college, and the fifth place was a place where returnees had started working with the support of the government reintegration assistance program. In these places every fifth returnee was given a questionnaire. Two data collectors were employed to assist illiterate people and those who found it difficult to respond in writing. In total 200 questionnaires were distributed, of which 168 questionnaires were returned (the response rate was 84 percent). The study did not include interviews with the families of returnees, traffickers, sending agencies, brokers, smugglers, or others affected by or engaged in migration to Saudi Arabia. Yet, these actors may have affected the experiences and future expectations of the returnees and therefore issues related to these actors are included in the study.

In addition to the survey, eight in-depth interviews were conducted with a selected number of returnees. Expert interviews were carried out with people working in organizations involved in the repatriation. These key informants included an expert working at the IOM office in Addis Ababa, government officials from the Ministry of Foreign Affairs (MOFA) and the MOLSA, and an expert at the Addis Ababa City Administration Labor Office. They were interviewed about their respective roles in relation to the repatriation process, the assistance provided, the measures taken to minimize the costs of migration, and the future plans of action in relation to repatriated migrants. Moreover, these stakeholders provided information on the general situation of return migrants from Saudi Arabia within the specific time period. Two focus group discussions (FGDs) were conducted with male and female returnees.

Background of the respondents

Age, gender, socioeconomic, and marital status of individuals influence the ways in which migrants experience their return (Ghanem 2003, 19; Ruben, van Houte, and Davids 2009,

916). In addition, socioeconomic and demographic characteristics may help to understand the reasons why people migrated, which may also have affected their possibility of employment and adjustment in the destination country (see Hammond 1999). In the case of Ethiopia, educational qualifications and gender are important variables affecting the type of work migrants are engaged in and their exposure to maltreatment and abuse. With regard to the gender of the respondents, 69 percent of the 168 respondents were female and 31 percent male. In terms of age distribution, the majority (87.7 percent) of the respondents were between the ages of 18–35; the number of respondents that were older was 13 percent. There were no respondents under 18, which may be related to the fact that minors are officially not allowed to migrate abroad and many young migrants change their age on their birth certificates.

The educational level of the interviewed returnees ranged from illiterates to college degree holders. Of the 168 respondents, 1.8 percent was illiterate, 5.4 percent were able to read or write, and 43.5 percent had only achieved elementary level. Those who had attended senior secondary education (9–12 years) comprised 22 percent; 29 percent had finished secondary school (completed grade 10/12). Only 3 percent graduated from a college. The fact that the large majority was not very educated affected the type of work they were engaged in and the possibility of employment upon return to Ethiopia. In addition, the educational level of returnees determined to some extent their access for assistance after their return home. For example, 30 returnees were given the opportunity to join the Health College in Addis Ababa. Moreover, lower educational levels can also lead to lower capacity to demand one's rights and increased susceptibility to deception.

In terms of religion, 36.9 percent of the respondents were Muslim and 51.2 percent were Orthodox Christians. Protestants comprised 10.7 percent of the respondents and only 2 of the 168 respondents were Catholics. In some cases labor migrants decide to change their religion in order to be accepted for migration, or they converted after having worked in a Muslim majority country. The data on marital status of the respondents indicate that nearly 60 percent of the returnees were single, almost 30 percent were married and the remaining 10 percent were previously married (separated, divorced, or widowed). Most of the single migrants were women (70 percent).

While lack of employment opportunities are often mentioned as the main reasons for migration, there was a considerable number of people employed prior to migration (31 percent) or they owned small businesses (22 percent). Interestingly, 18.4 percent were not yet part of the formal labor force (students and housewives). The remaining 28.6 percent had been unemployed. Those who had a means of income prior to migration said that they earned on average between 500–1000 ETB per month (25–50 USD). The fact that a considerable number of return migrants were employed prior to migration can be explained by their residence in Addis Ababa, where job opportunities are better than in the rural areas.

Migration motivations and trajectories

The major driving forces behind the migration of respondents were failure in education endeavors, a strong desire for success or change, hearing success stories of others (often from former friends or relatives who migrated from their locality to Saudi Arabia or the Gulf States), divorce, death of spouse or parents, the desire to be independent, underemployment, limited job opportunities and a low family income. Saudi Arabia was seen as an attractive destination for migration for a number of reasons, such as the relative easiness of accessing a residence permit (*iqama*), the minimum requirements of educational qualification and skills, the availability of free-visa or visa on demand (visa that can be collected with no other pre-condition) and the role of traffickers and smugglers in artificially creating demands. Economic transformations in Saudi Arabia created a shortage of labor in low paying, informal and dangerous sectors such as domestic work, construction, agriculture, and sex work (see Fernandez 2010; De Bel-Air 2014). Millions of foreign workers fill this gap, and traffickers and smugglers use this opportunity to persuade potential migrants to migrate to Saudi Arabia.

Before migrating, 45.2 percent said that they were informed about the type of work and the living conditions in Saudi Arabia. In-depth interviews revealed that even those who obtained advice and warnings from their relatives and friends were not interested in changing their decision. In many cases women want to test their chance though they had prior exposition and information about the destinations. 'Unless you experience it, you don't believe it' is the guiding principle of most migrants. However, a small majority (54.8 percent) reported that they had no prior information about life and work in Saudi Arabia. In addition, those who had prior information were asked about the accuracy of the information. From the 75 respondents who claimed they had prior knowledge, 54.7 percent said that the information they gained was misleading and deceptive. Working for multiple households and overwork (up to 24 hours), salary withholding, denial of food and rest, actual and attempted rape were things they had never been told about and they had never expected. Besides, most of those who followed legal routes were told that foreign recruitment agencies would follow up their condition and would protect their rights but in reality this never happened. Those who traveled by sea routes claimed that their voyage was painstaking and tedious which was beyond their expectations. Some of the respondents regretted that they were deceived by the understanding they had of Saudi Arabia. Likewise, some returnees said that their migration was a waste of time and believe that it is possible to earn the same salary in Ethiopia.

Ethiopian labor migrants use three main ways to go to Saudi Arabia: via work contract arranged by a Private Employment Agency (PEA), being smuggled over land and sea, and by obtaining a visa to go on *hajj* (a religious pilgrimage to Mecca). Visa for the *hajj* are only handed out to people older than 28 years. Hence, getting smuggled and going on a work contract basis are the two major means of migrating. Labor migration on the basis of a work contract is the major means to proceed to Saudi Arabia. A MOLSA report indicated that between July 2012 and July 2013, 161,787 Ethiopian migrant workers processed their migration to Saudi Arabia through Private Employment Agencies. The large majority (154,660 or 96 percent) was female; only 7,127 were male (4 percent).

The interviewed returnees had different motivations to choose a particular migration channel. The advantages of irregular channels were the costs (it is cheaper than migrating via PEAs), the fact that irregular migrants receive higher salaries, and the fact that the level of abuse is less because employers will also be hold accountable for employing undocumented migrants and are therefore more careful with their treatment. The availability of the services of local brokers who facilitate irregular migration was another reason mentioned. Some respondents mentioned that they did not have to do a health screening, which can be advantageous for people with HIV/AIDS. The advantages of migrating via

PEAs were that the pain of a long trip would be avoided (they would travel by plane), the positive feeling of being documented, and the possibility of getting protection from the Ethiopian Embassy and from the PEA (though agencies and embassies were in general described as not so helpful). Most of those who went to Saudi Arabia for *hajj* were working as undocumented migrants (freelancers). Freelancing is described as better because migrants can change employers since their passport will not be held by the employer or agency. The risk of freelancing is immediate deportation, which silences the migrants and gives them less power to negotiate with their employers.

A sudden return

In the Middle East, and in particular, in the Gulf Cooperation Countries, labor migrants work under temporary contracts specified for a particular period of time. Permanent settlement and citizenship rights are inaccessible for labor migrants. The general expectation is that once the contract is finished, labor migrants will leave the country unless their residence and work permits are renewed (Jureidini 2004, 3). Labor migrants who leave their employers without consent ('run away') and those unable to renew their residence permits become undocumented and liable for arrest and deportation. Migrants who entered the country on the basis of a *hajj* visa are expected to practice their religious missions. They are not allowed to engage in paid work and those who take up jobs are also liable for arrest and deportation. Migrants who came through irregular channels, are automatically denied residence and work permits unless they find a sponsor. From the information gathered we learnt that besides these conventional rules there were also people deported for 'other reasons'. These other reasons statistically represent a small number but reveal xenophobic sentiments ingrained in the minds of the people and officials of Saudi Arabia (see Jureidini 2004). Returnees and key informants mentioned a number of other factors related to the forceful expulsion in 2013–2014. One of them was that employment agencies in Saudi Arabia asked a huge amount of money to regularize the status of undocumented migrants. One returnee told us the following:

> I migrated to Saudi Arabia by buying a free visa. Before the tightening of the immigration rules I was paying 800 Saudi Riyal per nine months for a fake sponsor. After the tightening of the immigration rules the alleged sponsor asked me to offer him much more than what I used to paying to renew the visa. Because I was unable to pay that amount I stayed nine months without renewed visa till the expulsion.

Other factors attributing to the termination of labor and work permits included hatred of Ethiopian migrants and the fear of the expansion of Christianity. Some interviewees said that even religious leaders were involved in the crackdown operations. A male returnee told us that a religious leader came to his house, stole his money and assaulted him badly. Returnees that encountered racism and xenophobia said that they had not yet finished their contracts but felt forced to leave. Others said that they decided to leave when they saw the atrocities inflicted on fellow Ethiopians. Migrants who did not have documents were immediately deported but those that were working with false documents (for example those who had sponsors that they did not know) had to pay large sums of money in order to get released from their sponsors.

Deportees had in most cases little to no time to prepare themselves for their return. As a result, they encountered many challenges, which affected their return home. The survey results show that only 17.9 percent of the respondents expected Saudi Arabia to implement the planned deportation measures. These respondents waited for the day of the expulsion in order to save transportation costs to return back home. However, most of the deportees were planning to stay in Saudi Arabia. When they were suddenly arrested and deported they had no time to collect their belongings or to bring sufficient money home. Because of the sudden crackdown, many returnees were forced to leave Saudi Arabia empty-handed. The survey showed that only 20.2 percent brought their possessions and 24.4 percent brought some of their belongings. Nearly a third of the respondents indicated that their belongings were either confiscated or they were not given the opportunity to bring their belongings with them. Some of them even revealed being robbed of their money (up to 15 thousands ETB) by Saudis during the crackdown. A relatively large group (24.4 percent) said that they had nothing to bring home.

Almost all of the returnees had horrific experiences between their arrest and their return home. They were imprisoned for a number of weeks, and treated very badly. They could not change their clothes, and sometimes barely had something to wear; they got very simple food and had to sleep outside in the heat. Saudi guards and policemen were sleeping next to them and female returnees told us that they were continuously on the alert fearing to be raped. Many women were sexually harassed and raped, while men were beaten up. Some of the respondents said that their experiences during their imprisonment were worse than what they had ever experienced during their stay in Saudi Arabia. As a result, many deportees were traumatized when they returned to Ethiopia.

In short, the returnees were not at all prepared for their expulsion. They were planning to stay undocumented as long as possible and had no intentions to return to Ethiopia. The violent crackdown and the subsequent arrests and deportations gave them little to no time to prepare their departure. Some returnees were able to bring their personal belongings; others were arrested and deported without having the right to prepare themselves for their return.

Limited embeddedness back home

The sudden return of large numbers of migrants affected the entire country. The Ethiopian government suddenly had to take care of more than 160,000 returnees, who were in need of financial assistance, housing, employment, and health services. On a social level the sudden mass return affected the society at large; many returnees stayed in Addis Ababa because they did not want to return to their home villages empty-handed, they often had debts at home and did not want to face their families. In addition, a large number of the returnees had been traumatized and needed mental health care. Families were confronted with family members with serious mental problems, and were often unable to cope with them. In short, the scale of the mass return has been unprecedented, the government and the society at large lacked the capacity of dealing with such a high number of people in need of assistance on many levels. In this section we describe the economic, social network, and psychosocial embeddedness of the migrants following Ruben, van Houte, and Davids (2009).

Economic embeddedness

In the introduction of this paper, we cited Salam who said 'We were deported before we could experience the good sides of migration'. Just like Salam, many returnees failed to achieve their migration goals. Most Ethiopians migrate to help their families out of poverty and destitution. Family members are often involved in initiating and financing the migration project, and expect that their financial investment will be returned. Thus, remittances are expected and most returnees evaluated their migration based on the impact of their remittances on the lives of their family. Out of 168 respondents only 31 percent replied that they had achieved some or most of their goals while the majority (69 percent) said that they did not achieve any of the goals by migrating. Even fewer returnees in the second cluster replied that they were returning with debt since they had traveled through borrowing. A small percentage of returnees witnessed pervasive changes in the lives of their family (13.1 percent). 19.6 percent reported a partial change while 23.8 percent said that their remittances had only sustained family life. 25.6 percent stated that their remittances had not made any difference.

According to the interviewees, Ethiopian government officials in Saudi Arabia promised jobs and a sum of money after their expulsion but the key informant from the MOFA in Addis Ababa declined the alleged promise. Upon arrival the returnees assumed that the government would start to fulfill the promises but as time passed, the attention of the government declined and in some offices they were approached oddly. A female FGD participant indicated:

> Through the five months after the return we were going from office to office, yet nothing happened ... After we returned we are being idle and use the money we brought from Saudi Arabia and are again dependent on our family.

The type and timing of assistance provided to (return) migrants can substantially contribute to improving their lives after return (Ruben, van Houte, and Davids 2009). If returnees are not assisted to get training and find jobs upon their return, they may become a burden on their families and may once again seek employment abroad. The returnees that were residents of Addis Ababa prior to their migration, registered at the Addis Ababa city administration. This government office was involved in the reintegration process of returnees and launched two rounds of skills training and reintegration assistance. The support program started with six days psychosocial counseling and refreshment programs. After that returnees could choose from various skills training opportunities (such as food preparation, beauty salon, urban agriculture such as poultry raising, and producing construction material such as bricks), and receive one and half month skill training at six technical and vocational colleges. After finishing the training, they obtained a certificate. The respondents were satisfied by the training but frustrated about the follow-up.

The major problem in the reintegration process was access to credit services, the provision of working sheds, and the facilitation of trade licenses. Credit access and providing sheds became bottlenecks for the reintegration assistance provision. The credit institution in charge, the Addis Credit and Saving Institution, was not prepared to provide flexible credit services for returnees. Returnees had to present as collateral either a house blueprint or a person with sufficient capital, which for many was unfeasible. In addition, providing sheds or workshops was another problem. When the sheds were available, the problems with the credit facilities persisted, and returnees who managed to access credit or wanted to use their savings could not obtain sheds. Another problem was the lack of monitoring from the concerned bodies. Most sub-city administration offices were not prepared and interested in addressing the situation. A few sub cities tried to work toward a successful reintegration, which was confirmed by the interviewed returnees, but most of them were very frustrated about the assistance they received.

The social impact of return

A number of studies have discussed the impact of labor migration to the Middle East on marriage and family relationships (Dessiye 2011; Minaye 2012). The conventional understanding in Ethiopia is that women who worked in the Middle East were exploited and sexually abused, and therefore they are not seen as suitable marriage partners. In addition, married women's long-term absence may lead to divorce and separation. Hasena (39 years old), for example, discovered that her husband had married another woman in her absence. Yet, she was more upset about the fact that the money that she remitted to him had disappeared. She had planned to set up a small business upon return but now intends to migrate again. Many of the young women we interviewed in Addis Ababa said that they preferred to migrate again. They had not been able to find jobs and found their chances to get married minimal as a result of their low social status.

Returnees also spoke about the negative attitude of the society toward them. Social acceptance is crucial for a successful return (Van Houte and de Koning 2008). Social networks are important to become integrated in the society back home. Relations with other returnees are also essential in order to work through frustrations and traumatic experiences. 52 percent of the respondents reported that they had been able to secure strong relationships with their family and community after returning to Ethiopia. 30 percent of the survey respondents indicated that they had a weak relationship with their families and relatives. The remaining 18 percent stipulated having no relationship with their family at all. Zemzem (34 years old) returned after 14 years in Saudi Arabia and said that there was a clear relationship between sending remittances and the post-return relationship with her family:

> While I was in Saudi Arabia I used to remit often. After my return I was welcomed warmly by my family. I have a strong relationship with them and I believe this relationship happens partly because I was remitting. I know a friend who didn't remit and upon return she was not received warmly by her family.

Yet, there were also many returnees whose relatives were happy that they returned home. The stories of the violent crackdown and the subsequent treatment of arrested migrants had worried many people, and family members were often relieved when their beloved ones returned home alive. Salam had called her family when she was in the prison, and they told her that they preferred seeing her back in one piece than to receive her money. Many returnees said that they were relieved to be home, but very disappointed that they returned empty-handed. Their economic situation affected their psychosocial well-being, and a considerable number of respondents thought of migrating again.

Psychosocial problems

As described earlier, the days of the crackdown and expulsion were tied to a variety of horrific experiences, which affected the psychosocial state of the returnees to a large extent. The coordinator of the repatriation process described the situation upon arrival at the airport:

> Some of returnees were taking their clothes off and walked around naked. Some had mental problems but others hated the clothes they were wearing as they reminded them of what they had gone through.

Migrants with mental problems were referred to the only mental hospital in Addis Ababa, which was rapidly filled with returnees. The government lacked the capacity to take care of the large numbers of people that were in need of mental care. A number of Ethiopian non-governmental organizations took care of the traumatized returnees, hosting them in shelters and giving them psychological counseling. Yet, the magnitude of the deportation affected the country at large and many families had to cope with relatives that were traumatized. The fact that the returnees were forcefully expelled, and hardly had time to prepare their departure affected their mental state. They failed in realizing their migration goals; they had not been able to remit money or to save money to pay back their debts. This created a lot of tension and stress and mental problems. In addition, their experiences living and working in Saudi Arabia had a strong impact on their mindset. One of the female returnees said:

> Before leaving to an Arab country I was decent and respected the orders of my family but the exposure to the Arab way of life and experiencing bad things changed my conduct. After return, I don't have peace with my family. What they say, even if it is positive, to me it is negative. I am confronting them all the time and disagree with my family and I realize that I am behaving terribly.

A number of returnees also spoke about the problems related to the attitude of the society toward their return. They felt stigmatized and discriminated against, which affected their mental stability. As a result, they did not feel at home in Ethiopia and had no peace of mind. They had not intended to return home and their forceful expulsion affected their psychological embeddedness to a large extent.

Conclusion

The large-scale return of Ethiopian migrants from Saudi Arabia constituted a group of forced return migrants that were very badly prepared for their return. Cassarino (2004) stated that the way in which migrants are prepared for their return home, and in particular the way in which they are able to mobilize resources, are crucial for a successful return home. Most of the returnees had shown no desire to return to Ethiopia until the Saudi Arabia security forces began the crackdown. Within the seven months of the amnesty period, only 5,000 Ethiopians repatriated. According to Ghanem (2003) if returnees have no desire to return in the first place, it cannot be expected that they will easily reintegrate and view their country of origin as their 'home'. Our research results support these statements. While many of the respondents were happy to be home in the early days of their repatriation, because of the traumatic experiences during their arrest and imprisonment in Saudi Arabia, they were frustrated a few months later. They had expected more assistance from the Ethiopian government to establish their lives back home economically, yet they had only received attention in the first few months of their return. Almost all of them complained about the lack of opportunities and facilities to realize their aspirations to work or set up a business. Their economic embeddedness was thus very limited if not non-existent. Many respondents were depending on their relatives. This is in accordance with the findings of Ruben, van Houte, and Davids (2009) who also found that the returnees were economically not well-established, even years after their return. Yet, this limited economic embeddedness is a direct result of the fact that they were forcefully expelled and had no time to prepare themselves for their return. The psychosocial embeddedness of the Ethiopian returnees was also low. Many still struggled with what they had gone through in Saudi Arabia, and the fact that they returned almost empty-handed. Their psychosocial embeddedness was thus also related to the lack of preparedness for their return; they had not been able to mobilize resources and considered themselves failures. This also impacted on their social network embeddedness because they were unable to build up a social network back home, and relied heavily on their relatives. The fact that the Ethiopian government has not been able to improve the returnees' economic embeddedness has therefore wider implications than economically only. Many returnees may opt to migrate again, and in the absence of policies that protect migrants they will make use of irregular channels. They will be undocumented in the countries of migration and again run the risk of deportation.

Acknowledgement

We would like to thank Nathalie Peutz and Giulia Sinatti for their valuable comments on an earlier version of the paper.

Disclosure statement

No potential conflict of interest was reported by the authors.

Notes

1. The Saudi government had launched earlier policies that aimed to reduce foreign labor in favor of Saudi nationals (see De Bel-Air 2014, 4; RMMS 2014, 10). Yet, these efforts had limited result, which was mainly because Saudi nationals were unwilling to engage in low-skilled jobs, expected higher salaries and were lacking the skills and training required for much of the work in the private sector (De Bel-Air 2014, 5).
2. In the spring of 2015, the increasing death toll of migrants in the Mediterranean led to new debates about undocumented migrants and their possible return in Europe.
3. For training purposes, to process papers for the businesses they intended to set up, for meetings with government officials to ask for support, for work and for study.
4. The five areas were the Ethiopian Assembly Hall, the Yeka sub-city meeting hall, the Bole sub-city meeting hall, Misrak TVET and Gulele area, where some returnees started working through government support.

References

Cassarino, J. P. 2004. "Theorising Return Migration: The Conceptual Approach to Return Migrants Revisited." *International Journal on Multicultural Societies* 6 (2): 253–279.

De Bel-Air, F. 2014. *Demography, Migration and the Labor Market in Saudi Arabia*. Gulf Labor Markets and Migration. European University Institute and Gulf Research Center. http://gulfmigration.eu/media/pubs/exno/GLMM_EN_2014_01.pdf.

De Genova, N. P. 2002. "Migrant 'Illegality' and Deportability in Everyday Life." *Annual Review of Anthropology* 31: 419–447.

De Genova, N., and Peutz, N. eds. 2010. *The Deportation Regime: Sovereignty, Space and the Freedom of Movement*. Durham: Duke University Press.

Dessiye, M. 2011. "The Challenges and Prospects of Female Labour Migration to the Arab Middle East: A Case Study of Women Returnees in the Town of Girana, North Wollo, Ethiopia." MA thesis, Faculty of Psychology, University of Bergen.

Ellermann, A. 2009. *States against Migrants: Deportation in Germany and the United States*. Cambridge: Cambridge University Press.

Erlich, H. 1994. *Ethiopia and the Middle East*. Boulder: Lynne Rienner.

Erlich, H. 2007. *Saudi Arabia and Ethiopia: Christianity, Islam and Politics Entwined*. Boulder: Lynne Rienner.

Fernandez, B. 2010. "Cheap and Disposable? The Impact of the Global Economic Crisis on the Migration of Ethiopian Women Domestic Workers to the Gulf." *Gender & Development* 18 (2): 249–262.

Fernandez, B. 2013. "Traffickers, Brokers, Employment Agents, and Social Networks: The Regulation of Intermediaries in the Migration of Ethiopian Domestic Workers to the Middle East." *International Migration Review* 47 (4): 814–843.

Ghanem, T. 2003. *When Forced Migrants Return Home: The Psychosocial Difficulties Returnees Encounter in the Reintegration Process*. Oxford: Refugee Studies Centre.

Gmelch, G. 1980. "Return Migration." *Annual Review of Anthropology* 9: 135–159.

Hammond, L. 1999. "Examining the Discourse of Repatriation: Towards a More Proactive Theory of Return Migration". In *The End of the Refugee Cycle? Refugee Repatriation and Reconstruction*, edited by R. Black and K. Koser, 227–244. Oxford: Berghahn.

Human Rights Watch. 2013. *Saudi Arabia: Labor Crackdown Violence Ethiopian Workers Allege Attacks, Poor Detention Conditions*. Accessed December 30. http://www.hrw.org/news/2013/11/30/saudi-arabia-labor-crackdown-violence.

ILO. 2011. *Trafficking in Persons Overseas for Labor Purposes: The Case of Ethiopian Domestic Workers*. Addis Ababa: ILO Country Office.

IOM. 2014. *Emergency Post-arrival Assistance to Ethiopian Returnees from Kingdom of Saudi Arabia. Info Graphics*. Addis Ababa: International Organization for Migration.

Jureidini, R. 2004. *Migrant Workers and Xenophobia in the Middle East*. UNRISD Programme paper.

Kebede, E. 2001. *Ethiopia: An Assessment of the International Labor Migration Situation: The Case of Female Migrants*. GENPROM Working Paper 3, Series on Women and Migration. Geneva: ILO.

Minaye, A. 2012. "Trafficked to the Gulf States: The Experience of Ethiopian Returnee Women." *Journal of Community Practice* 20: 112–133.

Peutz, N. 2006. "Embarking on an Anthropology of Removal." *Current Anthropology* 47 (2): 217–241.

de Regt, M. 2010. "Ways to Come, Ways to Leave: Gender, Il/legality and Mobility among Ethiopian Domestic Workers in Yemen." *Gender & Society* 24 (2): 237–260.

RMMS. 2014. *The Letter of the Law: Regular and Irregular Migration in Saudi Arabia in a Context of Rapid Change*. Nairobi: Regional Mixed Migration Secretariat.

Ruben, R., M. van Houte, and T. Davids. 2009. "What Determines the Embeddedness of Forced-return Migrants? Rethinking the Role of Pre- and Post-return Assistance." *International Migration Review* 43 (4): 908–937.

Tafesse, M. 2014. "The Predicaments of Forced Return Migrants from Saudi Arabia." MA thesis, Department of Sociology, Addis Ababa University.

Van Houte, M., and M. de Koning. 2008. *Towards a Better Embeddedness? Monitoring Assistance to Involuntary Returning Migrants from Western countries*. Nijmegen: Center for International Development Studies.

The return migration experiences of Ethiopian women trafficked to Bahrain: ' ... for richer or poorer, let me be on the hands of my people ... '

Adamnesh Atnafu[a] and Margaret E. Adamek[b]

[a]School of Social Work, Addis Ababa University, Addis Ababa, Ethiopia; [b]Program in Social Work, Indiana University, Bloomington, USA

ABSTRACT

This study draws upon the return experiences of Ethiopian women trafficked to the Middle East. Understanding these experiences is critical to informing the design of effective government policy to mitigate obstacles to return and reintegration. This study was conducted in Addis Ababa with five women who were trafficked to Bahrain and later returned to Ethiopia. Action research was used to establish an inquiry group of women in order to produce a viable vision for successful reintegration. Despite initial high hopes, the returnees did not see migration as producing positive returns. All five participants agreed that their experiences in the destination were devastating and thus they were relieved to have returned to their home country. Nonetheless, reintegration was a difficult process for them. In addition to not accumulating enough savings to enable them to reintegrate economically, they all faced misunderstandings and impractical expectations from their families and community. The women suggested that adequate protection from law enforcement, facilitation of income-generating activities, and improved access to rehabilitation and medical services are important elements of successful return and reintegration. Effective return and reintegration policy is needed to ensure that trafficked returnees can become productive citizens in their home country.

Nowadays migration is increasingly viewed as temporary rather than permanent (Dustmann 2007). There are many reasons for migrants' return to their home country, including being unable to integrate in the host country, personal choice to return to one's home country, accomplishment of ambitions in the host country, and opportunities or pull factors in the home country (Ganga 2006). Forced return is also another factor critical in return migration. An example is the recent forced return of Ethiopian migrants from the Middle East. The Ethiopian government expected the number to be 30,000. However, by January 2014, the number of Ethiopian female returnees from Saudi Arabia had reached 150,000 (*The New York Times*, January 7, 2014).

Ethiopia is one of the countries in the world experiencing constant poverty. The causes for this poverty include social, political, economic, and environmental factors. Thus, many people opt to migrate to more developed countries in search of better opportunities for education and employment, and access to better living conditions. Consequently, those who are able to go to Western countries migrate to the west and those who cannot take the next best option to leave the country to go anywhere accessible. Some try to migrate through a legal process while others are victims of smuggling and trafficking.

Even though there is no reliable data on the number of migrants because of the challenge of tracking those who migrate illegally, according to the 2013 report of the Ministry of Labour and Social Affairs (MoLSA), the estimated number of female Ethiopian migrants who used Private Employment Agencies (PEAs) between July 2012 and July 2013 was 175,427. This number decreased from the previous year by 12,504 (the estimated number of female migrants between July 2011 and July 2012 was 187,931). This decrease reflects the heightened strictness of the government on PEAs' processing of migrant workers. Nonetheless, the number of Ethiopian domestic workers who migrate to the Middle East has increased by more than tenfold between 2010 and 2013. On the other hand, these data do not show the growing number who migrate irregularly using the 'desert and sea route' through the services of smugglers and traffickers. The most common destinations of Ethiopian women especially as domestic workers are as follows: Lebanon, Saudi Arabia, the UAE, Bahrain, Djibouti, Sudan, Syria, and Yemen while Djibouti, Egypt, and Somaliland are reported as the main transit routes of trafficked women (UNHCR 2009). Though the exact figures are not known since most women migrate illegally, police reports and other sources indicate that the number is increasing.

In Ethiopia, victims of trafficking are often women who migrate to the Middle East as domestic workers. According to Emebet (2006), the number of illegally trafficked women is increasing. Most of these women migrate to the destinations through illegal channels, leaving them with no legal power to protect their rights. They are usually victims of fraud, forced labour, and physical, sexual, and psychological abuse by their employers or by traffickers who take advantage of them (EWHRA 2009). A significant number experience traumatization and subsequently develop psychological problems during their stay. In addition, they face economic struggles to meet their basic needs. Many of these women are obliged to return to Ethiopia either by repatriation or by deportation.

The Refugees and Returnees Affairs (RRA) office in the Development and Inter-Church Aid Commission (DICAC) in Ethiopia is a programme that extends support to refugees and returnees. The activities of RRA include: providing essential supports (subsistence allowance, material assistance, and medication) for the urban refugee community and returnees, provision of training on income-generating activities and skill development to help refugees and returnees to become self-reliant, facilitating education, and rehabilitation and reintegration of returnees. Effective support methods can be planned properly after full awareness is gained about the experiences and needs of returnees, and with their participation in developing the services. However, much more needs to be done on the part of the Ethiopian government, NGOs, and private institutions, to support women's voluntary return and reintegration. Given the magnitude of the problem, and limited support systems, current efforts fall short.

One of the factors that contribute to the domination and perception of Ethiopian migrants as inferior and different is the fact that they have come from a developing nation (Wondwosen et al. 2006). In the host country, migrants who go abroad through illegal trafficking are more susceptible to oppression and different forms of abuse – physical, emotional, and sexual, especially in the case of women migrants (Lazaridis 2001).

According to Stewart (2005), trafficked women are susceptible to the development of physical and mental health problems because trafficking itself involves denial of human rights including the right to health. They are also vulnerable in protecting their own rights because of their weak socio-economic status. Most of the women who end up being trafficked are either not married or single mothers who have come from poor economic, educational, and social backgrounds. The women often experience different forms of abuse which result in health risks including the following: sexual abuse/rape; emotional abuse (insults and manipulation); physical injury such as bruising, broken teeth, and cuts and burns; sexually transmitted diseases and unwanted pregnancies which sometimes result in forced abortions; physiological problems such as anxiety and post-traumatic stress disorder; inability to recover and integrate into society; deprivation from food and sleep; and symptoms such as nausea, dizziness, vision disturbances, and body aches (Emebet 2006). The women work as sex workers, nannies, housemaids, strippers, and sometimes as waitresses. Many work for more than 18 hours a day seven days a week in order to pay their travel expenses which they owe the traffickers who hold their documents.

Hughes (2000) argues that trafficking women is a practice that has a huge market where large amounts of money are transacted. Because there is a supply and demand like in any other market, the demand comes from the receiving countries while the women from the sending countries are easily transported because most of them have a poor educational, economic, and social background. Usually the women are recruited through informal advertisements promising that they will be employed in a comfortable setting as waitresses, nannies, and house workers with a good salary. The women are persuaded by traffickers who are highly experienced in deceiving without revealing the genuine picture of the employment (Fernandez 2013). Another way of recruitment is through marriage agencies that target women who are eager to leave the economic desperation in their home country. These agencies arrange a meeting of the women with men who promise to marry them and take them abroad. The man then uses the woman for himself for some time and then gives her to another man who arranges for her to become a sex worker (Hughes 2000). Most of the times the woman is given false documents to enter the country of destination.

Many traffickers confiscate the women's legal documents until she pays off her debts of travel and service charges, which can amount to thousands in US currency. Sometimes, the women get accustomed to life in the destination country and try to persuade their friends and other women from their home country to join them. Oftentimes, they do not expect what they will face when they are trafficked to the destination countries. They lose control over their lives, they earn a very small amount of money which does not allow them to even consider going back to their country, and they sometimes become victims of extreme violence, at times ending in murder.

The women do not get legal support or protection and thus do not report violations of their human rights. Even if they report such abuses, they will not get sympathy and/or assistance from law enforcement. In fact, since they enter the destinations illegally, they are considered as criminals and face prosecution. At times, trafficking leads to commercial sex work (Jayagupta 2009). In addition to the abuse they faced in the destinations, these victims of trafficking, especially when they work as prostitutes, are blamed by society and even by their own community. This attitude of the community is one factor contributing to the leniency of legal actions taken against traffickers and criminals. The woman is blamed herself and stigmatized.

Regt (2007) examined the experiences of Ethiopian women who migrated to Yemen. The illegally trafficked women reach Yemen after a long and frustrating journey. To reach Yemen they must pay smugglers who transport them by boat across the Red Sea or through the Gulf of Aden. Unfortunately, after experiencing all of this trouble, the situation they get into is not what they have expected; instead, it is often worse than the situation in their home country. Though those who travel through arrangements of recruiting agencies face problems of low pay, psychological manipulation, and other forms of abuse resulting from the agents' deception. Those who are trafficked illegally face the most unfavourable situations. Their movement is restricted, they are often victims of violence including physical and sexual assault, and they are denied basic human rights like decent food and a place to sleep. Since their mobility is restricted, they cannot even change their place of work because their employers threaten to report them to the police.

Emebet (2006) argues that the issue of illegally trafficked Ethiopian women has not been given due attention by the responsible bodies. Recently, the government through the responsible organ, the MoLSA, has taken measures regarding both PEAs and public employment services (PESs) to lessen the incidence of illegal and irregular migration. For instance, the office has limited the categories of people who can find employment for a potential migrant abroad to close family members, namely mother, father, brother, and sister, which included friends and acquaintances previously. This service allowed traffickers to convince migrants that the process is legal and contracted through the MoLSA. At present, according to an official at the MoLSA, the potential migrant should first establish that the person who found the employment in the host country is a parent or a sibling. This person should then confirm at the respective Ethiopian Embassy or Consulate in the host country that there is evidence that they have the ability to receive and accommodate the potential migrant once in the host country. These provisions have lessened the use of PESs.

Although some effort is seen on the part of the government and other private initiatives regarding migration, not much is done to address the re-integration of returnees. One factor contributing to the lack of protection of women's rights is the absence of diplomatic representation in the countries where the women are mostly migrating. There should be contact persons in the consulates and embassies to represent the women in cases of violation of their human rights. One way to reduce the misfortunes is to launch an aggressive campaign to inform women in Ethiopia about the dangers of trafficking.

Returnees should also be assisted in their social and economic reintegration because most of them face serious difficulties (Brunovskis and Surtees 2012). Felege Wogen is an NGO established to work on the repatriation and reintegration of returnees. In addition to arranging safe return for the women, the organization also provides for the basic needs of returnees like shelter, food, short-term rehabilitation, support, medical service, and transportation to their permanent settlements after their return. Felege Wogen also raises funds for establishing income-generating activities/projects for the returnees. The Ethiopian Women Lawyers Association (EWLA) and International Organization for

Migration (IOM) also assist in the repatriation and reintegration of returnees. In addition to material provision, returnees need medical attention such as counselling for victims of trafficking who have experienced trauma. While the efforts of this NGO are laudable, they are insufficient to meet the needs of the growing number of returnees.

In addition to stigma, social problems include stigma from the society and blaming/unrealistic expectations from families, which returnees may not fulfil leading to unpleasant post-trafficking experiences (Brunovskis and Surtees 2012). Families and friends fail to provide support and reassurance to the victim despite the hope the returnees have upon their return. As a result of the trauma experienced at the destination, medical intervention may be necessary upon their return. In the study by Brunovskis and Surtees (2012), one victim's behaviour upon return was described as: 'She is crying all the time and cannot prevent herself from having aggressive manifestations. These are reactions or symptoms of severe post-traumatic stress. And the relatives do not understand and try to figure out why she's like that' (463).

In sum, the experience of trafficked women is devastating and has an impact on their well-being after their return. They are victims of different forms of abuse and are economically unstable because of their illegal status in the host countries. Thus, upon their return, a significant number of women are hopeless because of the trauma they experienced which results in failure to reintegrate into the home country. Many need assistance in the areas of health, economic support, and facilitation of their social reintegration. Though the responsible bodies are working on prevention of trafficking and protection of rights, the return and reintegration programme also needs significant effort and resources (UNIFEM 2002). Despite the call for attention to these issues, scientific research on the return and reintegration of trafficked women has been inadequate.

With these issues in mind, this study investigated the lived experience of illegally trafficked Ethiopian women who returned to Ethiopia in order to develop ideas of best ways to intervene to facilitate their reintegration. The research questions addressed by the study were: What are the experiences and meaning of return and reintegration for illegally trafficked Ethiopian women? What supports do returning migrants identify as being needed to facilitate their reintegration?

Methods

This exploratory study examined the experiences of five illegally trafficked Ethiopian women returnees from Bahrain, and identified the key areas where they require support. The purpose of this study was to understand the experiences of illegally trafficked Ethiopian women returnees, the meaning of returning and reintegration for these women, and to identify services/support that the women themselves identify as rehabilitation and reintegration. To accomplish the study objectives, a participatory research and co-operative approach was used. The anticipated result of such an approach was to form an inquiry group of women focused on how to support themselves and others who are in the same situation, and to create a long-range intervention plan. The goal was to build relationships and enhance the process of learning among the women.

Moreover, the research provided an opportunity to propose ways to enhance the support programmes based upon a deeper understanding of the women's real situation. Thus, the ultimate aim was to develop a broader and more integrated set of activities provided by support programmes, particularly the RRA, shaped by the reflections of the beneficiaries.

Action research is conducted with – not on – the illegally trafficked Ethiopian women who have been trafficked to Bahrain. The research was planned to be participatory following the cyclical steps of action research: process of an action, reflection and review of the action, plan new action, then finally come back to the process of the new action followed by the other steps (McAlpine 2005). Consequently, the first author facilitated the exploration of the lived experiences of the participants in the host country, the meaning of returning, identifying activities in providing support, and suggestions for actions.

This study was conducted with five trafficked women returnees in Addis Ababa. One criterion for selection was the place of migration. All participants were trafficked to Bahrain to work as domestic workers/housemaids. The other criterion was time of migration – participants were trafficked within the previous five years. A snowball method was used to identify study participants who met the criteria.

The first step was reflection and review of action and started from the researcher's initiation of the inquiry after convening the group of women. The action research method was implemented by applying the principles of collaborative recourse, reflexive critique, and dialectical critique as stipulated in O'Brien (1998). Throughout the process, the researcher took notes, recorded the observations of participants, took notes of responses by the participants, and finally recorded the outcomes. The meetings took place at a place convenient to all. Each session lasted for 90 minutes and all five participants were present for all sessions.

The researcher commenced the first meeting by explaining the objectives of the research, the process and method of the research, and by introducing the first stage of the process (O'Brien 1998). During the second and third meetings, the women were asked several questions about. The group shared experiences and the meanings of their experiences, followed by group discussions in the fourth and fifth meetings about the supports needed upon return. Participants wrote their ideas on index cards, which helped in identifying themes. The participants reflected on the ideas, critically offering their own interpretations, opposing and agreeing with ideas of others, respecting the credibility of the idea holder, and analysing the issues from different viewpoints.

The women preferred to discuss their experiences and the meaning of their experiences as a whole group. On the other hand, they preferred to discuss suggestions and assessment of support in mini-groups using index cards. They divided the group into two, conducted mini-group discussions, examined the discussions conducted in the mini-group in the whole group, and developed suggestions for support activities in facilitating their return and reintegration. Participants were enthusiastic and fully participated in the discussions and were eager to share their experiences with each other.

At the last meeting, the researcher shared her observations and reported the outcome of the process to the participants to get consensus on the content of the report. The report was initially prepared in Amharic and shared with the women. After receiving their feedback and consensus on the content, the report was translated into English.

The analysis of the data started with describing the process and the setting in detail. The researcher read all the notes, reports, and observations gathered during the interviews and conversations to obtain an overall sense of the data (Creswell 1998). These were recorded by the researcher from her observation and the participants themselves. Then emergent themes were identified which enables the researchers to determine patterns from the date.

The researchers respected the ethical requirements of confidentiality by using pseudonyms. Participants were reminded of their rights to withdraw at any time. Additionally, the participants were informed of their right to have equal participation in the research and equal access to the information generated from the research. In the section that follows, we discuss the sub-themes that emerged from our study.

Results

Profile and background of participants

The participants were first interviewed individually to gather background information. One participant was under the age of 18, so consent to participate was obtained from her legal guardian and herself. The other four were between the ages of 19 and 24 (see Table 1).

One participant was illiterate while two others were barely literate – having dropped out of school in the fourth grade. Two participants left school after they failed the eighth-grade national examination. All five participants were self-identified as Christian. This is an interesting dimension as all went to a Muslim country. Two participants were married with one child each, while the other three were unmarried. One was a single mother.

Concerning their economic background, all the participants stated that they came from poor families. Four of the five women were from the countryside, and one was from the capital city, Addis Ababa. All asserted that the income of their family was not enough to take care of the younger siblings let alone for an additional person like themselves. The married women stated that their husbands worked as a house-guard or in low-paying construction jobs. They did not have enough earnings to provide for their child and themselves. Of the participants, two were working as housemaids while the other three were not working at all. One of the participants, the single mother, came from the countryside to Addis Ababa to stay with relatives until her process of migration was completed.

Decision point to return: '... A blessing in disguise ...'

For the research participants, the decision to return to Ethiopia happened when the degree of the abuse they suffered reached beyond their capacity for tolerance. Of the participants, three returned to Ethiopia after three years in Bahrain. The other two returned after two and five years, respectively. None stayed long enough to obtain a legal work permit.

Two of the women did not finish paying their debt to their employer when they decided to return. They lost hope that they would ever be able to earn money in that condition. They could not go anywhere seeking another job in the country, because they were

Table 1. Profile of participants (*n* = 5).

Name	Age	Marital status	Number of children	Religion	Literacy	Time in the destination country
Almaz	22	Single	1	Christian	Fourth grade	Three years
Aster	24	Married	1	Christian	Fourth grade	Five years
Mastewal	19	Single	0	Christian	Eighth grade	Three years
Sinedu	21	Married	1	Christian	Illiterate	Three years
Tsige	17	Single	0	Christian	Eighth grade	Two years

illegal and did not know where to turn for help. Thus, the only choice they had was to return home. The other reason for deciding to return was when they could no longer tolerate the abuse they were experiencing. There was also a case of forced return. One of the women explained that she was reported to the authorities by her employer and was forced to return via deportation. However, she does not regret being returned as she said: 'it was a blessing in disguise'. All five lost hope of getting anywhere near their dreams – working to earn money and support their loved ones at home.

When deciding to return, all of them had an expired visa. This was the primary factor that led them to report to the police themselves, which enabled them to avoid any legal prosecution. Because they did not have the money to pay for their air ticket, the government had to pay their travel and deport them back to Ethiopia. The women know of others who still are being abused in Bahrain and who did not get the opportunity to return. The women in our study consider themselves lucky for returning safely. They felt fortunate to escape their situation while there are others who could not return for one reason or another.

The experiences of these women in Bahrain were very devastating. They experienced multiple forms of abuse. They were deprived of healthy food, adequate sleep, reasonable workloads, and freedom of movement. They were also victims of physical abuse such as beating, verbal abuse such as insults, and in some cases sexual harassment, all by their employers. Their experience damaged them both in the form of bodily injury and emotionally in terms of trauma.

Moreover, they were not able to be in touch with their families back home which added to their emotional stress. They were also misunderstood by their families for reasons like low level of awareness of their situation in Bahrain and high expectations in terms of earning potential. The women had poor family relationships partly because their employers limited their communication with others and partly because of their own fears of rejection.

Victims of trafficking often have no legal protection as they are illegal residents. Thus, the women did not have any protection from the government of Bahrain nor from other state organs or institutions. Thus, when the abuse and pain became intolerable, they decided to return at any expense. Unfortunately, they had not accumulated capital because their salaries were going back to the employer in one way or another to pay debts, etc.

Return: 'For richer or poorer, let me be in the hands of my people'

Each of the women shared their experiences of the process and meaning of return to Ethiopia. Almaz and Sinedu went directly to the police and reported their undocumented status while the other women did not know where to go and who to turn to. In the case of Aster, her employer reported her to the police and she was then apprehended from her work place.

The women felt a sense of relief once they arrived back in Ethiopia.

> I felt like I was escaping from a far away prison and coming back to my family. (Mastewal)
> I couldn't believe that I was coming back home until I entered a taxi with other Ethiopians who did not even know who I was and what I have been through – who did not follow my steps. I was still traumatized by the situation I was in while in Bahrain. I was even thinking that they (the employer) will wait for me at the Addis Ababa airport to take me back. (Tsige)

When the plane took off the land of Bahrain, I felt like something that has possessed me left me to fall off my shoulders. (Aster)

'Bikefam bilemam yagere hizb yigledelegn' which means 'for richer or poorer, let me be on the hands of my people'. (Sinedu)

Return for all five women including the one who returned against her will meant 'freedom – freedom of life'. The women shared about their return with passion and delight on their face. Return meant getting back their freedom to do what they would like, to eat and drink what they chose, to go wherever they want to go, and to get a good night's sleep in their own bed no matter how small and rough it is. Their unpleasant experiences in Bahrain led them to appreciate the situation in Ethiopia they left in the first place.

Nonetheless, the reaction from their families was not pleasant initially. First, their families expected much from them because they were considered as Ethiopians abroad – Diaspora – which is a status presumed to include wealth. When they returned without any savings, a negative reaction awaited them from their families and relatives. They were seen as persons who had migrated to improve their families' lives. Yet, after some time, this problem gets resolved as their families come to understand what they have been through and were even thankful for their safe return. The women were grateful that the emotional link with their families did not fade away; 'Your flesh and blood is always yours' (Aster).

Reintegration: 'I would rather face the evils of my country'

Regarding reintegration, the participants' comments revolved around three issues: economic reintegration, social reintegration, and psychological reintegration. Although the women were grateful for their safe return, they did not feel very hopeful about their future.

Primarily, lack of savings and income was a significant concern, leaving them dependent on family members. Sinedu, Tsige, and Almaz stated that they could not work as domestic workers because of the trauma they suffered in Bahrain that kept haunting them. On the other hand, they do not have sufficient funds to start up their own businesses however small. None of these women received any kind of support from the government, NGOs, or private institutions regarding facilitation of income generation. They added that if there was support available, they were not aware of it.

The women were not ready to get back on their feet and start working. They did not feel prepared to face the reality that they have to move on and work to earn their living. They also feel regret for the wasted years of their lives. They expressed regret thinking what their status now would be had they not left for Bahrain in the first place. Mastewal shared: ' ... I wish I did not take the step to go there. If I were here no one would have inflicted all those different forms of abuse ... Minim bihone agere lisekay' (Amharic saying meaning 'I would rather face the evils of my country').

Support services needed: 'I am still dependent'

Information/awareness

One of the main reasons for the women's unpleasant experiences upon return is lack of information or awareness about the work and living situation in the host country. Thus, the first aim should be prevention: preventing trafficking by making women aware of the real situation in the host countries and by providing information about the available opportunities in Ethiopia. The participants stated that they did not have any idea about Bahrain when they decided to leave – they did not have any knowledge of the Middle East. They also did not know who to contact or where to go when they had problems or were exploited and became victims of various forms of abuse.

The women did not know who to turn to in Bahrain. They were not aware of the available return processes and/or resources, if there were any. They did not know if there were services to facilitate their return when they decided they must leave. Tsige noted, 'I didn't know where to go or who to talk to because I didn't have a friend or family. Even if you know anybody, our employers will not let us contact anyone.' Thus, information was an important part of their discussion of needed support. In this regard, they suggested that the government, NGOs, and private institutions should avail information to women migrants, if possible, for them to be aware of what to do in case of violation of their rights. Women also need information about how to initiate return if they wish to return home.

Law and law enforcement

The participants shared about the protection they need from the law. From their lived experiences, they came to believe that traffickers should be stopped from sending women illegally to the Middle East. They regret that there was no one to warn them not to be involved in such means of leaving the country but now they desire to be examples for other women who wish to migrate to the Middle East.

Regarding their return and reintegration, they stated that the law and law enforcement have a significant role to play. They would like to see greater prosecution of traffickers as a form of compensation helping them psychologically integrate back home. Aster stated: ' … the law should be strict on the traffickers who deceived us. They told us that we were going to be rich once we get there. We did not even receive our money, the money we earned for our work properly'. The other is to make the exploiters in the host countries responsible for violating their basic human rights. Though this kind of allegation is difficult to exercise in another country, it may be possible if the appropriate negotiations are made by and between the two governments, that is, agreements based on international conventions of human rights.

Rehabilitation and medical attention

Being victims of trafficking, the participants stated that they also needed rehabilitation services including counselling. They required counselling services in order to overcome the trauma they experienced and continued to experience. They also stated that the physical abuse that they have experienced may have resulted in serious internal and external injury that they may have not realized at the moment. Since they were not able to get medical attention back in Bahrain, they needed to receive proper treatment upon their return.

Income generation

According to the participants, the most frustrating part of return is the lack of savings and capital to start life back in Ethiopia. These women do not have sufficient funds to engage in any kind of business unless they are willing to be employed as domestic workers. Aster expressed this as: 'I am still dependent, I need help to make a living because I haven't brought anything back home.'

One of the reasons for this is lack of skills and saleable talent for them to be employed in another setting. Thus, one activity that should be facilitated is provision of training for them to acquire certain types of skills through which either they start their own small business or can be hired by those requiring skilled labour.

Secondly, returnees need to be assisted in entering income-generation schemes. In addition to providing training to the returnees, the government, NGOs, and/or private institutions should facilitate fund-raising to provide seed money in the form of credit. This was emphasized by the participants. Almaz noted, 'we could start up our own small businesses if we get financial help like loans'. The women agreed this would assist them in integrating economically back in their country.

Organizing an advocacy association

The participants suggested that returnees be assisted in organizing themselves as an association. This will provide an opportunity to share experiences and help each other with different psychological and other needs. In addition, the association could contribute to public awareness large – in promoting the above suggested support activities. Finally, the women promised to initiate the establishment of an association of returnees from the Middle East and continue their advocacy efforts, taking this exercise as a starting point. In sum, the support activities the returnees need are dissemination of information about health and mental health care, support with income-generation activities/projects; counselling and rehabilitation services; the assistance of law and law enforcement; and finally support to create an association of returnees.

Conclusion

The literature on the experiences of trafficked women reveals that victims experience different forms of abuse – physical, sexual, and psychological/emotional (Stewart 2005). Most of these women came from poor socio-economic backgrounds and have a low level of education, which was also the case in this study. According to Stewart (2005), most women are single or single mothers. However, in this study, two out of the five women were married with children. Thus, this research revealed that even those with a husband and child make the decision to migrate despite the risk of becoming victims of trafficking.

Hughes (2000) argues that the trafficking of women is based on deceit which also applied to the women who participated in this research given that they all were given false information about the situation in the host country. The women in this study likewise were not paid as reported by Stewart (2005) and Regt (2007) who argue that the women are obliged to work for long hours but were not paid accordingly.

Similarly, regarding return and reintegration, and the support needed, the literature has identified the obstacles women face in returning and reintegrating back in their country. The results from this study are consistent with the literature as the findings show that the returnees face difficulties of financial instability (Araujo-Forlot 2002). They also face obstacles in their social and psychological reintegration. They need support to overcome the trauma they faced in the Middle East (Araujo-Forlot 2002; Emebet 2006). Similar to the findings of Brunovski and Surtees (2012), participants revealed that their families were not as understanding as they expected, which was one of the factors contributing to the difficulties of reintegration.

The participants in this study experienced many difficulties and were deprived of their rights in the host country. They experienced intense psychological distress because of the abuse inflicted on them by the employers in the host country. Thus, the last option – return – was chosen through a difficult process. After returning to their home country, the women faced additional obstacles to reintegrate as returnees. Despite the effort of the UN, the IOM, and other groups to fight illegal trafficking and violation of human rights, the frustrations and pain of these illegally trafficked women come from lenience in implementing such agreements in both sending and receiving governments.

Regardless of the struggles these Ethiopian women faced in re-integrating with the system and society, they nevertheless indicated that they were still happy to return home and be freed of all the abuse. Even though this study was based on a non-representative sample and generalizations may not be drawn, it can inform other more comprehensive studies on the subject. Because these women are not skilled and have not received any kind of training while in Ethiopia or in Bahrain, they were/are not able to be employed in another area of work – other than that of domestic labour. Their financial instability was a primary obstacle to successful reintegration back in Ethiopia.

The experiences and meaning of return for the women and their reintegration had both positive and negative implications. While their return experience was positive on one hand, their reintegration did have some negative aspects. In their experience of return, although the process of return was difficult for them, their return meant 'a green light for new life'. Most importantly, it meant regaining their freedom.

An important step in moving forward would be the dissemination of information on the voluntary return schemes (VRSs) in Ethiopia. Organizations like the IOM and the RRA in the DICAC have a variety of services for migrants, both legal and illegal. None of the participants were aware of the available VRS in Ethiopia. This kind of service helps in addressing stigma and emotional distress resulting from forced deportation, and helps migrants in arranging and covering the expenses of travel back to their country (Araujo-Forlot 2002).

According to Araujo-Forlot (2002), although there are laws with rigorous penalties for trafficking, the prosecution of traffickers has still been difficult due to lack of evidence. Hence, victims of trafficking do not get any compensation after facing all the violence and other frustrating experiences. Although the injustices they encountered may not be remedied, appropriate mechanisms should be put in place at least to redress the victims after their return. The IOM has been implementing effective programmes on return and reintegration of returnees through its offices (Jayagupta 2009). A project funded by the IOM in Thailand was proved to be successful focusing on two elements of reintegration – income-generating activities and psycho-social support (Araujo-Forlot 2002). On the other hand, NGOs can also act as mediators between the victims and law enforcement, government and other international donors in addition to providing the assistance themselves.

Voluntary return programmes are more advantageous for the returnees than forced return (Ganga 2006). Forced deportation will not take away the stigma and the obstacles of reintegration – economic and social, into consideration while voluntary return programmes facilitate these in advance. Hence, an effective return programme includes three elements: pre-departure, travel, and post-arrival conditions. This way the returnees' reintegration process would be less challenging in that information and counselling are provided to them before departing, return travel arrangements can be made for them before departure and during travel, and finally a post-arrival reception can be arranged to provide assistance based on their respective needs.

Considering the increasing number of Ethiopian migrants, the Ethiopian government should further develop policies to manage labour migration. The country should develop exit control mechanisms to restrict migrant workers leaving the country before they have clearance from the relevant authority responsible for labour migration as different labour-sending countries such as the Philippines, Bangladesh, India, and others (Khadria 2008). Regarding lack of information as mentioned by participants, there should be a campaign to disseminate information to potential migrants and families both in urban and rural settings.

Our research shows that migrants return mainly because of intolerable working conditions and continued abuse. Return and reintegration are important elements of migration that need to be addressed by the government. Migrant workers face socio-economic problems upon their return. Thus, access to sufficient resources, financial and psycho-social services is important to returning migrants. The government should initiate and facilitate the development of ways to provide such services and guidance for returning workers.

Steps to ensure effective return and reintegration policy include: systematic collection of data on returning migrants to inform migration policies of the country; borrowing best practices from other countries' return and reintegration policies and strategies, and open discussion forums and coordination among stakeholders about providing support to returning migrants. To gain deeper understanding of the issues related to returnees and reintegration, it would be useful for more cross-national comparisons thereby allowing researchers to examine the impact of different migration policies across countries. As the considerable number of irregular/illegal migrants suggests, the safe return and effectual reintegration of its citizens should be a top priority of the country.

Disclosure statement

No potential conflict of interest was reported by the authors.

References

Araujo-Forlot, A. 2002. *Prevention, Protection and Assistant Schemes to Victims of Trafficking: Policy and Examples of IOM Prevention and Return and Reintegration Programs*. Vienna: IOM.
Brunovskis, A., and R. Surtees. 2012. "Coming Home: Challenges in Family Reintegration for Trafficked Women." *Qualitative Social Work* 12 (4): 454–472.
Creswell, J. 1998. *Qualitative Inquiry and Research Design: Choosing Among the Five Traditions*. Thousand Oaks, CA: Sage.
Dustmann, C. 2007. "Return Migration, Investment in Children, and Intergenerational Mobility: Comparing Sons of Foreign- and Native-born Fathers." *The Journal of Human Resources* 13: 299–324.
Emebet, K. 2006. *An Assessment of the International Labour Migration Situation: The Case of Female Labour Migrants*. Women and Migration. GENPROM working paper 3. Geneva: ILO.

EWHRA. 2009. *ETHIOPIA: Ethiopian Women's Human Rights Alliance's UPR Submission*. Accessed February 20, 2010. http://lib.ohchr.org/HRBodies/UPR/Documents/Session6/ET/EWHRA_ETH_UPR_S06_2009.pdf.

Fernandez, B. 2013. "Traffickers, Brokers, Employment Agents and Social Networks: The Regulation of Intermediaries in the Migration of Ethiopian Domestic Workers to the Middle East." *International Migration Review* 47 (4): 514–543.

Ganga, D. 2006. "From Potential Returnees into Settlers: Nottingham's Older Italians." *Journal of Ethnic and Migration Studies* 32 (8): 1395–1413.

Hughes, D. 2000. "The 'Natasha' Trade – the Transnational Shadow Market of Trafficking in Women." *Journal of International Affairs* 53 (2): 625–651.

Jayagupta, R. 2009. "The Thai Government's Repatriation and Reintegration Programmes: Responding to Trafficked Female Commercial Sex Workers from the Greater Mekong Subregion." *International Migration* 47: 227–253.

Khadria, Binod. 2008. "Future of Migration from South Asia to the OECD Countries: Reflections on India, Pakistan, and Bangladesh." Paper prepared for the workshop on the future of international migration to OECD countries, OECD Paris, December 1–2.

Lazaridis, G. 2001. "Trafficking and Prostitution: The Growing Exploitation of Migrant Women in Greece." *The European Journal of Women's Studies* 8 (1): 67–102.

McAlpine, K. 2005. *Participatory Action Research: Local Causation of Primary School Drop-outs and Exclusion in Kilimanjaro Region*. Vol. 1. Moshi: Mkombozi Center for Street Children.

O'Brien, R. 1998. *An Overview of the Methodological Approach of Action Research*. Ontario: University of Toronto, Faculty of Information Studies.

Regt, M. 2007. *Ethiopian Women in the Middle East: The Case of Migrant Domestic Workers in Yemen*. Amsterdam: African Studies Centre.

Stewart, D. 2005. "Trafficking in Women: The Canadian Perspective." *Canadian Medical Association Journal* 173 (1): 25–26.

UNHCR. 2009. *Trafficking in Persons Report 2009 – Ethiopia*. Accessed March 2, 2010. http://www.unhcr.org/refworld/country,,USDOS,,ETH,,4a4214bc28,0.html.

UNIFEM. 2002. "Trafficking in Persons: A Gender and Rights Perspective." *Gender Matters Quarterly*, 1. Accessed March 2, 2010. http://www.unifem.org/attachments/products/traffkit_eng.pdf.

Wondwosen, T. B., N. Jerusalem, H. Seidler, and Z. Hanna. 2006. "International Migration: The Case of Ethiopian Female Migrants in Austria." *Journal of Social Science* 13 (1): 1–9.

Migration, gender, and mobility: Ethiopian–Israeli women's narratives of career trajectories

Yarden Fanta-Vagenshtein[a,b] and Lisa Anteby-Yemini[a,b]

[a]CNRS, IDEMEC, Aix-Marseille University, Provence, France; [b]Women Studies Research Center & Israeli Studies, Brandeis University, Waltham, MA, USA

ABSTRACT
Most studies on the Ethiopian community in Israel discuss the difficulties in its social, cultural, occupational, and educational integration. Too little attention has been paid to the young professionals in the community who are experiencing upward mobility and to the women in particular. As opposed to stereotypes of Ethiopian–Israelis as poor, uneducated, and marginalized, this article explores socio-economic advancement of Ethiopian–Israeli women in Israel. We look at their integration in the labour market and their professional mobility in the areas of arts, business, religion, the army, and education by analysing the factors that play a role in their success. This study allows us to explore Ethiopian women's worlds by looking at their background and the steps they have taken to succeed in their careers.

Introduction

Ethiopian Jews' forced and self-exile in Israel can be seen as an example of the globalization of Ethiopian migration in the world. Yet, as the second largest Ethiopian expatriate group (after the USA), few studies (except Kaplan 2010) compare or analyse Jewish migration from the perspective of Ethiopian diasporas because of a reverse narrative defining Ethiopia as the diaspora and Israel as the 'ancestral' home (Kaplan 2005). This article will, however, endeavour to contribute to a comparative study of Ethiopian diasporas by showing how complexity of identity as Ethiopian–Israeli successful women can be seen in a transnational dimension; through their maintenance of Ethiopian ethnicity and links to Ethiopia (via the internet, TV, travels, and circulation of Ethiopian goods), they resemble in many ways other women of the Ethiopian global diaspora.

The Ethiopian community in Israel numbers over 1,35,000, including 50,000 born in Israel; half are women; 29 per cent are under age 14 and 40 per cent of adults have only elementary education or less.[1] Most Ethiopian Jews lived in the northern highlands as non-literate peasants and artisans in a patriarchal society; they immigrated to Israel in two major waves, known as Operation Moses (1984–1985) through Sudan and Operation Solomon (1991) via Addis-Ababa. As a 'returning Jewish diaspora', they received immediate Israeli citizenship and government aid, such as free housing for the first year, Hebrew classes, vocational training, and subsidies to purchase homes. Yet, because of their low human capital and their concentration in specific neighbourhoods and schools, Ethiopian immigrants in Israel are often depicted as living under the poverty line, depending on welfare, failing in education, remaining unemployed or occupying unskilled jobs, and as being candidates for a foreseeable underclass and future ghettos (Ben-Eliezer 2004; Kaplan and Salamon 2004; Kimmerling 2001; Offer 2007). However alarming may be their situation, continually reporting on these issues also produces adverse effects, that is, essentializing, racializing, and stigmatizing the entire community. Those who remain understudied are the successful Ethiopian–Israelis integrated socially, professionally, and economically who become doctors, nurses, lawyers, journalists, educators, performing artists, entrepreneurs, diplomats, politicians, and rabbis. In the media, they are quasi-invisible, and instead of success stories, sensational coverage of murders, domestic violence, delinquency, and school dropout in the community prevails. Thus, if an Israeli–Ethiopian middle class is experiencing social mobility – notwithstanding reported discrimination – it still remains a neglected topic. Even less attention is paid to gender and no study except one (Walsh and Yonas 2012) has looked at upwardly mobile women of Ethiopian origin. This study seeks to add to the literature by looking at the role of family background, education, army service, marriage, identity, and discrimination in the immigrant women's achievements.

Academic studies display a notorious absence of research on Ethiopian–Israeli elites. Only one study deals with an educated population (Weil 1997); another explores class variations in de-stigmatization strategies of Ethiopian Jews in Israel (Mizrachi and Zawdu 2012) and recent research introduces standard of living and education as parameters for identity and integration (Amit 2012). Several studies do exist on women of Ethiopian origin, but without directly addressing their socio-economic success *per se*: Leitman (1995) researched the transformations in women's status from Ethiopia to Israel among three generations; Phillips Davids (1998) studied fertility patterns and changes in reproductive models from Ethiopia to Israel; Newman (2007) explored the transmission of past heritage and heroism through mother-to-daughter stories; Shabtay and Kacen (2005) edited a volume on women's transition from Ethiopia to Israel (with a focus on purity, pregnancy, birth, motherhood, health behaviours, intergenerational ties, army service, marriage patterns, and domestic violence) and presents a rather negative account of their integration; Salamon, Kaplan, and Goldberg (2009) investigated working-class Israeli–Ethiopian women's empowerment and economic control through rotating credit associations; and Weil (2004) offers an overview of women in Israel's Ethiopian community. Only Walsh and Yonas (2012) looked at successful Ethiopian women in Israel, focusing on factors explaining success and the role of ethnic identity. Thus, research on emergent Ethiopian–Israeli professional women deserves further research.

These lacunae also concern women of North African and Middle Eastern origin (*Mizrahi* in Hebrew) in Israel, for whom few studies have focused on upward mobility, partly due to academic marginalization (Motzafi-Haller 2001). Likewise, studies on professionally mobile migrant women worldwide are still lacking, despite the fact that migration theory has come to consider gender as contextual and power-laden (Donato et al. 2006). In the USA, recent theories consider that the 'new second generation' follows a 'segmented assimilation' model with three possible patterns: straight-line integration into dominant white middle class, downward mobility and assimilation into an urban underclass, or successful assimilation combining upward mobility with ethnic identity and solidarity (Portes 1994; Rumbaut 1994; Zhou 1997). These diverging paths are explained by contexts and resources, such as discrimination, location, strong co-ethnic community and intermarriage (Rumbaut 1994). Factors of successful incorporation include educational achievement, strong aspirations, language proficiency, native birth or arrival in youth, longer residency, lighter skin, higher family class, social networks, residence outside ethnic enclaves, and specific cultural values (Portes 1994). In addition, racial barriers may impede social mobility (Zhou 1997). Studies on young women of North African origin in France show that educational attainment and social mobility stem mainly from family mobilization and support (Belhadj 2006; Santelli 2001).

In our case, women of Ethiopian origin can be considered at a triple disadvantage in Israel: as women, as recent immigrants, and as immigrants from less developed countries, as has been suggested for *Mizrahi* women (Raijman and Semyonov 1997). According to segmented assimilation, Ethiopian–Israeli women should experience downward mobility because of differential opportunity structures such as low status in education, occupation, income; spatial segregation; low cultural, social and material capital; low rates of intermarriage and racism. In addition, the concept of intersectionality, referring both to interconnected identities (based on race, gender, class) and to the multiple discrimination they may lead to, is relevant here to understand strategies of empowerment of marginalized populations (Herrera 2013).

In this article, we explore what role gender plays in the mobility of women of Ethiopian origin and what factors, such as family or background (urban vs. rural), contribute to their success. Is access to resources and networks more difficult for women than for men? Do racial or gender barriers impede them or can being an Israeli–Ethiopian woman become an asset? Different ways of measuring professional mobility do not always assess cultural and social integration. For instance, are women married to non-Ethiopian Israelis better integrated socially? Or have women who married Ethiopian–Israelis and imposed new gender roles in the family and new attitudes towards working women inside the Ethiopian community achieved more? What it means to be a successful woman and for whom (the men, the Ethiopian community, Israeli society) should also be taken into account. We will also endeavour to understand how these women are tackling issues of race, gender, and class, and how they express multiple belongings such as Ethiopian, Jewish, and Israeli identities.

Methodology

This article is based on seven semi-structured in-depth interviews in Hebrew of two to three hours each, conducted by both authors together in the women's homes or workplace; all consented to be interviewed for the purpose of this research. We asked the women to narrate their life stories and experiences, focusing on their background before immigrating and on the steps they followed to build their careers in Israel. From the transcribed narratives, several themes emerged: family background and migration; education and military service; relations with spouses, children, and career; Ethiopian and Israeli culture and identity; discrimination and activism. We chose women who had succeeded professionally in various fields and who were willing to take time to talk with us. We selected them because they were at different stages of life and held various positions towards religion; their ages range from 28 to 55. Mostly from a rural background, they were living in different parts of Israel and immigrated between the 1980s and the 1990s. Some can be considered first-generation immigrants and those who immigrated younger, as the 1.5 generation (Rumbaut 1994). As a preliminary study on upwardly mobile women of Ethiopian origin, the purpose of this article is to challenge common stereotypes of Jewish women in Ethiopia, showing that some had high positions, relative freedom, and their own careers. Our research also aims, despite the small and carefully selected sample, to offer insights into women's experiences and strategies to overcome social, racial, or economic barriers in Israel and into self-reflections on their achievements. We hope that it will pave the way for future work on Ethiopian–Israeli elites by offering a 'success model' to study this community.

Diverse profiles of Ethiopian–Israeli women

Women of Ethiopian origin in Israel occupy jobs that are often at the bottom of the socio-economic scale. However, increasing numbers of women are also entering new occupations. In our sample, we found different profiles by occupation: business women, women in government and military positions, women in religious affairs and women in performing and visual arts.

Business women

A number of Ethiopian–Israeli women are succeeding in business and entrepreneurship, as in other migration contexts where self-employment and ethnic economy are paths to mobility (Waldinger, Aldrich, and Ward 1990). Some own stores and companies, some travel abroad for import/export and others sell goods through informal economy channels. Several women have opened hairdressing salons (including bridal services) and shops offering Ethiopian products such as food and spices, jewellery, clothing, incense, music, movies, and beauty aids or launched their own cosmetic brand for dark skin. Others developed small-scale enterprises selling traditional Ethiopian handicrafts or have set up and head self-help organizations, such as all-women credit associations (*eqqub* or *qubyé*) functioning in most neighbourhoods (Salamon, Kaplan, and Goldberg 2009). These associations, common in Ethiopia, offer the women economic freedom by granting cash sums used to purchase home appliances or plane tickets to Ethiopia (Anteby-Yemini 2004, 355). For example, Ziva[2] has owned for the past 12 years a hairdressing salon in a busy city in the Centre of Israel.

Women in military and government positions

Ethiopian–Israeli women are quite absent from the political scene, as opposed to the men, even though the first woman of Ethiopian origin was elected in 2013 as Parliament member for the centre-party *Yesh Atid*. However, women have key roles in public leadership, heading, and managing associations (sometimes unrelated to Ethiopian issues), serving on municipal boards, or participating as activists in community politics. Some also hold high positions in the army, the police or in government Ministries, as consul and ambassador abroad for the Foreign Ministry, in state projects for Ethiopian immigrants or as head of a public Israeli radio station. Even though most professionals are still found in the areas of health (nurses, care), social work, and education, there is a growing number of women lawyers, medical students, journalists and academics, a handful holding doctorates. Worke, for example, served in the Israel Defense Forces (IDF) as a high-ranking officer, and Abeba holds a high position in a government office.

Women in religious affairs

Religious women of Ethiopian origin receive even less attention; yet, they have gained recognition in the Orthodox world for their work in conversion classes for new immigrants and for their role as teachers, mediators, and educators in the state religious education system. As such, Tsahay has been actively engaged in religious affairs within her community.

Women artists

This is perhaps the arena where one hears most about successful Ethiopian–Israeli women, since they become prominent in fields such as television, theatre, film, or music. Top models are featured in Israeli and international fashion magazines; actresses and female musicians have gained national recognition, such as the winner of the 2011 TV song contest *Kokhav nolad* (equivalent of 'American idol'); film-makers, painters, and fashion designers are also being acclaimed and in 2013 a woman of Ethiopian origin won the Miss Israel beauty contest. Mulu, for example, is a sculptor, Alamnesh is an actress who appeared in Israeli TV programmes and performs at theatres, and Dvora is a successful singer.

Analysis and discussion of findings

Given these diverse profiles, can one determine the factors leading to socio-economic integration? Are there common characteristics explaining why these women succeeded and others did not? We will discuss some features that may influence these mobility trajectories.

Background and immigration

Five women in our study grew up in rural villages, in Tigray, Woggera, Wolqaït, and Armatcho regions or around Gondar, and their parents were farmers and artisans (fathers were often blacksmiths and mothers potters) with little or no formal education. One woman's (Tsahay) parents had attended school and were literate and only two, Worke and Abeba, came from an urban background (Gondar) where their parents had important positions (army officer, judge) and high socio-economic status.

Many had several siblings (between two and eight), who have also been successful in Israel. Women in these families held important roles, regardless of their urban or rural origin, either because of their education or because of their position. For instance, Mulu's grandmother herself sculpted figurines for tourists; Worke's mother owned a restaurant in Gondar; and Tsahay's mother read books and used to travel alone once a year to visit her sister in Addis-Ababa. These role models could be a determining factor in the women's high aspirations. In this respect, Newman (2007) found that in Ethiopian immigrant women's stories in Israel, mothers appeared not as victims, but as strong and heroic women, offering daughters an informal model of success and resistance, rather than failure. As numerous theories show, girls embrace the model of mothers as powerful, and not powerless (Newman 2007).

Achievements do not appear to be directly linked to the time spent in Israel, since among the women interviewed, some arrived in the 1980s, through Sudan, as young children or adults and others in the 1990s directly from Addis-Ababa. Conditions of migration were different in each case, but demonstrate the women's courage and determination. Abeba recalls:

> I decided in 1971, when I completed school at sixteen, to immigrate alone to Israel. Unfortunately I was denied an exit visa from Ethiopia as well as an entry visa by the Israeli Embassy. In 1984, I tried again, as an invited student to Israel, and this time the Ethiopian government accepted, under the condition I leave my husband and children in Ethiopia. It was a hard decision but I left and two months later they joined me in Israel.

Alamnesh recounts:

> I walked with my father and brothers three weeks to Sudan and arrived in a refugee camp. I saw people who had been waiting there for one year. No food, no life, nothing to do, no school; many died and there were many burials. After six months my father managed to get us out with bribes and I arrived alone in Israel.

Some studies show that second-generation mobility stems from family backing (Belhadj 2006; Santelli 2001). However, the fact that only two women immigrated with their families and the rest alone (though joined by their family later) did not hamper their successful schooling, even when family support was lacking and the separation added an emotional toll to resettlement. For example, Worke's mother sent her at the age of ten to Israel with an aunt with whom she lived. Later, Worke went to an Israeli boarding school.

Education and army experience

Studies have shown that education is the key to social mobility and integration. Among the women in our sample who were of school age in Ethiopia, all were educated in the Gondar area, showing the importance of formal education for these urban and rural girls and their parents. Even though there are no exact data on literacy rates among Ethiopian Jews prior to their migration, it is estimated to have been lower than those of the general Ethiopian population (36 per cent for men and 18 per cent for women in 1994)[3] because most Jews lived in remote villages far from schools. Nonetheless, in our sample, only one, Alamnesh, had not been to school:

> I was born in a small village near Gondar where I looked after the sheep and helped my mother at home. At eight, I was worried because I was not sent to school and I wanted to study. So I taught myself alone to read and write Amharic. My sisters were schooled in Ambober village, where they moved to, and later enrolled at the high school in Gondar.

Others began schooling at a later age, such as Tsahay, who grew up helping her father in the fields and her mother at home and only began school when she was twelve. Mulu took a more artistic path:

I lived with my maternal grandmother, who sculpted figurines in Wolleka. Art attracted me instantly and at ten an American woman taught me ceramics there; at eleven I was teaching others and at twelve I began selling my works to tourists[4]. But I also longed to learn in the Jewish school in the village and began going in the evenings. When I grew up, I left to teach sculpture at a nearby College.

Two women pursued secondary studies in Ethiopia and entered professions, demonstrating that they already belonged to an educated Ethiopian elite. In Israel, the younger women all attended either state religious schools,[5] boarding schools (*pnimiot*) or religious boarding schools for girls (*ulpanot*). Two obtained M.A. degrees from Israeli universities, one received a diploma from a private College, one is pursuing law studies, and another has obtained a Ph.D. Thus, contrary to some researchers' claims, the government did not marginalize all Ethiopian immigrant children by sending them to low-standard religious public schools. In Weil's study (1997), for instance, even though the graduates were schooled in the state religious system, mostly in non-academic tracks, they were pursuing academic studies. The educational trajectories of the women we met show that they sometimes attended prestigious religious institutions where they took general matriculation exams; the government's affirmative action policy enabled others to enrol in pre-academic programmes and enter higher education, as Alamnesh explains:

> When I arrived in Israel, I entered fourth grade in a boarding school, then switched to a religious boarding school for girls. In the meantime my parents arrived in Israel. I began a pre-academic program for Ethiopian immigrants at a large University. I dreamt of becoming a nurse or a social worker but in the end I studied psychology and continued graduate studies in organizational sociology to work in human resources or as a consultant. The pre-academic program was crucial because otherwise I would never have entered university and would not have encountered Israeli society and Israeli students with ambitions.

These examples demonstrate that even the women with limited schooling in Ethiopia attained high academic achievements, through immersing themselves in studies and aspiring to excel. It is also worth noting that today, more women than men of Ethiopian origin study for advanced degrees (Weil 2004). Furthermore, families often encouraged their daughters to study – whether in Ethiopia or Israel – and no woman mentioned her parents' opposition to her pursuing education. In contrast, this still remains an issue among young women of North African origin in France, whose fathers often refuse to let them study in higher education or favour the boys' education over theirs (Lacoste-Dujardin 1992).

Concerning the military, some women were not recruited because they were too old or because their religious schools discouraged it, as one woman claimed:

> If I had remained in the secular boarding school, I would have enrolled in the army; but because I finished high school in a religious school, there was pressure not to enrol, so I went directly to a pre-academic university program.

Others, like Ziva, did enrol in the compulsory two-year service for women, in contrast to her friends:

> I dreamt of enrolling in the army, but most of my friends either married and were exempted, or served in the National Service (*sherut leumi*) for religious girls instead. I decided to go into the

army. I still have good memories of my officer and did not feel any discrimination. I never thought that because I was Ethiopian I could not succeed.

Worke always dreamed of becoming an officer because of her deceased father (who had a high position in the Ethiopian army) and enrolled in a pioneer youth combat unit (*Nahal*), then proceeded to the officers' course which she completed successfully. Dvora's army service brought more than she expected: her acceptance in the military band of the Israeli Air Force paved her success to a musical profession. The army did help some future careers, as Shabtay (1999) found for male soldiers of Ethiopian origin. In other studies, however, few girls served in the IDF in the 1980s and 1990s, confirming that women soldiers were then still pioneering figures in the community.

Career, marriage, and motherhood

Making professional choices and beginning careers can be challenging and each of the women made decisions at different points in her life to pursue her ambitions. Ziva, who was studying accounting, switched to hairdressing when she was offered a job at a hair salon and sent for training to Dallas. She later opened her own hair salon and worked the first year until midnight every day. She is now a certified representative of an Afro-American brand of hair products and travels every year to the USA. She works with her sister, who also went for training to the USA. Her shop caters to black and white men and women who come for braids, dreadlocks, hair extensions, colouring, straightening, or to purchase beauty products (for black skin and hair). Ziva imports from the USA, England, and Ethiopia.

Tsahay, a mother of seven, also developed a new career. She began studying childcare in a high-ranking College when she arrived in Israel. She then moved to the South with her husband and worked in a factory, sometimes night shifts. Now she has recently become a religious educator for the government to teach Judaism in adult conversion programmes;[6] she also prepares young girls of the Ethiopian community for their *bat mitzvah*, is a counsellor for brides (*madricha kalot*), and also holds a diploma of ritual bath supervisor (*balanit*).[7] Tsahay feels that she is now fulfilling everything she dreamt of.

Worke, after a short career in the army, decided to study law at a prestigious college. She also presents Amharic programmes on Israeli public TV and on the Israeli–Ethiopian cable channel (ETV) and dreams of working in a government office or in the media. Dvora, after singing in the military band, began acting at national theatres, hosted a TV show and accompanied Israeli singers. She now performs for a children's theatre and has just released her first solo album. Alamnesh also switched to acting during her second year at university when she was accepted for a TV show audition. When she also got a part at a national theatre, she began taking private acting lessons to enhance her skills for a new career. Since, she has appeared in Israeli TV programmes for children, a series, and a reality show and also performs at theatres.

Mulu, mother of five, began sculpting again, when she lived in a mobile-home site after immigrating to Israel. 'One day, my daughter brought "play-dough" from the day-care and I made figurines that I sent back with her. That same evening five teachers came to visit and brought me clay'. Mulu began teaching sculpture at the site's community centre. She has now gained popularity among a circle of non-Ethiopians as a sculptor of small figurines recalling life in Ethiopia. Working mainly through associations to promote Ethiopian arts and crafts, she exhibits once a year at a popular venue. However, Mulu is frustrated working at home: 'Even if Israelis tell me I am a great artist, I have no publicity. I don't live in the right place for an artist'. Indeed, in her small apartment, in an overwhelmingly 'Ethiopian' neighbourhood in a town in the North, she does not feel she has sufficiently developed her career and wishes she could work in a studio and teach sculpting. As for Abeba, she succeeded in pursuing the career she began in Ethiopia (in social work), despite difficulties in her professional recognition in Israel and harsh conditions in the absorption centre upon immigrating. She now holds a high government position and claims: 'Despite the negative experiences, I never regretted coming to Israel'.

The women in our study are all married, two with non-Ethiopian Israelis; five were mothers and one a grandmother. None had an arranged marriage (even if this was the norm in Ethiopia), thus already suggesting changes among educated women in the Gondar area. However, being a single young woman was often challenged in Ethiopia, as Abeba recalls:

> I was the eldest of my family and the only daughter to study. I remember people asking all the time why I wasn't married yet and my father used to answer: 'I want her to be a horn and not a tail'. He always educated me to be a leader ... So I followed my father's advice and began studying.

Others contested their position in society, such as Alamnesh who refused to marry at 15.

Furthermore, all the women met their husbands on their own initiative, during their studies at university (Abeba, Tsahay) or at parties and social gatherings. This contrasts, for example, with French women of North African origin, whose families often still arrange their weddings or oppose marriage with non-Muslims (Lacoste-Dujardin 1992). Many remain single because they refuse both a traditional wedding and transgressing the exogamic taboo (Belhadj 2006). In addition, age at marriage is relatively late in our sample, at the end of the 20s, following studies and sometimes after securing careers, a trend also observed among educated non-Jewish Ethiopian women in USA and Europe (Abye 2004). If planned parenthood is widely practised, it is relevant that the one religiously observant woman has also the most children (seven), replicating fertility behaviours of Orthodox Israelis.

A few women interviewed claim that husbands of Ethiopian origin did not always understand their professional ambitions and preferred they spend more time at home, whereas others emphasized that their Ethiopian–Israeli husbands were the ones to support their work and career and help with childcare. When Abeba was accepted at University for graduate studies in Israel, her Ethiopian-born husband quit his job to care for their children while she went to study. Tsahay, a mother of seven, explains how her husband, who immigrated from Ethiopia before she did, supports her endeavours and helps with domestic chores: 'That's why I succeed'. On the whole, we did not find major differences in the narratives in the way gender roles were acted out between those who married men in Ethiopia, Ethiopian–Israelis in Israel and non-Ethiopian Israelis, even though some conflicts were no doubt left unmentioned.

As for juggling married life, motherhood and a career, some women admitted that it was harder to succeed, but did not consider marriage or children as an obstacle to advancement. They explained that those who do not succeed lack self-confidence and cannot conceive of work and a career after marriage. They believed that women of

Ethiopian origin are more courageous, more powerful, adapt quicker and succeed better than the men – even with the responsibilities of bringing up a family. Almost all claimed that excellence was their key to success; as one woman put it: 'I knew I had to be the best and could not count on anyone'.

If the women interviewed may represent radical changes compared to Ethiopian models of gender roles and women's status – because they achieved economic independence and careers, freely chose their husband, and often raised a family – we also learn from their life stories that such patterns existed in Ethiopia among women perceived as role models, be it grandmothers, mothers, sisters, or aunts.

Integration, culture, and identity

Among the women interviewed, most live in large cities or suburbs in the Centre of Israel, one in a development town in the South and one in a small city in the North. They all maintain intensive contacts with non-Ethiopian Israelis and many identify themselves first and foremost as 'Israeli women'. This is most clearly reflected through their lifestyles.

Almost all of the women dress in a secular Israeli fashion and one owns a dog – an uncommon pet in Ethiopian culture, but pointing to the adoption of Israeli norms. Many use products to uncurl, straighten or dye their hair, while others prefer to keep Ethiopian-style braids or wear colourful head clothes. Only Mulu still wears the Ethiopian white shawl (*natalla*) and long skirt that most older women wear. Tsahay's dress code denotes observant Judaism (long sleeves, long skirt, headscarf) and represents the minority of Ethiopian-Israelis who have integrated in Orthodox communities, speaking accordingly (using expressions such as 'Blessed Be God', 'with the help of God'), and schooling their children in the Orthodox education system.

However, most of the women schooled in religious schools drifted towards secular culture; Abeba even refused to send her children to a religious school in Israel and Dvora claimed that she left observant Judaism. This parallels Weil's (1997) observation: almost all her respondents defined themselves as traditional or religious, yet seem to have become more secular since leaving religious schools.

Despite the fact that some women retain a distinctive Ethiopian accent, they are all fluent in Hebrew and have acquired it often far better than other immigrant women (from the FSU, USA, or France). One can argue that mastering Hebrew is also a device to express their Israeliness vis-à-vis Russian speakers or African foreign workers (Anteby-Yemini 2004). Concurrently, Amharic is maintained through various media (magazine, radio, TV, music, movies, and internet) and events (concerts, plays). At least two women speak to their children in Amharic and teach them literacy in this language: Tsahay insists on teaching her seven children to read Amharic and use computer games to learn the language and Mulu's five children all speak Amharic and learn to write it through computer programmes. Thus, Amharic still plays an important role in these women's lives and is, in some families, transmitted to the next generation. Only for Dvora, is Hebrew the one vernacular she identifies with:

> The words of my songs are in Hebrew because that's the language we spoke at home and it's the most natural for me. I don't speak Tigrinya well (her parents' language), even if I understand it. I identify most with Hebrew.

The women were also influenced by globalization, and in particular by black global culture – through music genres or beauty models – as well as by transnational ties to Ethiopia or the USA (Anteby-Yemini 2005). For example, Ziva's hair salon conveys an eclectic style of Afro-American and Ethiopian cultures, from the colours of the storefront – identical to the Ethiopian flag – to the artefacts from Ethiopia on the walls, the Amharic-written products in the windows and the posters of Afro-American hairdressing models. These cultural flows are conveyed through the media, kin relations and high international mobility, since nearly all the women have travelled – to the USA, Europe, or Ethiopia – for professional or medical purposes, leisure or family visits, creating transnational networks.

For most of these women, links to Ethiopia remain strong and Ethiopian ethnicity plays an important function. Only two have Israeli first names; the others kept their Amharic ones, in spite of the State's practice of giving Hebrew names to new immigrants. More than half have been back to Ethiopia at least once. Many complained about the conditions, while others, usually the 1.5 generation, felt that they were not 'at home' there and became more conscious of their Israeliness. Travelling back to Ethiopia also offered the women novel constructions of race, class, centre/periphery relations, and nationality, as has been observed regarding migrants elsewhere (Glick Schiller, Basch, and Blanc-Szanton 1992). Ziva, for instance, has returned to Ethiopia twice, but explains: 'It's hard for me there, with the mentality ... I am spoiled. I need luxury and my comfort there ... ' Mulu has travelled to Ethiopia twice, mainly for health problems, and to the USA to visit one of her sisters who became a dentist there. Dvora has never been to Ethiopia:

> I'm very spoiled and I don't know how I would manage there ... I feel part of the Ethiopian community, but I don't have ties to Ethiopian culture; I feel completely Israeli. In fact, most of my friends are non-Ethiopian ... My songs are mainly influenced by Israeli music and culture. It's not because I'm of Ethiopian origin that I have to perform Ethiopian music!

Discrimination and activism

Some women brought up the topic of discrimination and claimed that they encountered outright racism, particularly in the religious sphere. One woman in a high government position even considered leaving Israel because of daily prejudices she felt were detrimental to her and her children. Mulu experienced injustice differently when she recalled that she used to sell her sculptures to Israeli stores but, because they took advantage of her as an Ethiopian immigrant, she stopped working with them. Abeba recounted how she experienced discriminatory treatment from Israeli academic institutions and went through long ordeals before being accepted for graduate studies. Tsahay stressed the racist attitudes of the ritual bath supervisors; instead of accepting racism, she resisted local discrimination by initiating national links with a non-Ethiopian–Israeli forum of religious-feminist women:

> It all began when the ritual bath supervisors didn't want to let us in because they didn't consider Ethiopian women as real Jews. So I approached an Israeli women's organization and a lot of noise was made about this affair. They supported me.

Tsahay wishes to fortify, through religious education, Ethiopian–Israeli youth, whom she thinks are not strong enough to face insults or discrimination. 'You need strength, even if it's hard'. Alamnesh observes: 'I feel discrimination when I am not invited to all auditions because I am black; I would like to go to auditions like anyone else' … In the performing arts, skin colour still determines casting and both women in this field felt discriminated when they were auditioned for 'Ethiopian roles' only. To come to terms with this, one of them is working on a script *without* specific parts for Ethiopians and is acting in a play any Israeli could perform. However, despite reports of discrimination against Ethiopian–Israeli professionals who are not hired or promoted because of their skin colour, the women's narratives did not specifically perceive racial identity as an obstacle to their advancement – except in acting – and did not consider that this played an important role in their career trajectories. Dvora goes so far as to jokingly argue, 'I don't even remember I'm Ethiopian!', explaining that she never saw her skin colour as an issue nor felt discriminated against. It has also been found that race does not hold an important place in the narratives of women of North African origin in France (Lacoste-Dujardin 1992) or of Ethiopian origin in USA and Europe (Abye 2004). Other studies, however, show that working-class Ethiopian–Israelis de-emphasize racial identity, whereas the middle class uses black global identity models (Mizrachi and Zawdu 2012) and suggest that upwardly mobile Ethiopian–Israelis feel the most racist attitudes towards them (Amit 2012), often because they continue to be seen as 'Ethiopians' by others (Walsh and Yonas 2012).

It is perhaps in the sphere of activism that the women most strongly affirm their citizenship and belonging as Israelis. By being active in associations, NGO's or government-sponsored programmes, they participate in civil society, especially concerning social issues such as education. Tsahay, who volunteers in her community to prevent domestic violence, and other women activists, with a feminist aim at empowerment, try linking discourses on feminism, religion, and racism; however, they do not call upon a radical feminist agenda nor do they draw on black feminist claims. In fact, few women of Ethiopian origin belong to feminist organizations or *Mizrahi* women's groups, which propose to represent 'women of color' in Israel, thus suggesting weak ties between Ethiopian–Israelis and feminist movements.[8]

Most women felt, nonetheless, that they were utilizing their knowledge and experience in their community, by being engaged with the youth in awareness projects, by conveying social messages and taking responsibility, such as writing in Israeli newspapers about spouse murder or performing for underprivileged audiences. Worke, for example, while studying in law school, leads a pre-army project to locate outstanding candidates of Ethiopian origin in high schools and accompany them through pre-academic preparation. 'With this project, I feel for the first time that I'm responsible for a revolution in the Ethiopian community. I think education is the most important thing'. Many are optimistic regarding the next generation and believe that young women can more easily succeed today, because they speak fluent Hebrew, already have role models and are aware of possibilities to fulfil their ambitions. Some women argued that despite difficulties stemming from ongoing lack of self-esteem and internalized self-limitation as a racialized group, as also found in other migrant contexts (Guenif Souilamas 2000), young girls in Israel now have the means to overcome these barriers. One woman explains:

> As a woman, I believe I can influence my community since many Ethiopian-Israeli women think they cannot succeed because they hold an idea of what women are expected to do. They only see marriage and that's it; for them, work means making concessions, giving up. The real problem is lack of self-confidence among the community's women, even those who grew up in Israel.

Another woman concluded: 'I knew that if I succeeded, people would look up to me'.

To cope with this, the social role of upwardly mobile women in the Ethiopian community is crucial, just as successful women of North African origin in France geared their work to their community and its youth for a similar goal (Belhadj 2006; Lacoste-Dujardin 1992). As such, Tsahay has created her own association for Ethiopian–Israeli women and also volunteers to organize activities in the Ethiopian synagogue of her town.

If affirmative action was not mentioned in most life stories, this policy did offer, to some extent, opportunities to enter higher education or advance in the military. Being a woman of Ethiopian origin was seen by some women as an asset and may explain why only two felt that race can hinder their chances to succeed. Dvora, for instance, thinks that it is easier to succeed as an exotic, good-looking Ethiopian woman than a man:

> It's because of fear of what people will think that some Ethiopian children fail; many are simply afraid; I believe success comes from the will to succeed and if someone does not think of herself as marginal, she will not be perceived and categorized as such ... I remember that as a little girl, I knew I wanted to have a career ... The environment is very important.

Two of her sisters have become musicians as well. Worke, on the other hand, does not think that her success is closely linked to being a woman of Ethiopian origin:

> It's more my past that pushed me forth. In the army, I was pushed ahead because I was an Ethiopian woman but you must also be excellent in your field. And it's more because of that that I succeeded.

Concluding remarks

Despite our limited sample, this article intends to shed light on integration and mobility processes of Ethiopian–Israeli women. The women we interviewed developed careers in spite of their rural background, low socio-economic status, lack of education in Ethiopia, or religious schooling in Israel. If integration is often determined by migrants' human and social capital, particularly education, professional experience, proficiency in the host language and social networks (Portes 1994; Rumbaut 1994), it is interesting to learn from the women's narratives what coping mechanisms and strategies they used to advance professionally. For example, cultural capital, such as Ethiopian values (respect for elders and authority, self-discipline, importance of education) was a resource, as for other migrants (Zhou 1997). Yet, the women's high aspirations, determination, and agency appear to have mostly shaped their mobility – factors that are often downplayed in migration research, but match the findings of Walsh and Yonas (2012) on Ethiopian women in Israel.

Race and gender may also affect advancement, by negative or positive discrimination. In our examples, few felt that because they were women of Ethiopian origin they could not succeed; some even believed that being an 'Ethiopian woman' is an advantage. In their narratives, racial identity did not frame their main experiences. Articulating gender and race with class is relevant too, since these women may not consider racial identity as an obstacle precisely because they are not working class. As black feminists have noted, 'social class differences among Afro-American women influence how racism is experienced' (Hill-Collins 2000). Thus, social constructions of race may differ for marginalized and upwardly mobile Ethiopian–Israeli women. Despite the fact that some did mention discrimination or resented being labelled 'Ethiopian women', many have succeeded outside of their own community and strive to become plain 'Israelis' ...

But if these women achieved social, cultural, linguistic, and economic integration, have they become for that matter Israeli women? They speak fluent Hebrew, live in non-Ethiopian neighbourhoods (except for two) and their self-presentation emphasizes Israeli identity, while globalized black models and Ethiopian ethnicity attest to complex identities. Patterns range from displaying an Ethiopian identity (Mulu), a hybrid bi-cultural Ethiopian–Israeli identity (Ziva and most of the others) to a sole Israeli identity (Dvora) where Ethiopianness appears as an 'optional ethnicity'. Similarly, Walsh and Yonas (2012) found that the integration of Ethiopian and Israeli identities accounted for the success of Ethiopian women they studied, and research on the 1.5 generation of upwardly mobile Russian–Israelis shows prevalence of hyphenated identities and a minority of 'regular Israeli' or 'Russian' identity models (Remennick 2003). Interestingly enough, the women rarely used Ethiopianness or blackness as an expression of identity politics, as opposed to youth of Ethiopian origin in Israel (Anteby-Yemini 2005; Ben-Eliezer 2004; Shabtay 2001). Furthermore, they do not consume mainly ethnic-based products (in contrast to older Ethiopian–Israelis) and ethnicity is performed through community involvement and linguistic maintenance. In contrast, among educated non-Jewish Ethiopians in France and the USA, loss of Amharic and lack of investment in teaching it to children were salient (Abye 2004, 348). Our observations, however, suggest different trends from former studies, where educated women of Ethiopian origin still lived in 'Ethiopian' neighbourhoods and led a segregated life, including restricted contact with non-Ethiopians and endogamous marriages (Weil 1997).

Recent studies argue that gender can explain higher attainment; yet, traditional role expectations in migrant families often complicate mobility (Donato et al. 2006). Upwardly mobile French women of North African origin still struggle to gain access to education and choice of spouse (Belhadj 2006; Lacoste-Dujardin 1992) and *Mizrahi* men in Israel fare better than women, partly because of compromises to maintain traditional family roles (Raijman and Semyonov 1997). In this respect, Ethiopian families have accepted, albeit reluctantly, Israeli secular patterns and seldom oppose girls' education, entrance in labour market, marriage plans or army recruitment (see also Walsh and Yonas 2012). The price is often paid by the men, whose status declined while the women's careers have not prevented them from marrying, raising children, and remaining connected to their community. In fact, Ethiopian–Israeli women are increasingly empowered and seem to have gained from migration more than men (Shabtay and Kacen 2005; Weil 2004).

Within the limitations of this preliminary overview, it is difficult to reach broad conclusions. However, the Ethiopian–Israeli women profiled in our study point to mobility trends diverging from common stigma of social, cultural, and economic marginalization and outline alternative integration models than those, predicted by some researchers, of segregation (Elias and Kemp 2010; Kimmerling 2001) and 'racially based stratification' (Offer 2007). As these women negotiate their Ethiopian, Jewish, Israeli, and female identities, they offer another reading of the intersectionality of race, class, and gender that might differ from that of men. They also show specific ways of constructing national belonging, citizenship, and ethnic identity as they consider Israel their 'home' and Ethiopia a diaspora. Finally, they attest to the emergence of Ethiopian–Israeli upwardly mobile women who should become the focus of a new area of academic studies that will also contribute to broader issues of gender, socio-economic mobility, and transnationalism in Ethiopian diasporas elsewhere.

Acknowledgements

We wish to thank all the women who were willing to share their life stories with us, as well as the anonymous reviewers and Fassil Demissie for their comments and Prof. Joan Roland for her careful reading of the manuscript.

Disclosure statement

No potential conflict of interest was reported by the authors.

Notes

1. Israeli Central Bureau of Statistics, Jerusalem, 19 November 2014 report on Ethiopian–Israelis.
2. All names have been changed.
3. UN data sheet for Ethiopia.
4. Figurines began to be made in the 1960s by Ethiopian Jewish women in Wolleka cf. Kaplan and Rosen (1996).
5. The Israeli education system consists of three networks: the state, the state religious, and the Ultra-Orthodox. Until 1995, Ethiopian immigrant children were systematically schooled in the state religious sector.
6. Ethiopian immigrants currently arriving to Israel are Falashmoras, a group that converted to Christianity several decades ago. They enter Israel through family reunification, according to the Law of Entry, and undergo a shortened conversion to be recognized as full-fledged Jews. See Seeman (2009).
7. Jewish observant women immerse in a ritual bath, the *mikveh*, after menstruation, to resume sexual relations with their husband; a supervisor (*balanit*) checks that they carry out the immersion properly.
8. On *Mizrahi* feminism, see Motzafi-Haller (2001).

References

Abye, T. 2004. *Parcours d'Ethiopiens en France et aux Etats-Unis: de nouvelles formes de migration*. Paris: L'Harmattan.
Amit, K. 2012. "Social Integration and Identity of Immigrants from Western countries, the FSU and Ethiopia in Israel." *Ethnic and Racial Studies* 35 (7): 1287–1310.
Anteby-Yemini, L. 2004. *Les paradoxes du paradis: les juifs éthiopiens en Israël*. Paris: CNRS Editions.
Anteby-Yemini, L. 2005. "From Ethiopian Villager to Global Villager: Ethiopian Jews in Israel." In *Homelands and Diasporas: Holy Lands and Other Places*, edited by A. Levy and A. Weingrod, 220–244. Stanford: Stanford University Press.
Ben-Eliezer, U. 2004. "Becoming a Black Jew: Cultural Racism and Anti-Racism in Contemporary Israel." *Social Identities* 10 (2): 245–266.
Belhadj, M. 2006. *La conquête de l'autonomie: histoire de Françaises descendantes de migrants algériens*. Paris: Editions de l'Atelier.
Donato, K., D. Gabaccia, J. Holdaway, M. Manalansan IV, and P. Pessar. 2006. "A Glass Half-Full? Gender in Migration Studies." *International Migration Review* 40 (1): 3–26.
Elias, N., and A. Kemp. 2010. "The New Second Generation: Non-Jewish Olim, Black Jews and Children of Migrant Workers in Israel." *Israel Studies* 15 (1): 73–94.

Glick Schiller, N., L. Basch, and C. Blanc-Szanton. 1992. *Towards a Transnational Perspective on Migration: Race, Class, Ethnicity and Nationalism Reconsidered*, Vol. 645. New York, NY: Annals of the New York Academy of Science.

Guenif Souilamas, N. 2000. *Des "beurettes" aux descendantes d'immigrants nord-africains.* Paris: Grasset/Le Monde.

Herrera, G. 2013. "Gender and International Migration: Contributions and Cross-Fertilizations." *Annual Review of Sociology* 39: 471–489.

Hill-Collins, P. 2000. *Black Feminist Thought: Knowledge, Consciousness and the Politics of Empowerment.* New York, NY: Routledge.

Kaplan, S. 2005. "Tama Galut Etiopiya: The Ethiopian Exile Is Over." *Diaspora* 14 (2/3): 381–396.

Kaplan, S. 2010. "Ethiopian Immigrants in the United States and Israel: A Preliminary Comparison." *International Journal of Ethiopian Studies* 5 (1): 71–92.

Kaplan, S., and H. Rosen. 1996. "Created in their Own Image: A Comment on Beta Israel Figurines." *Cahiers d'Etudes Africaines* 36 (141): 171–182.

Kaplan, S., and H. Salamon. 2004. "Ethiopian Jews in Israel: A Part of the People or Apart from the People?" In *Jews in Israel: Contemporary Social and Cultural Patterns*, edited by U. Rebhun and C. Waxman, 118–148. Hanover: Brandeis University Press.

Kimmerling, B. 2001. *The Invention and Decline of Israeliness.* Berkeley: University of California Press.

Lacoste-Dujardin, C. 1992. *Yasmina et les autres: filles de parents maghrébins en France.* Paris: Editions la Découverte.

Leitman, E. 1995. "Migration and Transitions: Three Generations of Ethiopian Women." In *Between Africa and Zion, Proceedings of the First International Congress of the Society for the Study of Ethiopian Jewry*, edited by S. Kaplan, T. Parfitt, and E. Trevisan Semi, 166–178. Jerusalem: Ben Zvi Institute.

Mizrachi, N., and A. Zawdu. 2012. "Between Global Racial and Bounded Identity: Choice of Destigmatization Strategies among Ethiopian Jews in Israel." *Ethnic and Racial Studies* 35 (3): 436–452.

Motzafi-Haller, P. 2001. "Scholarship, Identity and Power: Mizrahi Women in Israel." *Signs* 26 (3): 697–734.

Newman, R. 2007. "La survie dite par les femmes: récits de mères et filles juives d'Ethiopie." In *Les juifs d'Ethiopie: de Joseph Halévy à nos jours*, edited by D. Friedmann, 193–210. Paris: Editions du Nadir.

Offer, S. 2007. "The Ethiopian Community in Israel: Segregation and the Creation of a Racial Cleavage." *Ethnic and Racial Studies* 30 (3): 461–480.

Phillips Davids, J. 1998. "Fertility Decline and Changes in the Life-Course among Ethiopian Jewish Women." In *The Beta Israel in Ethiopia and Israel: Studies on the Ethiopian Jews*, edited by T. Parfitt and E. Trevisan Semi, 137–159. Richmond: Curzon Press.

Portes, A. 1994. "Introduction." *International Migration Review* 28 (4): 632–639.

Raijman, R., and M. Semyonov. 1997. "Gender, Ethnicity and Immigration: Double and Triple Disadvantage among Recent Immigrant Women in the Israeli Labor Market." *Gender and Society* 11 (1): 108–125.

Remennick, L. 2003. "The 1.5 Generation of Russian Immigrants in Israel: Between Integration and Socio-Cultural Retention." *Diaspora* 12 (1): 39–66.

Rumbaut, R. 1994. "The Crucible Within: Ethnic Identity, Self-Esteem and Segmented Assimilation among Children of Immigrants." *International Migration Review* 28 (4): 748–794.

Salamon, H., S. Kaplan, and H. Goldberg. 2009. "What Goes Around, Comes Around: Rotating Credit Associations among Ethiopian Women in Israel." *African Identities* 7 (3): 399–415.

Santelli, E. 2001. *La mobilité sociale dans l'immigration: itinéraires de réussite des enfants d'origine algérienne.* Toulouse: Presses Universitaires de Toulouse.

Seeman, D. 2009. *One People, One Blood: Ethiopian-Israelis and the Return to Judaism.* New Brunswick: Rutgers University Press.

Shabtay, M. 1999. *Best Brother: The Identity Journey of Ethiopian Immigrant Soldiers.* Tel-Aviv: Tcherikover (Hebrew).

Shabtay, M. 2001. *Between Reggae and Rap: The Integration Challenge of Ethiopian Youth in Israel*. Tel Aviv: Tcherikover (Hebrew).

Shabtay, M., and L. Kacen, eds. 2005. *Mulualem: Women and Girls of Ethiopian Origin in Spaces, Worlds and Journeys Between Cultures*. Tel-Aviv: Lashon Tzaha (Hebrew).

Waldinger, R., H. Aldrich, and R. Ward, eds. 1990. *Ethnic Entrepreneurs: Immigrant Business in Industrial Society*. Newbury Park: Sage.

Walsh, S., and A. Yonas. 2012. "Connected to my Roots but Moving Onwards: successful Ethiopian Women in Israel." *Society and Welfare* 32 (3): 317–346 (in Hebrew).

Weil, S. 1997. *Graduates of Ethiopian Origin of the Education System in Israel 1987-89: Past, Present, Future*. Jerusalem: Institute for Innovation in Education, Hebrew University (Hebrew).

Weil, S. 2004. "Ethiopian Jewish Women: Trends and Transformations in the Context of Transnational Change." *Nashim* (8): 73–86.

Zhou, M. 1997. "Segmented Assimilation: Issues, Controversies, and Recent Research on the New Second Generation." *International Migration Review* 31 (4): 975–1008.

Bole to Harlem via Tel Aviv: networks of Ethiopia's musical diaspora[†]

Ilana Webster-Kogen

School of African and Oriental Studies, University of London, London, UK

ABSTRACT

One of the fastest growing sources of domestic labor in the Global North is Ethiopia, whose female population travels to North America, Europe, and the developed Middle East to work for remittances to send home. Once these migrants settle in cities such as London, Abu Dhabi, Tel Aviv, Rome, or Toronto, they organize themselves into cultural enclaves that navigate their positionality, namely the state, religious practice, and their bodies. While scholars are occasionally interested in the explicit security ramifications of absorbing these migrant workforces, they pay less attention to the cultural forces propelling citizenship, and to migrants' relationship with their home culture. This gap in knowledge is counterproductive, because scholars and policy-makers will have trouble assessing the Ethiopian migrant population's perspective through interview material alone. The Ethiopian values of honor and respect for authority dictate a hesitance to criticize explicitly, so the population's feelings about marginality rarely emerge in discussion about labor. This taboo curtails the effectiveness of typical ethnographic methods (e.g. interviewing). Rather, this article examines Ethiopian music as a prism through which migrant musicians navigate the complex web of religious, ethnic, national, and embodied identities in their new surroundings. In this article, I present findings based on participant-observation of Ethiopian live music in North American and Middle Eastern diaspora cities (New York, Washington, DC, Tel Aviv, and Dubai), and argue that the populations are linked through the multidirectional cultural influences of Ethiopian diasporic popular music. I will argue that Ethiopian migrants' music offers a stable, alternative form of political discussion to more overt discussions of contested identities, and that these discussions reshape cultural boundaries. By considering performance techniques such as choice of language for lyrics, and the incorporation of Ethiopian or local dance style into music videos that are distributed over the Internet, one begins to understand how the rapidly expanding transnational network of Ethiopian migrants conceptualizes itself as an emerging global source of labor in cosmopolitan urban centers.

[†]Bole2Harlem, whom I implicitly reference here, was a band of Ethiopian-American musicians in New York, who disbanded in 2008 after bandleader Tigist Shibabew died suddenly. The band's syncretic style foreshadowed many of the stylistic musical pairings I discuss in this article.

Introduction: Ethiopians moving across worlds

Returning from a research trip to Addis Ababa in April 2013, I spent a long evening in the departures terminal of Bole airport. I waited in terminal 1, which serves non-African destinations. Expecting to see London, Rome, Washington, Tel Aviv, and Toronto on the departures board, cities that dominate academic and media characterizations of the Ethiopian diaspora, I found geographic homogeneity: Kuwait City, Riyadh, Dubai, and Doha. The list went on, with multiple nightly flights to Jeddah, and Abu Dhabi flights departing more frequently than all of the Europe-bound flights combined. All told, more than half of the departures from Addis Ababa in the international terminal went to the Persian Gulf, which at just a few hours away, is neither a travel hub nor a stop-off point for most of these passengers.

After researching the music of one Ethiopian micro-diaspora for several years, I saw a vastly different visual image of Ethiopia's 'age of migration' (Castles and Miller 2008) unfolding before me at Bole. Long lines of almost-entirely young female travelers to Jeddah were en route to their new jobs in domestic labor (see Fernandez 2010, as well as De Regt 2010 for discussion of the precarious conditions for Ethiopian female laborers in the Gulf).[1] Supplemented by a male labor force of security guards, the Ethiopian population in the UAE alone is over 100,000, although it receives little attention since Ethiopians are far outnumbered by South and Southeast Asian migrants. And yet, the cultural dynamics of this increasing population of mostly-female labor migrants offers a fascinating counterexample to my own work on music and migration in which researchers conceptualize migrants as 'bifocal' (Vertovec 2007, 150), or keeping one eye on home and another on host culture. Rather, this rising force of labor migrants represents a series of arrows pointing to multi-sited and often seemingly disconnected new diasporic peripheries, with cultural endeavors like music demonstrating the degree to which migrants can live both 'there' and 'here'.

Scholars have examined the Ethiopian micro-diasporas of Washington (Shelemay 2009), Tel Aviv (Herman 2012), Toronto (Danso 2002), London (Palmer 2012), and Seattle (Chait 2011; Scott and Getahun 2013) in the context of their host societies, but the literature is missing a sense of how these micro-diasporas fit together (efforts being addressed for the first time by Kaplan 2010). My research thus examines the intersections of overlapping subjectivities of religion, politics, and citizenship among Ethiopian musicians across the transnational network, with a focus on the sometimes-harsh distinctions between labor migration and the establishment of diasporas. The rising presence of Ethiopians in the Gulf makes apparent that current paradigms of researching diaspora do not account for the Ethiopian experience, not least because these migrants are not citizens and they are not subject to the integrating forces of the nation-state (see Lyons in Mandaville and Lyons 2012). In particular, the concept of bifocality (Vertovec 2007) fails to acknowledge the splintering of migrant families, and the hierarchical geopolitical circumstances that send individuals to one place or another, all of which makes people look across and virtually instead of in straight lines.

Moreover, such scholars as Madrid (2012) and Rommen (2011) have argued effectively that musical redefinitions of migratory and diasporic spaces offer a richer understanding of human encounters and movements, particularly with redefining relationships with home culture. Therefore, my research argues that mapping the Ethiopian soundscape on the ground offers an explanation of the directionality of cultural influence, and an in-depth exploration, following the work of Getahun (2006) of where certain migrants go, how they live when they get there, and which other populations they are in contact with. While the logistics of life for a domestic worker in Beirut might differ vastly from those of an Eritrean asylum seeker in Rome, or a professional in Los Angeles, their musical song texts might invoke the same narratives of mobility and distance for all three. And while my research encompasses the contrasting positionalities of citizens, expatriates, labor migrants, and refugees (see Braziel 2008a or Clifford 1997), this article focuses on the circuitous route of mostly-female singers on the diasporic tour scene. I will highlight some striking points of confluence between their repertoires, as a sort of musical counterpart to the new multidirectional migration map on display at Bole airport.

Intrigued as I was by the Bole departures board, I was surprised by the ubiquitous evidence of multidirectional Ethiopian migration flows (see Cohen 2008) as I traveled across the diaspora through 2014. From Dubai to Rome to Harlem, I observed the erosion of borders between musical styles, musicians in each case occupying the overlapping spaces that home and host society share. In this article, I describe a series of concerts I attended in 2014 that illustrate the consolidation of the Ethiopian diaspora into a set of interdependent migrant enclaves, and how musicians are participating in a 'transnational remapping' (Braziel 2008b, 5) of Ethiopian cultural boundaries.

First, I will examine a concert in New York City by Ester Rada, an Ethiopian-Israeli soul singer (see Parfitt and Semi 1999 or Seeman 2009 for discussion of the terminology applied to Ethiopians of Jewish lineage and Israelis of Ethiopian lineage). In describing Rada's performance, I contend that she draws from the musical style and cultural geography of the Black Atlantic, effectively singing in code about the Ethiopian experience in 'white' societies. Then, I will describe preeminent singer Aster Aweke's first concert in Tel Aviv in May, and the arrival in Jerusalem of ambassadors of the groundbreaking *Ethiopiques* CD series. In the process, I will argue that Ethiopian-Israelis reconnect with the Ethiopian diaspora through an imagined, embedded historical connection with Jerusalem. Third, I will focus on Wayna Wondwossen's summer 2014 tour promoting her most recent album, arguing that she navigates multiple subject positions (Ethiopian, Ethiopian-American, African-American) through her musical style. I would not discuss hip hop in this article, both because its mobilizing power is explained in-depth elsewhere (see Charry 2012) and because Ethiopians enjoy extra international credibility in soul and reggae thanks to the Rastafari attention on Ethiopia. As such, although hip hop deserves attention for its contribution to contemporary wax and gold literary themes (see Levine 1965 and Webster-Kogen 2011), the Ethiopian imprint on soul and reggae is more prominent than it is in the global hip hop scene. Throughout my analysis, I will argue that these multidirectional musical influences track the movements of people according to the constantly shifting status of Ethiopians across their host societies, and that musicians actively reshape cultural boundaries on behalf of displaced populations.

Ester Rada: connecting the Atlantic

One irony of the commercial success of soul singer Ester Rada is that her international breakthrough escaped the notice of Ethiopian music enthusiasts. Her first major international platform was neither Womex (the 'World Music' expo where she performed in

November 2014) nor the Festival of a Thousand Stars in Arba Minch (southern Ethiopia), but at the popular Glastonbury Festival in the UK in 2013. Indeed, the audience could have been forgiven for not recognizing her as Ethiopian-Israeli, since she has taken substantial steps to portray herself as generically Afrodiasporic. Yet this Ethiopian singer who was born to religious parents in a controversial Jewish settlement in the West Bank has earned deserved acclaim back in Tel Aviv among bohemian secular elites, since she has crossed over to the pop industry by eliminating any performative shibboleth of Israeliness that might limit her rise on the soul scene. In my discussion of Ester Rada's work, I will argue that an Ethiopian-Israeli musician has drawn successfully from a set of Afrodiasporic musical styles, and in the process, initiated a career on a transnational soul scene that would be inaccessible to the more socially privileged (non-Ethiopian) Israelis whom she would count among her cohort in a national performance context. Despite an early life peppered with discrimination as an Ethiopian in Israel well documented in interviews in the popular media, and a pro-reconciliation/anti-occupation political agenda, Rada has capitalized on an ambiguous ethnic performative self, and garnered acclaim across North America and Europe.

Critics describe Rada's music as 'Ethio-soul',[2] or a contemporary pop style influenced by Aretha Franklin and Nina Simone. She draws occasionally from Ethiopian source material, and particularly from Ethiojazz standards from the Addis Ababa of the 1970s (see Falceto 2002). Apart from these occasional songs in Amharic, her lyrics are written entirely in English, and even in concert in Tel Aviv, she often speaks to the audience in English. In addition to her formidable deep voice, which sounds like a blues singer's, she is a lithe dancer, incorporating *Eskesta*[3] in the Amharic numbers. In examining her musical style, I will posit that she has broken into the transnational soul scene by portraying herself as an Afrodiasporic musician, thereby downplaying her Israeli origins and invoking her Ethiopian roots. I will argue that for Rada, reggae and soul music serve as 'transformative performance' (Brown, Kuwabong and Olsen 2013, 64) that facilitate a process of 'becoming black', (Wright 2004), or engaging the African diaspora through music that implies the Black Atlantic experience of suffering. I argue that Rada uses song style to establish an alternative history for Ethiopian migrants, particularly those whose political status in their host country is demeaning.

In one of her first stops on a 40-city tour of the USA and France, Rada performed at Madison Square Park in New York City on 25 June 2014. As a stop on an album tour, the playlist included several original hits from her 2014 eponymous album, plus songs from her 2013 EP *Life Happens*. In concert, Rada is energetic, although she comes off as somewhat aloof because she does not banter with the audience in English. Instead, she has mastered a script that she mobilizes between songs to an audience that can only be described as enthralled. I will describe three of the songs from her eight-song set to demonstrate how Rada constructs an Afrodiasporic self for her audience, whether it is European/American, Israeli, Ethiopian, or in the case of this performance, a fairly even distribution of each.

A standard of Rada's in-concert repertoire is Nina Simone's 'Feeling Good', which she includes as part of a three-song Simone medley. Nina Simone is an important figure in a lineage of black women in America who proclaimed emancipation of their voices and bodies through music (see Hayes and Williams 2007) – and as an expatriate, enormously popular in Europe – and she is a major influence on Rada.[4] Rada re-interprets the song in

Ethiojazz style, changing the tempo to 6/8, and adding brass instead of the dirge-like string introduction. She begins by asking the audience how they feel. She responds with a solo gospel/confessional 'I'm feelin' good' opening line. On the anacrusis, the band jumps into an Ethiojazz 6/8 exposition of the motive. The Ethiojazz section returns at each chorus, and it features the saxophone, trombone, and trumpet, the instrumentation and tonality producing the iconic Ethiojazz sound.

The verses alternate between soul and reggae. At the end of the chorus, the ensemble slows down and Rada's voice syncopates the lyrics: 'Birds flyin' high/You know how I feel,'[5] For the first two lines of each verse, Rada's ballad style is accompanied by a deep, funky bassline. At the third line, the ensemble slows further, and the syncopation creates a reggae effect. As she approaches the anacrusis, she reverts to Ethiojazz for the chorus.

The particular combination of multidirectional Afrodiasporic influences in 'Feeling Good' creates a collage effect. Rada incorporates Hebrew language only when absolutely necessary (when the audience cannot answer back in English); Ethiopian musical conventions that are accessible to her audience; and African-American musical cues. These strands are clearly delineated, but they demonstrate Rada's performance goal: to represent Ethiopian music faithfully, and to earn accolades from a soul audience, while retaining discretion about her Israeli upbringing. Moreover, no matter how diverse Ester Rada's musical influences are, the Afrodiasporic collage dynamic of multidirectional stylistic influences replicates itself in each of her songs, including in her original material.

Rada's best-known original song, 'Life Happens' (also performed at Madison Square Park), offers the same mix of Ethiojazz and soul, but alternates between styles rather than fusing them.[6] The song follows a pop structure, but moves between Ethiopian and Afrodiasporic genres: first, an Ethiojazz opening (performed in the official video on a *massenqo*[7]) which lasts two measure and repeats, with the four-measure section opening each new verse. Next, she sings a four-line verse in minor key, in a throaty soul style in her lower vocal register. Finally, the chorus modulates to major for four measures, eventually cycling back to the Ethiojazz section, with a brief gospel-style vocal passage punctuated by rhythmic hand-clapping and homophony at the end of the song.

The video for 'Life Happens' mirrors her vocal performance style strikingly. Each four measures or so, Rada changes her clothing, alongside the musical instrument she plays, invoking iconography of Addis Ababa in the 1960s or key moments in African-American popular music: a 1960s style shift dress (reminiscent of Swinging Addis [see Falceto 2002]); a saxophone; a flute (which sounds more like an Ethiopian *washint*); a massenqo/west African prints and headdress; and an electric bass. The visual image of an Ester-self from the 1960s, the 1970s, and the 1980s, playing different instruments, in different modes of ethnic dress, needs no explanation beyond the aesthetic statement of collage-like multidirectional influence coming from Ethiopia, the USA, and Jamaica (but not from Israel). The video expresses her combination of eras, regions, tone colors, and melodic structures through an easy-to-grasp visual medium, and it is effective and compelling for the diverse audiences who follow her work.

Nonetheless, not all of Ester Rada's material is easy listening for her American audience. She closed the New York show, like many of her concerts, with the Ethiojazz standard 'Nanu Nanu Ney',[8] which many members of her audience would recognize whether they are Ethiopian, Israeli, or Ethiopian-Israeli (see Webster-Kogen 2014 for discussion of the song's appropriation by Israeli pop musicians). Unlike her Nina Simone covers, her interpretation of Mulukun Melesse's song is conservative, with her seven-piece backup band capturing Ethiojazz tonality more adeptly than any non-Ethiopian ensemble I have seen.[9] She adds little in the way of improvisation or vocal ornamentation to her performance, but she dances Eskesta during the chorus, to rapturous audience response.

By choosing 'Nanu Nanu Ney' as the Ethiojazz standard she typically covers on her touring circuit, Rada makes an oblique political statement that is easily lost on most listeners because it is so understated. She has chosen an Ethiopian popular classic that any Ethiopian would recognize, as well as any card-carrying world music aficionado (since the song leads off the first volume of *Ethiopiques*). But Israelis would recognize the song, too, since it was sampled controversially by multiethnic band The Idan Raichel Project in 2005, who used a short passage in the introduction to the song 'Mima'amakim' on the album of the same name. Rada, on the other hand, sings the entire song, implicitly critiquing the powerful songwriter/producer Idan Raichel's somewhat more curatorial/cannibalistic approach to referencing Ethiojazz. As she explains:

ER: Idan Raichel did something really nice, because there was never anything like this in Israel. And I got quite emotional, and went to hear the original song. And I loved it. And I thought that someone had to do the original. Because it's an amazing song. Not to do, like *that* to Idan Raichel [makes a stabbing motion] ...

IWK: You do the whole song, and you dance, and the audience loves it, and it's great.

ER: That's what I wanted. It's something that the audience knows, and a lot of people think that Idan Raichel wrote the song, so I wanted people to know that it's an Ethiopian song, that it has an origin, that it's a complete song, even that's a good [outcome] in my opinion. And people have really liked it. It's been on the radio a lot in Israel. It's the first time a full Ethiopian song has been on the air in Israel. (Interview, Jaffa, 5 March 2015)

By closing her syncretic performance with the one Ethiopian song that Israelis and world music fans might reasonably know, she asserts the importance of Ethiopian music in her largely African-American-influenced style. In the process, after drawing a set of lines between herself and the USA and Jamaica, and occluding the lines between herself and Israel, she settles on incorporating Ethiopia into an imaginary map of stylistic influences.

When considering all three songs –'Feeling Good', 'Life Happens', and 'Nanu Nanu Ney' together, Rada's audience might recognize that she has inverted the particular racial prejudice imposed upon Ethiopian migrants in Israel by actively embracing blackness ('becoming black' as per Wright's 2004 formulation) and associating with its cultural vanguard. I argue that the multidirectional set of musical influences in Rada's on-stage repertoire represents a reconfiguration of a narrative of Ethiopian-Israeli marginality and citizenship that was unstable for decades. These three songs, their syncretic style and accompanying visual and gestural imagery, represent an embrace of Afrodiasporic performance style that connects musicians directly to their African roots and diasporic kin, cutting them off from the political structures that disempower them in their host society.

Aster in Tel Aviv, *Ethiopiques* in Jerusalem

Ester Rada's international profile makes her the Ethiopian-Israeli solo singer with the widest audience, but she is not the most popular musician among her fellow Ethiopian-Israelis. The population of 135,000 Jews of Ethiopian extraction, scattered across the

State of Israel, and especially on the Mediterranean coast between Haifa and Ashkelon, listens primarily to music from 'back home'. During my fieldwork in Tel Aviv in 2009, as young people showed me their 'clippim', or the downloaded playlists on their mobile phones, I learned that young people are just as attached to Ethiopian music as their immigrant parents are. Fortunately for them, they possess two resources that their parents did not in the early days of migration to Israel in the 1980s and 1990s (for discussion of the journey, see BenEzer 2002): the internet as a resource for staying in touch (Levine 2004), and a touring circuit that, as of 2014, now includes Tel Aviv. In this section, I contend that Israel joined the Ethiopian diaspora in 2014, as evidenced by the arrival of Aster Aweke and, soon thereafter, of *Ethiopiques*. I argue further that the musical performance itself navigates the boundary between Ethiopian and Israeli culture for a group that has been historically marginalized by both.

During the awkward early days of my fieldwork in Tel Aviv in summer 2008, when I did not know any better, I occasionally asked Ethiopian-Israelis whether they enjoyed living in Israel. Prompted by a literature that focuses overwhelmingly on Ethiopian-Israeli marginality on racial grounds (Anteby-Yemini 2004), on religious grounds (Kaplan 1992; Seeman 2009), and ultimately, because of class prejudice (see Parfitt and Semi 2005), I wanted to understand how musicians process this marginality. Unfortunately, little of value can be gleaned from such a direct question, especially given the legendary Ethiopian habit of avoiding social conflict. The realism of the common Ethiopian joke, that there is no word for 'no' in Amharic, forcing Ethiopians to answer affirmatively for everything (see Leslau and Kane 2001), presents a challenge to ethnographic methods, particularly interviewing. However, even before I learned how to converse with my informants, I learned that talking about music could substitute for many of the socio-cultural questions I had about life in Israel. In particular, I found that many Ethiopian-Israelis did not consume Israeli music at all, listening almost exclusively to music produced in Ethiopia or the diaspora.

Aster Aweke, the most prominent Ethiopian female musician today, is herself a product of a home–diaspora flux. She left Ethiopia during the DERG (see Shelemay 1991 for discussion of musical life during that period), produced her first albums in London, lived in Washington, DC, settling in Los Angeles (and later returning to Ethiopia), and travels to virtually every city with an Ethiopian population, including Abu Dhabi and Dubai in 2011. Like the latter, some of these diasporas remain subject to strict limitations on citizenship and often harsh labor conditions, but Aster[10] tours wherever migrants with disposable income open up a market for Ethiopian culture. Even so, until 2014 she had not visited Israel, where a mostly-Jewish population lives in a state of perpetual liminality on account of suspicion from both Ethiopians and Israelis (see Shelemay 1986 for the polemics over tracing Ethiopian Jewish lineage). This population remained off the radar of musicians like Aster for decades; I frequently asked my informants to comment on the isolation of Ethiopian-Israelis from the Ethiopian diaspora to little avail. In that case, I will discuss Aster's inaugural trip to Tel Aviv promoting her album *Ewedihalehu*, and unpack the wider ramifications for Ethiopian-Israelis of connecting to a wider Ethiopian musical network. I will argue that the arrival of mainstream Ethiopian musicians in Tel Aviv and Jerusalem demonstrates the beginning of Ethiopian-Israeli acceptance into the Ethiopian diaspora, but that this is the end result of a long-term process of working through the confusing migration context whereby Ethiopian-Israelis left one diaspora (Jewish) to enter a new one (African).

Aster's long-awaited debut performance in Israel took place on 5 May, which fell in 2014 on *Yom Ha'atzmaut*, Israeli Independence Day, and the promotion of her arrival reveals the sometimes-conflicting dynamics of Israeli nationalism and diasporic solidarity driving the Ethiopian-Israeli population today. In the video,[11] Aster arrives at Ben Gurion Airport, greeted by fans and accompanied by band members. This staging is a recognizable homecoming trope in Israel; nationalist composer Naomi Shemer penned the classic El Al airlines advertisement in the 1970s, 'Latoos El Al', or 'To fly El Al', that concludes with, 'V'kama tov lashuv habayta, ve'eizeh yofi shetisayta, lehitraot', or 'And how great is it to return home, and it's wonderful that you travelled, see you soon.' The image of arriving at Ben Gurion implies homecoming, and the Israeli flag flashing across the screen in the video promoting Independence Day implies that Aster is coming home rather than visiting.

The timing of Aster's concert contributes to the significance of her arrival. Like most Israeli citizens apart from anti-Zionists among 1948 Palestinians and ultra-Orthodox populations (see Shafir and Peled 2002), young Ethiopian-Israelis spend their Yom Ha'atzmaut evening celebrating in the streets, and the following day off work grilling in the park. The day is organized around the collective celebration – again, apart from the citizens for whom 1948's effects were detrimental (see Kanaaneh and Nusair 2012) – of the nation, and national dance, anthems, and nostalgic folk songs constitute the soundscape of the quasi-festival. Ethiopian-Israelis take patriotism seriously, and until the launch of a protest movement against marginality and police brutality in April 2015, they were the ethnic group most heavily invested in wearing their Zionism openly (see Herman 2012 for discussion of patriotism as a reconfiguration of Ethiopian 'honor'). So to spend Yom Ha'atzmaut at an Aster Aweke concert represents a variation on the nationalist narrative, one where ethnic roots are actively celebrated as a component of national/ist celebration. Despite ongoing struggles for acceptance, that have reached a boiling point and widespread media attention in 2015, Ethiopian-Israelis can publicly acknowledge Ethiopian culture as a part of their celebration of Israeli citizenship.

The imagery in the video is an important mechanism in promoting a nationalist perspective on diasporic consolidation, indicating that an arrival abroad can be a homecoming, too. The footage of Aster's arrival; her being greeted with flowers and adoration; and the Israeli flag waving across the screen, portrays an image of homecoming, that Aster is perhaps more of a pilgrim than a guest, and that her visit to the biblical Holy Land is part of a historical connection between Ethiopia and Jerusalem. For Ethiopian musicians, the arrival in modern Israel evokes the fourteenth century Ethiopian foundation epic, the *Kebra Negast*, in which Prince Menilek returns to Jerusalem to meet, and usurp his father King Solomon (Levine 1974). Indeed, the implicit connection of Ethiopians to the biblical Holy Land (see Ullendorff 1968) recurs in the concerts of 2014, as I witnessed in Alemu Aga's rather emotional tribute during his concert in Jerusalem in September 2014.

Aster's confirmation that Israel had become a part of the Ethiopian diaspora network was bolstered in September 2014 by the arrival of an equally illustrious enterprise, *Ethiopiques*. This influential CD series produced by Buda Musique in France is a combination of classic records on re-release, and modern or contemporary material, produced by Francis Falceto. In the absence of a wide body of literature on Ethiopian music, Falceto is perhaps the most authoritative Anglo-European voice about Ethiopian music, and he is equally respected in Ethiopia as in the diaspora. His records are a staple of the bootleg CD trade, highlighting the tension between official channels and an informal market:

> IWK: In terms of coming to Jerusalem, there are a lot of different aspects that are interesting. There's the Christian history perspective, there's the fact that there's a community here, there's the fact that some of the musicians whose discs you've produced live here ... What's the most interesting to you?
>
> FF: I'd like to stay here several weeks.... And I'd like to go to Tel Aviv ... I'm collecting bootlegs of *Ethiopiques*. I would love to bring them from here just for fun. And I was brought one from Vietnam once – *Ethiopiques* 1!
>
> IWK: Do you want me to pick up a couple for you at X in Tel Aviv?
>
> FF: For my collection! That would be nice of you ... Can you believe that I found bootlegs of Mahmoud [Ahmed, the best-selling musician on *Ethiopiques*] sold *in Mahmoud's music shop?!* (Interview, Jerusalem, 11 September 2014)

He was invited to speak at the Jerusalem Sacred Music Festival, to complement a concert by Alemu Aga, the *beganna* (lyre) player from disc 11 of *Ethiopiques*. This set of events serves, as Aster's concert did, as a potential tribute to the upward mobility and climbing cultural capital of Ethiopian-Israelis, but the performances catered to an Israeli elite demographic, highlighting a set of power relations and hierarchical structures that, somewhat ironically, exclude Ethiopian-Israelis.

The *Ethiopiques* events bear some striking differences from Aster's performance, although the dynamic of diaspora consolidation brings the two together. Whereas Aster's concert was oriented toward an Ethiopian audience, including her verbal invitation in Amharic and the disconnect of spending Independence Day with her, the *Ethiopiques* event was directed toward a wider, if equally socially homogenous Israeli audience. I posit that the arrival of *Ethiopiques* in Jerusalem reveals the place of Ethiopians in Israeli society from a different angle, one of sustained invisibility.

I had been to *Ethiopiques* mini-festivals twice before: in June 2008 at the Barbican Centre in London and in Paris in February 2011. Francis Falceto facilitated both festivals, and he told me in an interview that they can really only happen when a wealthy arts complex (or, as in 2013, Harvard University) sponsors him, since the series does not earn much money. Album sales revenue goes directly to the musicians in Ethiopia, so trips to Europe are lucrative and desirable ways to bolster album sales. So for Falceto as for the musicians he promotes, the trip to Israel was especially anticipated because it would potentially bring the musicians face to face with the seat of the Orthodox Church, and with their controversial perceived champion in Israel, Idan Raichel.

I approached this momentous event with trepidation, since it bore the fault lines of Ethiopian-Israeli life that were, at the time, opaque to most Israelis but apparent to researchers. The issues that spurred my apprehension later became some of the guiding issues of the protest movement in spring 2015. I was skeptical that there would be any Ethiopians in the audience at the elite venue, Mishkenot Shaananim, since Ethiopian-Israelis social mobility is slow. I was not sure that Alemu Aga was the most representative musician in this context; he is a Christian musician playing religious music, and would not have a following among Ethiopian-Israelis. I gathered that the program was put together without considering an Ethiopian audience. Moreover, I was not certain that a mostly-Israeli audience would understand Alemu Aga's music nor were they going to be prepared for his reaction to performing overlooking the Old City walls.

Above all, I was nervous that a member of the Idan Raichel Project would turn up at Alemu Aga's concert, causing him to demand a decade worth of royalties from them for sampling his song 'Tew Semagn Hagere' uncredited (see Ramboteau 2007). Or worse – they would not show up. As I prepared for the concert, I considered the actual wrongs committed against Ethiopian-Israelis versus the perceived slights that perpetuated their marginality.

The concert on 10 September confirmed my apprehension, but the event was a success for the audience and for Alemu Aga himself. The crowd, a mostly elderly audience of affluent Jerusalem professionals and intellectuals, applauded politely, but did not love the music. Aga himself was so moved by the setting – so close to the seat of his Church – that he was unusually soft-spoken in his conversation with the audience. Nonetheless, they warmed to his personality; they might not have understood what he meant theologically when he explained that a song in liturgical Ge'ez was about 'the futility of life', but this left-leaning audience in a contested city understood the sentiment. Mostly, though, I was disconcerted by two elements of the concert: first, no one attended from the Idan Raichel Project. Raichel samples Aga's music in his first hit, 'Bo'ee', which brought him monodirectional economic benefit. This event would have been an opportune moment for members of the Project to meet the musician sampled in their most popular song, and to potentially subvert a paradigm of north–south appropriation for commercial gain. Aga did not perform 'Tew Semagn Hagere' that evening, and leaving the best-known piece of his repertoire out of the playlist constitutes a powerful commentary on the cultural dynamics that brought him to the festival.

Second, there was not a single Ethiopian-Israeli in the audience. This was a disappointment if not a surprise: Alemu Aga's music is associated with the Ethiopian Church, and the Jewish Ethiopian-Israelis would have little emotional connection to the lyre played outside of churches during Lent. Indeed, after a long-fought battle for religious acceptance, any association with the Church could be actively detrimental to their citizenship status. At any rate, the venue was some distance from any substantial Ethiopian population, and it was marketed as a bourgeois cultural event, so it would not have reached the typical networks of circulation and distribution such as Ethiopian-Israeli Facebook groups, or the walls of south Tel Aviv that advertise local gigs. The elitism of the event demonstrated that this concert was not so much a redistribution of opportunity nor a gesture toward inclusion, as a retrenchment of privilege of insiders at the expense of the less powerful. Although Ethiopian-Israeli acceptance in the Ethiopian diaspora owes some credit to upward mobility and the disposable income that comes with integration, diasporic inclusion also rests, in part, on the continued reality of frequent Ethiopian exclusion in their host society.

Wayna: performing Africanness on U street and Lenox avenue

The most obvious diaspora destination for an Ethiopian musician is Washington, DC, the home of the most prosperous Ethiopian diaspora in the Global North (see Chacko 2003 or Shelemay 2009). And in Washington, few performance venues have the cache of the Howard Theatre, a legendary African-American music venue located just off U Street, the epicenter of Ethiopian life in Washington DC (and only a few blocks from restaurant Dukem). Washington is an important stop in the circuit because 'DC Ethiopians' comprise the most established Ethiopian diaspora, some of its members having left Ethiopia with their assets in the last days of Emperor Haile Selassie's reign in the mid-1970s.[12] They mix with the African-American population of Washington, DC, but they remain distinctive with Orthodox religious rituals,[13] hairstyles, and diet. I was excited to see Wayna, a favorite Ethiopian-American musician perform there on 21 June 2014. But as I will describe, her reception was chilly that evening, and as I followed her album tour over the course of the summer at prestigious African-American venues up and down the East Coast of the USA, I concluded that the popularity of a migrant musician can emanate as much from the personal narrative demonstrated in audience engagement as in song style itself. The three Wayna concerts that I attended were virtually identical in terms of playlist, but the audience reaction swung wildly according to Wayna's attention to migration narratives. Therefore, this section will argue that the most 'successful' case of Ethiopian integration (in African-American culture) illustrates the pitfalls and opportunities of coming to identify with one's host culture.

The venues around Washington that offer live Ethiopian music are in a state of flux today, transforming themselves as the Ethiopian migrant population ascends in social status. Dukem, the restaurant that has offered regional folk music performances twice a week for years, launched a jazz night in 2013. Today, a curious visitor is as likely to find a Japanese-American singer as a Gurage dancer. As Washington, DC gentrifies, the long-established Ethiopian population is achieving upward mobility at a faster rate than the African-American urban population at large (see Hopkinson 2012 for an especially moving discussion of the effects of gentrification on African-American music in the city). As a result, people like Wayna – Ethiopians who grew up in Washington and have little trouble fitting in as American, but whose parents are motivated by mobility – are prospering in an economy that increasingly separates them from the black working class. In the case of the USA, I contend that the cultural capital of African-American culture, and the social capital of Ethiopian family values (i.e. upward mobility) conflict directly at the level of musical style.

Wayna is among the most prominent DC Ethiopian musicians, performing soul music that is not recognizably Ethiopian. The DC Ethiopian community follows her career closely, but she has self-consciously expanded her reach beyond both her city and her fellow migrants – I have little doubt that she would have had immense trouble reaching her current level of commercial success if she performed songs in Amharic or with Ethiopian instruments. As Wayna told me:

> Initially, I was playing mainly for African-Americans because my music was soul music. But what I found was that the Ethiopian community was so excited about seeing something different that they'd come out and support me, so even when I was brand new and nobody knew what kind of music I was doing, I could fill up a club because people were interested … One very sweet thing about our culture is people are proud of people doing something different, daring. I appreciate that. But that main challenge is turning those people who are interested in me for patriotic reasons into actual fans. (Interview, Washington, DC, 30 July 2014)

She has established a fan base by developing a musical vernacular that African-American audiences relate to. In the process, she has replaced the tonality and instrumentation of Ethiojazz, Azmaris (traditional bards) and even Aster with rock instrumentation and the occasional Latin percussion instrument, rendering her style a creative renegotiation of Ethiopian status in the USA.

Wayna identifies as a soul singer, but I hear some Ethiopian influence in the high register of her vocals. As she confirms:

> I've just realized this on the last album. Although I've had producers say, 'Oh, that's the Ethiopian in you doing this or that' ... but there are certain things. First of all, the rhythm, the choice of 6/8 is a big part of it, and then the pentatonic scale is something that, I guess hearing it in the background [growing up], I would naturally gravitate towards. And then, on this project specifically, we incorporated the massenqo. (Interview, Washington, DC, 30 July 2014)

This influence is lost, though, on a listener who is not searching for Ethiopian tonality, and it is her lyrics that focus most obviously on her Ethiopian family and status as an immigrant. Most of this material emphasizes the experience of feeling out of place, and integrating as a personal triumph. This theme recurs on each of her three albums, *Moments of Clarity Volume 1* (2004), *Higher Ground* (2008), and *The Expats* (2013). Each album makes reference to movement through physical space or spirituality, often intertwining the two and demonstrating the fluidity between the physical location and emotional state of migrants.

The Expats was recorded in Toronto, in a confirmation of Carment and Bercuson's thesis of Canada's rise in the world through migration (2008). The theme of moving across diasporic space is present in her work even if she sings in English in a throaty soul style that contrasts with Aster's high-pitched ululating style. She seemed a natural choice to open for Lira, the prominent South African soul singer, at the Howard Theatre, on 23 June, because as she told the audience, 'I'm from the continent, too – I'm from Ethiopia.' By bringing in Wayna to open for Lira, the Howard offered an imagined geographic contiguity that evening – to present two African female soul singers – to somewhat tepid results. The audience, well-dressed African-American professionals with a smattering of South Africans around the room, bought tickets to hear African music, and they were underwhelmed by Wayna's repertoire, murmuring that her repertoire was similar to the music their children listen to on their phones. Wayna recognizes this dynamic among Ethiopians, too; as she explains:

> When more Ethiopians started coming [to Washington in the 1990s], there was separation in that community, too, because I had become American, so they would call me that – 'the American'. My uncle would be like, 'Ah, you're just an American', like I'm so different from them. (Interview, Washington, DC, 30 July 2014)

Like Wayna's family, the Howard audience was more impressed by Lira, who sang a short number in Zulu and told the audience about her journey into music after apartheid. The audience coded Wayna's performance style as African-American, rendering her too integrated to be exotic in this context. Seeing her upstaged on U Street by a visiting soul singer from Africa who was portraying herself as 'authentic' and foreign, illustrated the complexities and limitations of multidirectional influence for Ethiopian songwriters and performers, defined by Shelemay as the tension between 'descent and dissent' (2011).

Within the month, though, Wayna transformed her reception among audiences. On 21 July, she performed a nearly identical set list at New York jazz venue The Blue Note in Greenwich Village. She played a late set at 10.30 p.m., and her delivery was exuberant. The audience's response was warmer this time, perhaps because of her revised personal narrative. As Lira did at the Howard Theatre, she talked about her personal journey, and described the process of giving up professional security for creative fulfillment. The audience demanded an encore.

Wayna's monologue between songs was one prong of her audience engagement: she also made minor adjustments to the playlist that demanded audience encouragement. For the duration of her tour, she incorporated the song 'Mama's Sacrifice', from her first album, which narrates the difficulties experienced by her single mother. As Wayna moves between the sung chorus and the narrated verses, detailing the lengths of maternal devotion, the affective power in the room emanates from the audience reaction. Embracing her proximity to the African-American tradition, Wayna presents herself in this context as part of the jazz tradition (pausing between verses for applause as though after an instrumental solo), with a clear homage to the gospel confessional tradition.

By the time she arrived in Harlem on 15 August, Wayna had perfected her delivery of the mini-bildungsroman. She performed at Ginny's Supper Club on Lenox Avenue, the speakeasy partner business beneath Ethiopian-Swedish chef Marcus Samuelsson's restaurant, Red Rooster. Red Rooster is a major catalyst for gentrification on Martin Luther King Jr. Boulevard, with most of the restaurant's patrons white professionals and young families. Downstairs, the atmosphere had lower lighting and a more local demographic (perhaps fans of Bole2Harlem, the now-defunct band I reference in this article's title). Yet both my assumption and Wayna's that most of the crowd was African-American was incorrect. 'Who here's from Ethiopia?' she called out as she began her set. She was surprised (as was I) by the number of people clapping, and answered, 'Wow, a lot of you, actually!' And she took a moment to thank Washington-based *Tadias* magazine – the editors were sitting at the front table. The fluidity for Wayna and her audience between Ethiopian, Ethiopian-American, and African-American identities became apparent at Red Rooster, as her musical style came to adhere to a personal narrative.

Of the three Wayna concerts I attended through summer 2014, the one at Ginny's was the most warmly received by the audience, despite three virtually identical playlists. Rather than focusing on qualitative differences between performances, the audience responded increasingly effusively to her enthusiastic delivery between songs of a personal narrative of moving from Ethiopia to Washington, and overcoming hardship to live her dreams as a musician. What I noted at the Howard Theatre as the bifocality of an Ethiopian musician who has settled in Washington successfully transformed into a multidirectional performance style incorporating jazz, gospel-style confession, and pan-Africanism. Accepting her in-between status, Wayna blended her repertoire with her personal narrative, emphasizing the dynamic process of defining herself to her audience. In Wayna's spread from local to national prominence, her ability to perform Africanness, and to present herself as an African who has 'made it' in America, is central to her ability to navigate cultural boundaries at the East Coast's most prestigious African-American music venues.

Conclusion

In the months of spring 2008, I attended an *Ethiopiques* concert for the first time (marketed to World Music audiences), first heard 'cultural' music at Dukem (regional folk music marketed at Ethiopians of any ethnicity in Washington, DC), and commenced my research in Tel Aviv (a subculture catering to one small section of Israeli society). Considering these events in concentric circles of transnational audiences to specialized ones, it seems that it was still possible as recently as 2008 to conceive of individual diasporas as unique in circumstance and absorption strategy. Only a few years later, the urban centers of the

Ethiopian diaspora have consolidated into a network of mutually dependent enclaves of cultural production and consumption. The combination of Ethiopian musical events I witnessed around the world in 2014 – Ester Rada becoming Europe's most famous Ethiopian pop star, Aster Aweke being greeted at the airport as through she has returning home and *Ethiopiques* playing in Jerusalem, and Wayna's reception at elite African-American venues – confirms the consolidation of disparate Ethiopian diaspora cities into a circuit of stops for cultural ambassadors. Despite often being invisible in their adopted cities as an underclass, these migrants are engaged across borders with one another, musicians redefining the boundaries between home and host society.

Moreover, what happens today in one diaspora city affects other diaspora cities – and life back in Ethiopia – more immediately and acutely than ever before. For Ester Rada to have 'made it' in America means success in Tel Aviv, too. The arrival in Israel of *Ethiopiques* and Aster Aweke translates to recognition that Ethiopian-Israelis are part of the diaspora. And Wayna increases her credibility as an African musician by emphasizing a personal narrative of striving in the vein of South African singers. The often imperceptible influences of each diaspora on one another adds up, eventually, to a 'transnational remapping' (Braziel 2008b, 5), or a consensual engagement of migrants coming to terms together with their position in their host society.

Notes

1. A literature of Ethiopian migration to the Middle East is still in its earliest phases, but scholars are increasingly acknowledging Ethiopia's status as a main sending country for labor in the Gulf. Part of the reason that they are not given as much attention as Filipina domestic workers, or Nepalese construction workers, is that they are a semi-hidden segment of the labor force, doing manual domestic labor in Saudi Arabia, the UAE, and Qatar (plus Lebanon and Yemen). Ethiopian women migrate in somewhat higher proportion than men because since they are sent to school in lower numbers, their career prospects in Ethiopia are lower, too (see De Regt 2010). When they arrive in the Gulf, they occupy the bottom of the hierarchy of domestic labor.
2. The press calls her music 'Ethio-soul,' which effectively means Ethiopian music fused with soul.
3. Ethiopian shoulder dancing.
4. See the 'bio' section of Rada's website: http://www.esterrada.com/ (Accessed on 5 May 2015).
5. https://www.youtube.com/watch?v=SmFvgBUGH9Y (Accessed on 10 May 2015).
6. https://www.youtube.com/watch?v=c_QFQCvdtyw (Accessed on 5 May 2015).
7. The massenqo is a one-stringed spike fiddle played by folk poets (Azmaris) in northern Ethiopia. For a discussion of the moral characteristics associated with instruments, see Kebede (1977).
8. https://www.youtube.com/watch?v=EGLNRfUmCs0 (Accessed on 5 May 2015).
9. Foreign musicians often struggle with Ethiopian tonality because it emphasizes notes considered dissonant in Western pop music, such a tritones and minor seconds.
10. Since Aster is known by her first name only to her fans, I will henceforth refer to her as Aster.
11. https://www.youtube.com/watch?v=eW0xGLlr9bg (Accessed on 5 May 2015).
12. See Kaplan (2010) and Shelemay (2009) for details of migration patterns. There is certainly evidence of Ethiopians moving south to Kenya and South Africa, but my work focuses only on movements north to Europe, North America, and the developed Middle East.
13. At the same time, DC Ethiopians are converting to Pentecostalism at about the same rate as in Ethiopia (see Kay 2009).

Disclosure statement

No potential conflict of interest was reported by the author.

References

Anteby-Yemini, Lisa. 2004. *Les Juifs Ethiopiens en Israel: Les Paradoxes du Paradis*. Paris: CNRS Editions.

BenEzer, Gadi. 2002. *The Ethiopian Jewish Exodus: Narratives of the Migration Journey to Israel 1977–1985*. London: Routledge.

Braziel, Jana Evans. 2008a. *Diaspora: an Introduction*. London: Blackwell Publishing.

Braziel, Jana Evans. 2008b. *Artists, Performers, and Black Masculinity in the Haitian Diaspora*. Bloomington: Indiana University Press.

Brown, Benita, Dannabang Kuwabong, and Christopher Olsen, eds. 2013. *Myth Performance in the African Diaspora: Ritual, Theatre, and Dance*. New York: Scarecrow Press.

Carment, David, and David Bercuson, eds. 2008. *The World in Canada: Diaspora, Demography, and Domestic Politics*. Montreal: McGill University Press.

Castles, Stephen, and Mark J. Miller. 2008. *The Age of Migration: International Population Movements in the Modern World*. Basingstoke: Palgrave Macmillan.

Chacko, Elizabeth. 2003. "Identity and Assimilation among Young Ethiopian Immigrants in Metropolitan Washington." *American Geographical Review* 93 (4): 491–506.

Chait, Sandra M. 2011. *Seeking Salaam: Ethiopians, Eritreans, and Somalis in the Pacific Northwest*. Seattle: University of Washington Press.

Charry, Eric, ed. 2012. *Hip Hop Africa: New African Music in a Globalizing World*. Bloomington: Indiana University Press.

Clifford, James. 1997. *Routes: Travel and Translation in the Late Twentieth Century*. Cambridge, MA: Harvard University Press.

Cohen, Robin. 2008. *Global Diasporas: An Introduction*. London: Routledge.

Danso, Ransford. 2002. "From 'There' to 'Here': An Investigation of the Initial Settlement Experiences of Ethiopian and Somali Refugees in Toronto." *GeoJournal* 56 (1): 3–14.

Falceto, Francis. 2002. *Abyssinie Swing: A Pictorial History of Modern Ethiopian Music*. Paris: Shama Books.

Fernandez, Bina. 2010. "Cheap and Disposable? The Impact of the Global Economic Crisis on the Migration of Ethiopian Women Domestic Workers to the Gulf." *Gender and Development* 18 (2): 249–262.

Getahun, Solomon Addis. 2006. *The History of Ethiopian Immigrants and Refugees in America, 1900–2000: Patterns of Migration, Survival, Adjustment*. New York: LFB Scholarly Publishing.

Hayes, Eileen M., and Linda F. Williams, eds. 2007. *Black Women and Music: More than Blues*. Urbana: University of Illinois Press.

Herman, Marilyn. 2012. *Gondar's Child: Songs, Honor and Identity among Ethiopian Jews in Israel*. Trenton, NJ: Red Sea Press.

Hopkinson, Natalie. 2012. *Go-Go Live: The Musical Life and Death of a Chocolate City*. Durham, NC: Duke University Press.

Kanaaneh, Rhoda Ann, and Isis Nusair, eds. 2012. *Displaced at Home: Ethnicity and Gender among Palestinians in Israel*. Albany: State University of New York Press.

Kaplan, Steven. 1992. *The Beta Israel (Falasha) in Ethiopia, From the Earliest Times to the Twentieth Century*. New York: New York University Press.

Kaplan, Steven. 2010. "Ethiopian Immigrants in the United States and Israel: A Preliminary Comparison." *International Journal of Ethiopian Studies* 5 (1): 71–92.

Kebede, Ashenafi. 1977. "The Bowl-Lyre of Northeast Africa. Krar: The Devil's Instrument." *Ethnomusicology* 21 (3): 379–395.

Kay, William. 2009. *Pentecostalism*. London: SCM Press.

Leslau, Wolf, and Thomas Kane, eds. 2001. *Amharic Cultural Reader*. Wiesbaden: Harrassowitz.

Levine, Donald. 1965. *Wax and Gold: Tradition and Innovation in Ethiopian Culture*. Chicago, IL: University of Chicago Press.

Levine, Donald. 1974. *Greater Ethiopia: the Evolution of a Multiethnic Society*. Chicago, IL: University of Chicago Press.

Levine, Donald. 2004. "Reconfiguring the Ethiopian Nation in a Global Era." *International Journal of Ethiopian Studies* 1 (2): 1–15.

Madrid, Alejandro L., ed. 2012. *Transnational Encounters: Music and Performance at the U.S.-Mexico Border*. New York: Oxford University Press.

Mandaville, Peter, and Terrence Lyons, eds. 2012. *Politics from Afar: Transnational Diasporas and Networks*. New York: Columbia University Press.

Palmer, David. 2012. "'It's as if You Were Being Dropped from the Moon': Exploring Ethiopian Cultural Paces and Well-being through Oral Histories with Ethiopian Forced Migrants in London." *Oral History* 40 (1): 67–78.

Parfitt, Tudor, and Emanuela Trevisan Semi, eds. 1999. *The Beta Israel in Ethiopia and Israel: Studies on Ethiopian Jews*. Richmond: Curzon.

Parfitt, Tudor, and Emanuela Trevisan Semi, eds. 2005. *Jews of Ethiopia: the Birth of an Elite*. London: Routledge.

Ramboteau, Emily. 2007. "Searching for Zion." *Transition* 97: 52–89.

Regt, Marina de. 2010. "Ways to Come, Ways to Leave: Gender, Mobility, an Il/legality among Ethiopian Domestic Workers in Yeme." *Gender and Society* 24 (2): 237–260.

Rommen, Timothy. 2011. *Funky Nassau: Roots, Routes, and Representation in Bahamian Popular Music*. Berkeley: University of California Press.

Scott, Joseph W., and Solomon A. Getahun. 2013. *Little Ethiopia of the Pacific Northwest*. New Brunswick, NJ: Transaction Publishers.

Seeman, Don. 2009. *One People, One Blood: Ethiopian-Israelis and the Return to Judaism*. New Brunswick, NJ: Rutgers University Press.

Shafir, Gershon and Yoav Peled. 2002. *Being Israeli: The Dynamics of Multiple Citizenship*. Cambridge: Cambridge University Press.

Shelemay, Kay Kaufman. 1986. *Music, Ritual, and Falasha History*. East Lansing: Michigan State University Press.

Shelemay, Kay Kaufman. 1991. *A Song of Longing: an Ethiopian Journey*. Urbana: University of Illinois Press.

Shelemay, Kay Kaufman. 2009. "Music of the Ethiopian America Diaspora: A Preliminary Overview." In *Proceedings of the 16th International Conference of Ethiopian Studies: July 2–6, 2007*, Trondheim, Norway, edited by Svein Ege, Harald Aspen, Birhanu Teferra and Shiferaw Bekele, 1153–1164. Wiesbaden: Harrassowitz.

Shelemay, Hay Kaufman. 2011. "Musical Communities: Rethinking the Collective in Music." *Journal of the American Musicological Society* 64 (2): 349–390.

Ullendorff, Edward. 1968. *Ethiopia and the Bible*. London: Oxford University Press.

Vertovec, Steven. 2007. "Migrant Transnationalism and Modes of Transformation." In *Rethinking Migration: New Theoretical and Empirical Perspectives*, edited by Alejandro Portes and Josh DeWind, 149–180. New York: Berghahn books.

Webster-Kogen, Ilana. 2011. "The Azmari Paradox: Ethnicity, Identity, and Migration in Ethiopian-Israeli Music in Tel Aviv." PhD diss., SOAS, University of London.

Webster-Kogen, Ilana. 2014. "Song Style as Strategy: Nationalism, Cosmopolitanism and Citizenship in The Idan Raichel Project's Ethiopian-Influenced Songs." *Ethnomusicology Forum* 23 (1): 27–48. doi:10.1080/17411912.2013.879034

Wright, Michelle M. 2004. *Becoming Black: Creating Identity in the African Diaspora*. Durham, NC: Duke University Press.

'No place like home': experiences of an Ethiopian migrant in the host country and as a returnee to the homeland

Adamnesh Atnafu[a] and Margaret E. Adamek[b]

[a]School of Social Work, Addis Ababa University, Addis Ababa, Ethiopia; [b]Program in Social Works, Indiana University, Bloomington, IN, USA

ABSTRACT

Using an in-depth interview with an Ethiopian returnee who lived abroad for 17 years, this study examined both integration and reintegration experiences. For this returnee, the experience of migration was psychologically costly. Challenges in the host country included acquiring a resident permit, overcoming language barriers, and contending with oppression and marginalization. Being treated unequally was a major push factor for his return to Ethiopia. Despite his relief upon reentering his home country, he faced challenges which made reintegration difficult, including the inefficiency of government offices, lack of a work ethic, time mismanagement, and the unsystematic processes in a developing country. To facilitate integration and reintegration processes, more effective policy responses of both the host and home countries are needed. Developing countries should not miss the opportunity to capitalize on the potential contributions of returnees who are committed to bringing about positive change in their homeland.

Background to the study

> Still I feel some pity for an exile
> Like somebody sick,
> or a prisoner.
> A refugee has to walk a dark road,
> And foreign bread has a bitter
> Flavour. (Anna Akhamatova 1889–1966)

Each year thousands of Africans migrate to other countries, particularly to the USA and Europe. Migration is often triggered by unfavorable conditions such as political disorder, civil unrest, economic difficulties, governmental oppression, and/or environmental calamities (Buuba 2007). According to Richardson (2007), nowadays, migration has become more of a freedom of movement issue rather than being a process to avoid crisis. Despite its vast resources, Africa is considered a disadvantaged region with low economic development – a primary reason for the ongoing out-migration (Van Dalen, Groenewold, and Schoorl 2005). Whether the migration is forced or desired, most people migrate in search of a better life than they had in their country of origin. While a number of studies have examined African migration, including Ethiopian migrants (e.g. Papadopoulos et al. 2004; Wondwosen et al. 2006), none have examined the experiences of Ethiopian returnees, other than refugees. It is therefore the purpose of this piece to reveal the integration and reintegration experiences of an Ethiopian migrant who voluntarily returned to his home country after living abroad for several years.

Various processes related to globalization including technological growth, urbanization, and increased economic ties between countries are believed to make the choice to migrate reachable for a broader range of individuals. However, Czaiki and de Hass (2014) question commonly held assumptions about globalization, diversification, and migration. Through a detailed analysis of global migration patterns between 1960 and 2000, Czaiki and de Hass (2014) concluded that though 'liberalization and globalization processes seem to have increased access of people living in poor countries to the international migration "game"' (318), they have not leveled the playing field. Refuting the theory that globalization and migration have made the world 'flat', Czaiki and de Hass (2014) document a pattern of migration that is increasingly skewed, favoring some regions and countries over others. The impact of these larger economic and social forces on the experiences of migrants and returnees needs careful consideration.

In trying to understand decisions to migrate, one should consider not only the geographical context, but also the characteristics of the migrants. In a study of German migrants choosing to migrate to New Zealand, Burgelt, Morgan, and Pernice (2008) found that weak family ties contributed to the likelihood of migration. In addition,

> Participants who grew up with opportunities to explore natural environments and travel developed curiosity, fantasy/imagination, knowledge/skills, and self-confidence. Curiosity and imagination made these participants thirsty for new experiences to find out more about their selves and to achieve a better understanding of the world around them and a better life. (287)

In Ethiopia, the main reason that people migrate to more developed countries is to search for a better life abroad. In a study of attitudes toward migration among Ethiopian medical students, Wakgari and Aklilu (2012) reported that over half of their 600 study participants aspired to emigrate to the USA or Europe after earning their degrees. Similarly, Silvestri et al. (2014) reported that 28 percent of nursing and medical students surveyed in eight Asian and African countries, including Ethiopia, had intentions of immigrating after graduation. According to Aluttis, Bishaw, and Frank (2014), the migration of healthcare professionals from low- to high-income countries, facilitated by the opening of borders through globalization, has become so extensive that questions of justice in relation to the health care of populations in the global south are increasingly raised. Despite globalization, the opportunities for migration – whether outgoing or return – are hardly equal.

Avenues for emigrating vary and may include going through family ties or other networks, marrying someone from another country, or applying for the US DV (diversity) lottery (Adamnesh 2006). Increasingly, smugglers and traffickers act as extra-legal travel agents – hiding people, supplying false passports, or bribing immigration officials (Fernandez 2013). A significant number of Ethiopians also use business meetings or conferences as an avenue for migration. The travel costs, including accommodations and visa fees, are often covered by the sending organizations. The business travelers stay in the destinations for a while and apply for asylum while working illegally until they get their work permit (Adamnesh 2008). People may have close family members or friends who have already settled abroad which is an important pull factor. Most of the time the settlers help the newly arriving migrants in their integration process by providing accommodations and useful information about employment and the new culture (Adamnesh 2006).

Host societies typically see newcomers in a different way than they see their own citizens. Migrants may be viewed either with curiosity, with anxiety, or sometimes with disdain (Richardson 2007). Such views make it difficult for the migrants to integrate smoothly within the host society. Migrants often feel oppressed and discriminated against. Yet, most integration efforts focus on resolving practical issues such as getting asylum applications approved and facing the hassle of making a living until work permits can be acquired (Cvetkovic 2009). Much less attention is given to the psychosocial adjustment of migrants.

One often overlooked challenge related to integration is defining one's identity. In identity formation after migration, migrants have to reconcile the culture and values they brought from their home with those they encounter in the host country (Bathala 2005). Creating a new blended identity without losing one's culture of origin is an important step in immigrants' integration with the host society, which could be an important factor in the success of reintegration after return (Cvetkovic 2009).

It is difficult to measure the extent of out-migration and return. However, available data indicate that the Ethiopian migrant stock increased from 1970 to 1990, and then declined between 1990 and 2010 (Table 1). One explanation for the change is that more migrants returned to Ethiopia after 1990, slowing the growth rate. However, it is still not known whether this decline is due to the return of migrants, fewer Ethiopians migrating abroad, or both.

The exact number of Ethiopian returnees is not known because there is no complete statistical data recorded by government offices. According to Adamnesh (2008), a

Table 1. Ethiopian migrant stock abroad from 1970 to 2010.

Indicator	1970	1980	1990	1995	2000	2005	2010
Estimated number of international migrants at mid-year (both sexes)	394,582	40,192	1,115,390	794,667	662,444	555,021	547,984
Estimated number of refugees at mid-year	20,500	10,930	741,965	370,777	227,824	108,399	91,082
Population at mid-year (thousands)	29,823	37,062	51,040	60,007	68,525	74,661	84,976
Estimated number of female migrants at mid-year	171,197	183,840	548,106	376,069	311,823	260,787	257,945
Estimated number of male migrants at mid-year	223,385	220,352	607,284	418,598	350,621	293,234	290,039
International migrants as a percentage of the population	1.3	1.1	2.3	1.3	1.0	0.7	0.6
Female migrants as percentage of all international migrants	43.4	45.5	47.4	47.3	47.1	47.1	47.1
Refugees as a percentage of international migrants	5.2	2.7	64.2	46.7	34.4	19.6	16.6

Indicator	1970–1975	1975–1980	1980–1985	1985–1990	1990–1995	1995–2000	2000–2005	2005–2010
Growth rate of the migrant stock (percentage)	−0.1	0.6	7.3	13.7	−7.5	−3.6	−3.6	−0.2

Source: United Nations, Department of Economic and Social Affairs, Population Division (2009)

number of returnees may be missed because many do not inform the authorities about their intent to resettle in Ethiopia. In addition, the documentation of returnees was only recently standardized electronically. Another factor contributing to the uncertainty of numbers of returnees is the fact that there is no system to account for those who re-migrate. Adamnesh (2008) explains:

> Data collected by the Recording and Travel Document Production Department of the Immigration authority, which is an office that provides Ethiopians by origin who have returned back and want to work in Ethiopia, a residence and work permit (the yellow ID card), is the only way to track returnees who reported back in the country. Still the data cannot be taken as complete representing returnees for the fact that Ethiopian migrants also return back to Ethiopia before changing their citizenship to the host country, where they do not need the yellow card when they return. Thus, there are also returnees who may not be registered in the immigration office as they do not come to claim the yellow card. (30)

Taking the number of Ethiopian returnees who take the yellow card every year as a reference, the number of returnees seems to be increasing each year by 30 percent. This includes those who came back from the top destinations: the USA and Canada, Europe, Israel, the Gulf States, and Australia (Adamnesh 2008).

The most important factors determining decisions to return to one's homeland may be unfavorable conditions in the host country, social and familial networks/attachments, and retirement or early retirement (Ammassari and Black 2001). Those who experience unfavorable conditions in the host county, especially those who are still living there illegally, find it far more difficult than living in their homeland (Rodriguez and Egea 2006). Moreover, if obstacles in the home country no longer exist, the migrant may decide to return home. Or, returnees may decide that the challenges in their home country are more tolerable than the discrimination experienced abroad.

Various reasons are given by some migrants to justify not returning to their home country, including being of working age, the slow accumulation of capital, concern about taking children to the home country where there might not be a good educational system, and fear of political instability (Ganga 2006). In a study of immigrants from Chile who migrated to Sweden, one migrant explained: 'I couldn't go back to the old days. Chile is a country that lacks both democracy and security … We didn't want our children to grow up there … ' (Cvetkovic 2009, 114).

Some migrants want to return to their homeland after they have accumulated capital – either social or financial. Some desire to reconstruct their homeland with the capital they have accumulated. As one returnee expressed:

> Nowadays, the hardest thing is that hope vanishes … Let us love our land, we will water it with our sweat and dig with all our strength, with courage. The light of hope shall guide us, we will harvest and build. Only us can borrow the routes of the sky, the land and the water without being chased like an outcast or pariah. We will no longer be travellers without luggage. Our callous hands will find others in warm handshakes of respect and shared dignity … (Buuba 2007, 215)

Upon return, migrants may have different expectations depending on their individual characteristics. Some may say that the homeland has changed and it does not feel like home anymore, while others wish that the culture and values of the people would change as they themselves have changed and wish to fit in (Rodriguez and Egea 2006). On the other hand, people in the homeland may have changed in many ways, which may cause some returnees to feel like they are not home. In a study which uncovered the unsuccessful reintegration of Iraqi refugees who had immigrated to Denmark, one returnee stated:

> We were told that much had changed, so we knew that the country had changed beforehand. But we had never thought that the people could change, yet when we returned we discovered that we were dealing with completely different people to the ones we left behind. (Riiskjaer and Nielsson 2008, 5)

While living abroad the migrants themselves often change, acquiring the modern culture of the West and a changed value structure. As a result, they may no longer fit into their own society as before especially if the homeland people have retained their original culture and values. Thus, after experiencing life with democracy, freedom of speech, efficient services provided by government offices, and a better standard of living, many returnees whose origin is a developing country face difficulties in readapting to their homeland (Cvetkovic 2009).

Another factor contributing to challenges in reintegration may be the home society's attitude toward returnees. Sometimes, returnees are treated as strangers and foreigners, which contributes to feelings of being an outsider (Cvetkovic 2009). If returnees are known to have come back from the West, they are assumed to be wealthy and may become targets of robbery and other crime (Riiskjaer and Nielsson 2008). Despite these problems, some returnees become accustomed to the fact that the homeland is a developing country and adjust accordingly. Others cannot handle the stress and re-migrate.

Adamnesh (2006) found that Ethiopian returnees also face troubles in their sociocultural reintegration in trying to rebuild bonds with the community. Some experience the feeling of being unwelcome which may also explain their association with other returnees (Adamnesh 2006). There may be a wide gap between returnees' expectations and the reality back home. Having lived for a time in a developed nation, returnees may face difficulties in accepting the bureaucracies, the work ethic of people, the mismanagement in different offices, and other challenges that are typical in a poor country (Adamnesh 2006). Nonetheless, for most returnees the difficulty of reintegrating lessens or even vanishes over time.

Purpose

This study was conducted to investigate the experiences of an Ethiopian migrant who lived abroad for 17 years and had been back in his homeland for 3 years. Learning in-depth about such experiences may help policy-makers better understand the challenges return migrants come across in attempting to reintegrate into their home country as contributing and happy citizens.

Method

This study examined the lived experiences of an Ethiopian return migrant including his migration abroad and his reintegration upon return to Ethiopia. In this instrumental case study, the respondent was asked to describe his reasons for migration, his experiences in the host country, his motivation for returning, and finally his reintegration experiences in the homeland. The study aimed for an in-depth understanding of the experience of the returnee including the meanings he attached to migration and to his return to his homeland. The purpose was thus to shed light on returnees' experiences to inform policies that can facilitate a smooth transition for migrants and returnees.

The respondent was selected through purposive sampling and was identified through an associate of the first author. Selection criteria were based on the need to examine a case with clear boundaries (Creswell 1998) and in this case the criteria were a returnee, who has migrated to the West, lived there for not less than ten years, and has been back in Ethiopia not less than three years – long enough to experience both the nature of life in the host country and the homeland society after return. The respondent was selected to participate following the first contact with the researcher because he matched the inclusion criteria, agreed to the interview schedule, and ensured his availability in case the researcher needed more information. The interview questions were designed in a manner to get in-depth information about the informant's lived experience of life before migration, after migration, and after return, mainly focusing on his life events and his reactions to those events. The interview was conducted in English in a private room at the interviewee's place of business. The interview was tape-recorded and lasted for 90 minutes.

The informant fully consented to participate in the interview. He was provided with detailed information regarding the study – its purpose and method, as well as his rights to privacy and confidentiality and signed the informed consent as per the requirements of ethical standards of research (Reamer 2013). The identity of the informant was protected by use of a pseudonym.

Data analysis

Because the study involved an instrumental case study, the analysis began with a detailed description of the case and its setting (Creswell 1998). The data were transcribed after the interview. As an initial stage of data analysis, the transcripts were read several times (Yin 2003). Along with the transcripts, the researcher also read through all the notes collected during the interview to obtain an overall sense of the data (Creswell 1998). This helped in framing the themes that were identified. The relationships/order of the themes was determined by establishing a pattern of the beginning, the mid-point, and the end of the story. Finally, a draft report was written in response to the research questions, showing how the researcher developed broader interpretations of the meaning of the case, analyzed the data, and compared the case with existing literature considering the context, experience and meanings of the case (Creswell 1998).

Results

The participant, Elias, was 44 years of age at the time of the interview and had lived abroad for 17 years. He returned to Ethiopia three years before the interview took place. He initially decided to live abroad due to political and economic instability in Ethiopia. He found his experience in the host country frustrating at times and meaningful at others. He described his life after returning to Ethiopia as one of relief despite the challenges he sometimes encountered.

Motives for leaving

Elias stated that he had a happy childhood and there was nothing that he would complain about his way of living. His father worked as a prison administrator and earned enough income to support the family. In addition, as an only child, he was well provided for. He noted, 'I was the only child and my mother and father used to see me as God's precious gift for them. They gave me all I wanted.' After graduating from college with a degree in building and technology, Elias started working at an organization where he got the chance to go to Sweden for a seminar. This opportunity initiated the idea of living abroad. Though political and economic instability of Ethiopia were push factors, friends also influenced Elias to stay in Sweden when the seminar ended. Elias was 24 at the time. It was not an easy choice but, as Elias explained, he decided not to return to Ethiopia:

> It was very difficult for me to decide that way. I was thinking about my girlfriend and my family as well. But despite all the worries I had and the fact that I was going to be apart from my loved ones, I decided to stay there.

Obstacles and opportunities in the host country

In Sweden, Elias faced many obstacles in trying to live and work to survive. One of the problems was getting a resident permit which is a requirement for one to legally work in Sweden. Since the process was very long, he had to work without the government's knowledge in order to support himself. Trying to make a living from a low-paying and illegal job was very difficult. The other problem he had in Sweden was the language barrier. He could not learn the language fast enough to integrate smoothly with the local people. In general, he was unhappy with his life in Sweden. As Elias explained:

> I realized that living in Sweden was going to be difficult for me as the permit was taking long. Then I started thinking about moving to another part of Europe instead of staying in Sweden. I had and still have friends in England.

After three years in Sweden, Elias' friends convinced him to move to England. He found life in the UK more comforting than in Sweden. In England, even if one does not have a resident permit, he/she is allowed to work. Being able to communicate in English also made life easier for Elias. He found a job easily and started to make a living on his own. At this point, Elias felt he had succeeded:

> After working in the restaurant and also the cafes for about 7 or 8 months, I started processing my driving license and license for taxi driving. I passed and got both licenses in not a very long time. Then I started working as a taxi driver employed by one taxi agency. After working there for about 2 years or so, I bought my own taxi and started to earn more money. I have been doing this until I moved back to Ethiopia.

Oppression and other disturbing experiences

According to Elias, the people in Sweden see migrants as inferior to the dominant host population. In addition to other problems, the language was not easy to learn, aggravating the adjustment problems even more. Elias experienced a feeling of inequality and oppression while living in Sweden:

> It was clear that they didn't like us. They are not comfortable when we sit next to them. Even in public shops, they speak in Swedish knowing that I can't speak Swedish. I knew these people could talk in English but they just want to get rid of you. You don't get equal access to things as people of their own. They used to serve them first and come to us even in a restaurant.

Elias stated that life was better in England. There he did not experience obvious discrimination or oppression from the host society. He was living in London where there was a significant number of people from different ethnicities. But he still felt some discrimination and inequality even there:

> There is a significant number of minorities living in London. Since it is the capital, most migrants are concentrated there, also close to the native people. So racism or discrimination was not apparent in an obvious manner. But still you can feel it inside. You can see and understand when someone is real with you or not. They were obliged to deal with us due to the situation I mentioned. The fact that there are other many migrant workers who live in London made the Londoners accept us even if they didn't like it. Though it was not as obvious as in Sweden, the discrimination was still there.

Apart from the feeling of being oppressed, Elias experienced other forms of frustration. Leaving his loved ones behind was very difficult. In the first years of his migration, he felt lost. The strain on his close relationships with his parents and his girlfriend back in Ethiopia were the most bothersome factors. There was nobody as close to spend time with which was disturbing to Elias. He expressed the frustrations as:

> I felt lonely. Coming from Ethiopia, where people eat together, get along for coffee, have drinks together and have fun together, I couldn't handle living alone in this country. By living alone, I don't mean living in the same house per se, but people by your side. Getting, calling them to have coffee, calling them to have lunch or dinner, you don't have that kind of life there. You work day and night, you will get tired and then you go to sleep.

The other challenge with living abroad to Elias was not being able to have those things that he was accustomed to at home. Living abroad, he had to do many tasks by himself from cooking to doing his own laundry and cleaning his house. This was unpleasant to him since in Ethiopia, he never had to do such housework. He was frustrated at first but then got used to the idea:

> I couldn't get used to the system there fast because in Ethiopia as you know, what we are used to is to hire a housemaid to do everything for you. The cooking, the laundry, the house cleaning and every kind of work in the house is done by the housemaid. You hire them for not big salary and they do everything for you. When you live abroad, such things will not be there for you. If you want to hire a housemaid, you will have to be very rich which I was not.

It was also frustrating for Elias to work as a taxi driver since he had a university degree and thus considered himself a professional. However, he accepted it as a way of living – a sacrifice made to earn more than he earned back home.

On the other hand, Elias acknowledged that his migration had benefits as well. One of the benefits he mentioned is that it taught him how to be self-sufficient and independent in terms of taking responsibility in the family. The other benefit was the assets he accumulated because of his work in the host countries. Elias was also grateful he has been able to provide the opportunity of a better education for his son who was born in London.

The return

Elias had a plan to return to his country at some point. What he did not know is that he was going to return at the time he did. He had plans to return as soon as he accumulated enough assets to start up a good-paying business in Ethiopia. He wanted to return to

Ethiopia after his son went to college and no longer needed his support. However, in the meantime, he separated from his first wife in England – an Ethiopian – and that changed his plan. He immediately decided to move back to Ethiopia:

> If my marriage is dissolved, then I might not be able to raise my child the way I wanted. So I thought and felt there is no point in staying there for another time. It was a difficult decision since I had to leave without my son. I didn't want my son to come with me to Ethiopia throwing away his opportunities in England. But I made the decision anyway.

By returning to his homeland after 17 years, Elias felt relieved and happy. His strong relationships with his family and friends in Ethiopia reinforced his attachment to his homeland:

> The feeling was like 'no place like home'. Nobody can take your home from you. When the plane touched the ground, I knew that I came back to live here in Ethiopia and it was like 'Efoy agere' [efoy is a word of relief like saying thank God and agere means my country].

Socialization/reintegration with home people after return

Upon his return, Elias started up a restaurant business, among others, as he had planned. As he had anticipated, he had accumulated enough capital while working in England to start up his business back home. Elias described his reintegration process as successful. During his stay in England, he traveled often to Ethiopia for holidays and vacations. Thus, it was not difficult for him to reintegrate with the home people. He acknowledged that he has changed over the years but was able to fit into his home society by accepting their differences:

> It is true that I have a changed value to some of the things I used to believe in, those that are still believed in by most Ethiopians including my family. But still I respect those values and beliefs of others even though they are not mine anymore. The other is that as I was coming here often like twice a year for holidays and vacations; I was not completely detached from the community. I also have friends who have come back to Ethiopia after living abroad for many years. I associate most with these kinds of people. It is undeniable that you will be more comfortable to hang out with those who have lived abroad as I have. But it doesn't mean that I had problems of re-integrating.

On the other hand, Elias admitted that he had some difficulties accepting the way things are done in a developing country. After being away for so many years, living in a developed country, it was not easy for Elias to simply accept the way things are done in a very poor country. The way people understand work, the way they view time, and other important issues affecting daily life were frustrating to him at first. In addition, the bureaucracy in government offices, the time mismanagement, and the work ethic of the people were a source of frustration for Elias. Nonetheless, in the end he is happy that he decided to return and stay in Ethiopia:

> Whether you have everything you need abroad, whether all your asylum applications went through and you are accepted as a legal resident, whether you became rich or poor, whether you have friends there or not, whether you pass all the hassle and you are integrating well with the host society, or whether you are having difficulties in reintegrating with the homeland society or not, there is 'NO PLACE LIKE HOME'.

Conclusion

The motivation to live abroad came about for the participant primarily because of push factors at home. However, his first years in the host country were not very promising as the initial integration process was stressful. He faced various inequalities and suffered from exclusion from the workforce because of immigration processes. Socially, he felt oppressed and marginalized by the people in the host country. After 17 years abroad, he returned home and experienced great relief. Though they cannot be taken as representative, Elias' experiences are consistent with the literature illustrating the experiences of other migrants trying to make a life in a host country and ultimately deciding to return to their homeland.

In addition to the usual obstacles encountered by the informant in getting a resident permit and learning the language in the host country, Elias faced oppression and challenges with identity formation. Similarly, Wondwosen et al. (2006) reported that when asked about their experiences abroad, many migrants note the immigration hassle, discrimination by the native people, and feelings of loneliness in the host culture. Likewise, Elias felt oppressed by the inequality he experienced during his stay. He felt lonely and stressed by the way of life in the destination country. Leaving behind his loved ones and not integrating successfully were very stressful for him. Yet, because the primary phase of integration eventually worked out, that is, language and immigration difficulties, the opportunities to save enough capital to start up a successful business back home were realized.

Studies of immigrants in Sweden (Cvetkovic 2009) and Denmark (Riiskjaer and Nielsson 2008) illustrate that returnees as well face problems in socializing or reintegrating with the homeland society. Returnees with changed values may be treated as strangers and foreigners that may contribute to feelings of alienation. They may be considered as wealthy and so become targets of crime. In this study, the data did not reveal this kind of treatment from the home country. Despite some challenges, returning home was an elating experience for Elias. For some other returnees, the challenges at home may drive them away, pushing them to re-migrate.

To develop a more comprehensive understanding of returnee experiences, research is needed with Ethiopian returnees who are diverse in terms of gender, class, age, and education. Since this was a case study, the findings cannot be generalized to other Ethiopian returnees. The story of the informant may not fit with other Ethiopian migrants living abroad who decided to return to their homeland. An enhanced understanding of returnees' experiences can inform the development of more effective and integrated policies and systems of support to assist returnees in reintegrating into their home society with fewer difficulties.

The UN and regional groupings such as EU and OECD advocate that developed countries provide the necessary support for migrants to integrate both in the workforce and in general society (Richardson 2007). Despite the efforts of the UN and other groups, immigrants continue to face oppression, inequality, and difficult integration processes in host countries. Sometimes the host countries blame the migrants themselves for their unwillingness to learn the language and so become better integrated (Wondwosen et al. 2006). However, with the slow application process and lack of support, immigrants get frustrated and may be in a dilemma about whether or not to stay. That was the experience of the study participant that pushed him to re-migrate from Sweden to England before his return to Ethiopia.

Understanding the experiences of Ethiopian migrants in host countries may assist in designing appropriate policies to protect migrants from oppression. The UN and other groups such as the EU should be constantly informed about the experiences and frustrations of these migrants for them to respond accordingly. Governing bodies should be challenged to implement established policies which are intended to support immigrants. Instead, governments worldwide, including Ethiopia, are stepping up efforts to upgrade the 'management' of national borders (Andrijasevic and Walters 2010). The challenges for migrants seem to be growing worldwide, and not only in global north nations. Tobias (2012) argues that the spread of neoliberal economic practices and policies has spurred growing resistance to migration even within sub-Saharan Africa.

The Ethiopian government is making efforts to attract Ethiopian migrants all over the world to return home by providing favorable conditions for initiating new businesses. Efforts to improve access to livelihood opportunities in Ethiopia could attract the Ethiopian Diaspora to be active participants in development endeavors (Adamnesh 2008). We recommend strengthening such government initiatives and developing new ones to create and enhance a favorable working and living environment, facilitate sustainable delivery of assistance post-return, and offer more attractive incentives to support reentry. Returnees themselves could be tapped to offer input directly to government officials or through returnee associations to ensure the success of reentry initiatives. To enhance Ethiopia's social and economic development, Melaku (2009) recommends that priority be given to establishing 'research and training institutions dedicated to international economic law and policy issues' (350). Returnees could be recruited to provide leadership or to advise such development-oriented organizations. The social aspect of repatriation should also be considered in facilitating returnees' reintegration so that their social functioning will be realized in support of the country's development.

Though returnees potentially have much to offer to improve living conditions and development in their home country, without an understanding of their experiences, their hopes for their country, and their personal aspirations, their contributions may never be realized. Developing countries should not miss the opportunity to capitalize on the potential contributions of returnees who are committed to bringing about positive changes in their homeland. Interested returnees can be invited to advise policy-makers regarding social or economic policies that may spur development. The expertise of returnees gained from living abroad, coupled with their commitment to their homeland, represents a powerful synergy that can be tapped to strengthen and invigorate opportunities at home, perhaps even stemming the push to migrate.

Disclosure statement

No potential conflict of interest was reported by the authors.

References

Adamnesh Atnafu. 2006. *Aspects of Ethiopian Return Migration*. Unpublished manuscript. Addis Ababa: Institute of Regional and Local Development Studies, AAU.
Adamnesh Atnafu. 2008. *Facets of Ethiopian Out-migration and Return: The Case of Ethiopia*. Unpublished. Addis Ababa: Envisioning Ethiopia.
Aluttis, C., T. Bishaw, and M. W. Frank. 2014. "The Workforce for Health in a Globalized Context-Global Shortages and International Migration." *Global Health Action* 7. doi:10.3402/gla.v7.23611.

Ammassari, S., and R. Black. 2001. *Harnessing the Potential of Migration and Return to Promote Development: Applying Concepts to West Africa.* Brighton: Center for Migration Research, University of Sussex.

Andrijasevic, R., and W. Walters. 2010. "The International Organization of Migration and the International Government of Borders." *Environment and Planning D: Society and Space* 28: 977–999.

Bathala, C. 2005. "Issues in National and Cultural Identity: The Case of Asian (East) Indian Migrants." *Managerial Law* 47 (¾): 139–151.

Burgelt, P., M. Morgan, and R. Pernice. 2008. "Staying or Returning: Pre-migration Influences on the Migration Process of German Migrants to New Zealand." *Journal of Community & Applied Social Psychology* 18: 282–298.

Buuba, D. B. 2007. "Africa: Setting for Human Migration." *Convergence* 11 (3–4): 211–217.

Creswell, J. 1998. *Qualitative Inquiry and Research Design: Choosing among the Five Traditions.* Thousand Oaks, CA: Sage.

Cvetkovic, A. 2009. "The Integration of Immigrants in Northern Sweden: A Case Study of the Municipality of Stromsund." *International Migration* 47 (1): 101–131.

Czaika, M., and H. de Hass. 2014. "The Globalization of Migration: Has the World Become More Migratory?" *International Migration Review* 48 (2): 283–323.

Fernandez, B. 2013. "Traffickers, Brokers, Employment Agents and Social Networks: The Regulation of Intermediaries in the Migration of Ethiopian Domestic Workers to the Middle East." *International Migration Review* 47 (4): 814–843.

Ganga, D. 2006. "From Potential Returnees into Settlers: Nottingham's Older Italians." *Journal of Ethnic and Migration Studies* 32 (8): 1395–1413.

Melaku Geboye Desta. 2009. "Accession for What? An Examination of Ethiopia's Decision to Join the WTO." *Journal of World Trade* 43 (2): 339–362.

Papadopoulos, I., S. Lees, M. Lay, and A. Gebrehiwot. 2004. "Ethiopian Refugees in the UK: Migration, Adaptation, and Settlement Experiences and Their Relevance to Health." *Ethnicity & Health* 9 (1): 55–73.

Reamer, F. G. 2013. "Ethics in Qualitative Research." In *Qualitative Research in Social Work*, edited by A. E. Fortune, W. J. Reid, and R. L. Miller, 2nd ed., 35–60. New York, NY: Columbia University Press.

Richardson, J. 2007. "Migration: New Urgencies Replace Traditional Welcome." *The Foresight* 9 (5): 48–55.

Riiskjaer, B. H.M., and T. Nielsson. 2008. *Circular Repatriation: The Unsuccessful Return and Reintegration of Iraqis with Refugee Status in Denmark.* Policy Development and Evaluation Service. Geneva: UNHCR.

Rodrıguez, V., and C. Egea. 2006. Return and the Social Environment of Andalusian Emigrants in Europe." *Journal of Ethnic and Migration Studies* 32 (8): 1377–1393.

Silvestri, D. M., M. Blevens, A. Afzal, B. Andrews, M. Derbew, S. Kaur, M. Mipando, et al. 2014. "Medical and Nursing Students' Intentions to Work Abroad or in Rural Areas: A Cross-sectional Survey in Asia and Africa." *Bulletin of the World Health Organization* 92: 750–759.

Tobias, S. 2012. "Neoliberal Globalization and the Politics of Migration in Sub-Saharan Africa." *Journal of International & Global Studies* 4 (1): 1–16.

United Nations, Department of Economic and Social Affairs, Population Division. 2009. *Trends in International Migrant Stock: The 2008 Revision* (United Nations Database, POP/DB/MIG/Stock/Rev.2008).

Van Dalen, P. H., G. Groenewold, & J. J. Schoorl. 2005. "Out of Africa: What Drives the Pressure to Emigrate?" *Journal of Population and Economics* 18: 741–778.

Wakgari Deressa, and Azazh Aklilu. 2012. "Attitudes of Undergraduate Medical Students of Addis Ababa University Towards Medical Practice and Migration, Ethiopia." *BMC Medical Education* 12: 68–79.

Wondwosen, T. B., N. Jerusalem, H. Seidler, and Z. Hanna. 2006. "International Migration: The Case of Ethiopian Female Migrants in Austria." *Journal of Social Science* 13 (1): 1–9.

Yin, R. K. 2003. *Case Study Research: Design and Methods.* 3rd ed. Thousand Oaks, CA: Sage.

Index

Note: **Boldface** page numbers refer to figures and tables, n denotes endnotes

action research method 124
activism 144–5
Addis Ababa Bureau of Labor and Social Affairs 109
Addis Credit and Saving Institution 114
Africa, human trafficking in 47–8
African and Black Diaspora: An International (ABD) 7
African migration 166–7
African Watch Report 4
Arab League States 99
army, women in 136–7, 139–40
Aster Aweke 155–9

blocked mobility hypothesis 78
business travelers 167–8
business women 136

Chile, migration in 169
Civil Service Ministry 15
cross-border migration 57

DC Ethiopians 159–60
DC Taxicab Commission 82
Denmark, Iraqi refugees immigration to 170
Derg (military regime) 10, 43
diaspora bond 15, 63
diaspora engagement policies 15, 60, 63–4
diasporas, definition of 12–13, 15
disadvantage theory 77, 78
discrimination 143–4
District of Columbia Taxicab Commission 81
domestic workers **7,** 7–8, 44, 50
drivers of Ethiopian migration 26–7

ECC *see* Ethiopian Community Center
economic diplomacy 11
economic embeddedness 114–15
economic migrants 6
ECSDC *see* Ethiopian Community Services and Development Council
educational needs and immigration 167
EEPCO *see* Ethiopian Electric Power Corporation
embeddedness: definition of 106; economic 114–15; psychosocial 107, 116; social network 115
entrepreneurialism in 'Jeppe' 27–8
EPRDF *see* Ethiopian Peoples' Revolutionary Democratic Front
Eritrean People's Liberation Frontforces 12
ESA *see* Ethiopian Student Association
Eskesta 153
ESUNA *see* Ethiopian Students Union in North America
Ethio-Eritrean war (1998–2000) 11, 12, 14
Ethiojazz 153–5
Ethiopian Community Center (ECC) 17
Ethiopian Community Services and Development Council (ECSDC) 17
Ethiopian diaspora 6–7; engagement policies 63–4; mass displacement and emergence of 5–6, **6**
Ethiopian Electric Power Corporation (EEPCO) 63
Ethiopian Embassy in Kuwait 100–1
Ethiopian emigrants: categories 16; economic theory of 13; network theory 13; organizing principle in 11; overview of 10–12; political antagonism, challenges of 20–1; population 14, 18–20; rural–urban 12; transnational interaction, centrality of politics in 18–20; transnationalism and state policies of 21–2; in USA 17; in Washington DC 16
Ethiopian Investment Agency 15
Ethiopian–Israeli women: activism 144–5; army experience 139–40; background and immigration 137–8; business and entrepreneurship 136; career 140–1; culture and identity 142–3; discrimination 143–4; economic integration 142–3; education 138–9, 145–6; lifestyle 142; married life

INDEX

and motherhood 141–2; military and government positions 136–7; overview of 133–5; religious affairs 137; TV artists 137
Ethiopian musical diaspora: Aster Aweke 155–9; overview of 151–2; Rada, Ester 152–5; Wayna Wondwossen 159–62
Ethiopian Orthodox Church 18, 19
Ethiopian People's Revolutionary Democratic Front (EPRDF) 5, 11, 13, 21
Ethiopian People's Revolutionary Party (EPRP) 4
Ethiopian returnees: inequality and oppression 172–3; motives for leaving 171, 174–5; obstacles and opportunities 172; readapting, difficulties in 170, 174; reasons for returning 169, 173–4; research data analysis 171; selection of respondents 170–1; sociocultural reintegration 170, 174; statistical analysis on 168; yellow card holders 169
Ethiopian Student Association (ESA) 17
Ethiopian Students Union in North America (ESUNA) 10
Ethiopian taxicab drivers: autonomy 85; community's involvement in business 82; ethnic economies and entrepreneurship 77–9; ethnic occupational niches 79–80; flexibility 85–6; immigrant drivers 80; second-generation progress 84–5; self-sufficiency 85; socio-economical mobility 83–4; in Washington DC 80–2
Ethiopian women labor migrants to Kuwait: domestic workers migrants 100–1; government policies and legislations 95–6; international migration of 94–5, 97–8; migrant workers situation in Gulf 98–9; migration-related Ethio-Kuwaiti relations 101–2; protective policies 96; regulatory and restrictive policies 96; theoretical framework 91–4
Ethiopian Women Lawyers Association (EWLA) 122–3
Ethiopian women trafficked to Bahrain: action research 124; decision point to return 125–6; forced return 119; health risks 121; income-generation schemes 128–9; information/awareness 127–8; law enforcement 128; organizing advocacy association 129; participants profile **125**; participants reintegration 127; poverty 119–20; rehabilitation and medical attention 128; return to Ethiopia 126–7; victims of trafficking 120, 123; women's legal documents 121
Ethiopiques 157–8, 163
Ethio-soul 153, 163n2
ethnicity 20, 143, 146
ethnic occupational niches 79–80
Europe, trafficking of African women 48–51

Ewedihalehu 156
EWLA *see* Ethiopian Women Lawyers Association
Expats, The 161

Falashmoras 147n6
Feeling Good 153–4
Food and Agriculture Organization 94

GCC *see* Gulf Cooperation Council
gender violence 37
genfo 34, 40n7
German migrants 167
globalization and migration 1, 167
Global Report on Trafficking in Persons (2009) 48
Government of Ethiopia 63
grand renaissance dam (GERD) 15
Gulf Cooperation Council (GCC) 96, 98–100
Gulf Cooperation Countries 112

Hagan, Jacqueline 27
Higher Ground 161
host societies: finding community 34; unfavorable conditions in 169, 172; view of migrants 168
human trafficking *see* trafficking of Ethiopian women

ICMPD *see* International Centre for Migration Policy
identity formation, migrants 168
Idir 31, 40n5
ILO *see* International Labour Organization
internal migration 4–5
International Centre for Migration Policy (ICMPD) 48
International Labour Organization (ILO) 49–50, 95, 97
international migration 12, 13
International Organization for Migration (IOM) 16, 122–3
International Remittance Services (IRS) 15
IOM *see* International Organization for Migration
Iraqi refugees, immigration to Denmark 170
IRS *see* International Remittance Services
Israel, Ethiopian immigrant women in *see* Ethiopian–Israeli women

Jeppe 27–8, 40n4
Jerusalem, *Ethiopiques* in 157–8, 163
Johannesburg, Ethiopian migrants in: crime and corruption 35–6; disconnection and reconnection 28–30; drivers of migration 26–7; family expectations 38; finding community 34; gender violence 37; Jeppe,

INDEX

entrepreneurialism in 27–8; life events in absentia 33–4; loss and longing 32–3; monetary benefits 36; networks theory of migration 30–1; overview of 25–6; phoning home 30; promise of South Africa 28; research assistance 39n1; social capital 31–2, 34–5; social freedom and vigilance 36–7

Kafala system 96, 99, 108
Kuwait: Ethiopian Embassy in 100–1; labor migrants to *see* Ethiopian women labor migrants to Kuwait

life events in absentia 33–4
Life Happens 153, 154

Mahbers 31, 40n6
MIDA *see* Migration for Development in Africa
middleman minority 77
migration, definition of 42, 47
Migration for Development in Africa (MIDA) 16
mikveh 147n7
military-socialist government in 1991 11
Ministry of Foreign Affairs (MOFA) 14
Ministry of Labor and Social Affairs (MOLSA) 15, 44, 95, 96, 108, 111, 122
mixed embeddedness 78
Mizrahi women 135
MOFA *see* Ministry of Foreign Affairs
MOLSA *see* Ministry of Labor and Social Affairs
Moments of Clarity Volume 1 161
monetary benefits 36

Nanu Nanu Ney 154–5
Nations, Nationalities, and Peoples 11, 20
neoclassical macro-economic theory 91–2
neoclassical micro-economic theory 92
Netherlands, Ethiopian migrants in: dependent variables 64; Ethiopia's diaspora engagement policies 63–4; independent variables 64–5; knowledge of diaspora policies 65–7, **66, 68**; overview of 60; participation in policies **66**; regression analysis, policy knowledge 67, **69–70**, 71; state-diaspora relations 62–3
networks theory of migration 13, 30–1, 93

organizing principle 11

Palermo protocol 48
PEA *see* Private Employment Agency
PESs *see* public employment services
phoning home 30
'politics as profession' 22

Private Employment Agency (PEA) 111–12, 120, 122
prostitution 47–9
protective policies 96
psychosocial embeddedness 107, 116
public employment services (PESs) 122

racially based stratification 146
Rada, Ester: Feeling Good 153–4; Life Happens 153, 154; Nanu Nanu Ney 154–5
rational choice theory 46
Red Terror program 4, 10, 81
Refugees and Returnees Affairs (RRA) 120
Regional Mixed Migration Secretariat (RMMS) 108
regulatory policies 96
Renaissance Dam Bond 63
restrictive policies 96
RMMS *see* Regional Mixed Migration Secretariat
RRA *see* Refugees and Returnees Affairs
rural–urban migration 12

Saudi Arabia, Ethiopians returning from: economic embeddedness 114–15; forced return migration 105–7; methodology 109; in Middle East 107–8; migration motivations and trajectories 110–12; overview of 104–5; psychosocial embeddedness 116; respondents 109–10; return to Ethiopia 112–13; social network embeddedness 115
Saudi Ministry of Labor 105
secessionist war 4
sexual exploitation 48
sexual workers 47–9
Simone, Nina 153
social capital: in Johannesburg 31–2; in work-dominated environment 34–5
social freedom 36–7
social network embeddedness 115
South Africa, immigration to 26–8
Sweden: inequality and oppression in 172–3; obstacles and opportunities for migrants 172

Tel Aviv, Aster Aweke in 155–9
Tewdros Adhanom 14
Tigrian People's Liberation Front (TPLF) 12
Trafficking in Persons Report 2014 47
trafficking of Ethiopian women: to Bahrain *see* Ethiopian women trafficked to Bahrain; case studies 52–5; domestic workers 44, 50; family background 50; Inter-Ministerial Committee on 51; internal trafficking 49; International Labour Organization report 49–50; Ministry of Labour and Social Affairs 44; overview

INDEX

of 42–5; Palermo protocol 48; sexual workers 47–9
Trafficking Victims Protection Act 47
transnational governmentality 62
transnationalism 12, 21–2

United Nations High Commission for Refugees (UNHCR) 26
United Nations Population Division 1
UN 2008 Revised Population Database 3

vigilance 36–7
villagization scheme 5
vocal diaspora 22

Washington: Ethiopian migrants in 16–18, 22; Ethiopian music in 159–60; Ethiopian taxicab drivers in 77, 80–2
Wayna Wondwossen 159–62
women artists 137
women education 138–9, 145–6
work-dominated environment, social capital in 34–5
World Migration Report 43
World Systems approach 92–3

'Yellow Card' policy 63, 70–2, 169
Young Ethiopian Professionals (YEP) 18